How to Get the Best Home Loan

D1444333

How to Get the Best Home Loan

Second Edition

W. FRAZIER BELL

John Wiley & Sons

New York • Chichester • Weinheim • Brisbane • Singapore • Toronto

Copyright © 2001 by W. Frazier Bell. All rights reserved.

Published by John Wiley & Sons, Inc.

Published simultaneously in Canada.

This publication is designed to provide accurate and
authoritative information in regard to the subject matter covered.
It is sold with the understanding that the publisher is not engaged
in rendering professional services. If professional advice or other
expert assistance is required, the services of a competent
professional person should be sought.

Library of Congress Cataloging-in-Publication Data:

Bell, W. Frazier, 1950–
    How to get the best home loan/W. Frazier Bell.—2nd ed.
        p.   cm.
    Includes index.
    ISBN 0-471-41511-1 (pbk: alk. paper)
    1. Mortgage loans.   I. Title.
    HG2040.15.B45 2001
    332.7´22—dc21   00-066255

Printed in the United States of America
10 9 8 7 6 5 4 3 2 1

This book is dedicated to my wife, Harriet, who has suffered through my many years in the real estate industry.

ABOUT THE AUTHOR

Mr. Bell has been involved in many facets of the real estate industry since 1973. A graduate of the University of Virginia, he has been a builder and a Real Estate Broker, and is currently a mortgage banker in Charlottesville, Virginia. He has been a Direct Endorsement Underwriter for FHA loans, past president of the local mortgage bankers association, and taught Real Estate Finance at Piedmont Virginia Community College. When he is not chasing mortgages, he is chasing trout in the nearby Blue Ridge Mountains.

CONTENTS

A FABLE

Once there was a man who lived in a cave. It was a nice cave—not the best, but it suited his needs. One day another man came along who decided he wanted this cave. In the normal manner of business at that time, he demonstrated this desire by beating the owner over the head with a club. Now, the owner liked his cave, but he knew he could find another one that he liked just as well without much trouble. So, it only took one bashing over the head to convince him to give the cave to the man with the club.

Without undue hardship he soon located another, better cave. It had added amenities such as a spring (indoor plumbing), a deep pit (trash compactor), and a beautiful view of the valley. Settling in, this man and his family enjoyed their new and improved environment for several years, as the neighborhood grew and new people moved into the area. One day a newcomer to the area saw the appeal of this particular abode and expressed an interest in perhaps trading something of value for it. The owner was perfectly content and resisted the advances of this potential homebuyer. After being bashed over the head five or six times, he decided that maybe the cave really was not worth that much, and he moved again.

Being a little more shrewd than most of his neighbors, he decided that if he wanted to keep a home long enough to appreciate its true value, he would have to find something other than the standard cave. So, he cut down some trees and built a crude but secure hut. The nice thing about this particular structure was that he could build it where he wanted to live and not be limited to living only where he could find a cave. He could also have all of the necessities of life close by. He found a nice spot on the bank of a stream where he could get water and bathe, gather firewood and game from the forest, and still have a beautiful view.

Other families saw the advantage to having a hut by the water, and the neighborhood began to sprout huts of various designs and sizes. Because he could see that additional features would make his home more comfortable, our homeowner added a wing for the children and another hut in which to house the assorted animals they kept.

Since there was plenty of room, and everyone could build exactly what they wanted, there was little need to bargain for someone else's hut. The family grew. The father died, and the oldest son took possession of the hut. As each generation grew up and passed the property along, improvements and modifications were made to make the property more comfortable. A fireplace was built, boards were laid over the dirt floor, and cracks in the walls were chinked. More rooms and fireplaces were added. Unfortunately, these fireplaces tended to burn almost as readily as the firewood. The little hut by the stream was reduced to ashes on numerous occasions, only to be rebuilt each time a little bit bigger and stronger, and with a functional utility to meet the ambiance of the times.

As the times changed, so did people's tastes. And, as will happen, the house had just burned down again. The couple had been eying one of the homes built in the new, two-story brick style, and they lost no time in having plans drafted and put into shape. Soon, there arose from the ashes a splendid example of good taste in architecture. Everything was of the latest design, including brick fireplaces to minimize the chance that this would only be a temporary shelter.

As time passed, more and more people built by the water, leaving fewer desirable locations. Because good sites were harder to find, they became more valuable. About this time our family found itself in a precarious financial situation, brought about by the eldest son's penchant for cockfighting (his bird soon became Sunday dinner). Having the premier location in the area and one of the most admired homes, the family soon had an offer—in those days considered quite generous—from people of more prosperous means who were looking to buy a home reflecting their higher station in life. Deciding that they really did not need such a grand home, and that they would be able to clear all debts and still have enough remaining to purchase a smaller, but comfortable home, our family sold the house for $2,000 plus five barrels of the finest tobacco. With this they would eventually establish a trading company and in later years have a home more opulent than the original. However, our story concerns the recently sold manor.

The new owners took great pride in their new home and improved upon it at every opportunity. Surrounding land was bought and the property became one of the larger, more profitable estates in the region. This property was handed down from generation to generation; occasionally a few acres were given to one of the children for them to build their own smaller, but compatible home near the great house.

During the early part of the twentieth century there came a time when the current heirs to the estate did not produce any children. In their later years they decided to sell the family home and retire on the resulting fortune of $70,000. The local bank gave the purchasers a loan of $20,000 at 3% to be paid off in 10 years. The new owners enjoyed the property until the stock market crash of 1929 forced them to sell the property for $30,000.

The new owners paid cash. They were shrewd, evinced by their ability to survive and flourish during the Depression. They acquired new properties until the estate contained well over 4,000 acres of prime land stretching all the way to the edge of the local town. By the 1950s, however, the good genes running in this family had begun to play out. Portions of the farm were sold to pay debts and maintain the style of living to which they had become accustomed. Other parcels were subdivided, and row upon row of small, tasteless, ranch-style homes were built. These homes were bought by members of the new rising middle class for prices ranging from $10,000 to $12,000, depending on whether you wanted a carport and wall-to-wall carpet. The purchasers would put 10% or more down and finance the balance at 5% for 15 or 20 years. Their annual incomes were about $4,000 to $6,000.

The manor home was soon surrounded by large numbers of houses of every design known. Paved roads, curbs, and storm sewers replaced the old country road that had run through the farm. By this time, the original property consisted of the manor home and various parcels of land scattered throughout the growing urban sprawl. The upkeep of the main house had become increasingly expensive, and it was showing a great deal of deferred maintenance. In the early 1960s the owner decided to sell it to a prosperous young doctor with a growing family. The house and three acres sold for the princely sum of $27,000. The physician added another $4,000 in renovations. The bank was happy to lend money to someone that it knew would be making large sums of money within the next few years. The doctor put down 10% and financed the remainder at 6% for 30 years.

The doctor's family grew up in the home, went to college, and then moved on to new areas and greater challenges. The parents found themselves living in a house with 12-foot ceilings, five bedrooms, a study, a family room, living room, dining room, large eat-in kitchen, three and a half bathrooms, a two-car garage, and a large dependency building. They sold the house and its three acres in 1980 for $200,000 and moved into a townhouse that they bought for $70,000, paying cash and taking the one-time exemption from the capital gains tax. The purchaser of the manor house borrowed $120,000 and financed it at 9% for thirty years. The purchaser's income was about $44,000 per year.

The scattered parcels of land retained by the previous owners were slowly developed over the years. In the mid-1960s one 25-acre parcel was developed into twenty-one lots that sold for $3,000 apiece. By 1980 these lots were worth $18,000 each, and new lots in the more prestigious area were selling for $50,000 each. By 1989 the $18,000 lots were worth from $35,000 to $50,000, the $50,000 lots were selling for $135,000 to $175,000, and the $70,000 townhouse was worth $130,000. New homes with three bedrooms, two bathrooms, a living-dining room (known as a "great room" to increase sales appeal), and an eat-in kitchen crammed into 1,200 finished square feet on an unfinished basement were selling for $100,000 to $200,000, depending on location.

To finance these homes, purchasers put down from 5% to 50% and borrowed the remainder from numerous different lending sources, with mortgages that were at a fixed interest rate for fifteen to thirty years, five- to ten-year balloon loans, at adjustable rates, or even loans that charged you more interest than you were paying (known by the innocuous name of "negative amortization"). Between 1980 and 1989, interest rates ranged from 8.5% to 17%. Purchasers' incomes ranged from $28,000 to $65,000, depending on the price and the interest rate.

Our original manor home, now on three acres, was worth $550,000. If you put down 20%, financed the remaining $440,000 at 10.5% for thirty years, you would need to earn about $15,000 to $16,000 per month to qualify for the loan. Some people have begun to live in caves again.

How to Get Best Home Loan

INTRODUCTION

When I wrote the first version of this book, the mortgage industry was just on the verge of significant changes. In the past 9 years mortgage lending has evolved from the Flintstones to the Jetsons. Since about 1995, the changes have been absolutely extraordinary. We have moved from multiple verifications by mail to by fax to alternative documentation to email. Underwriting has been turned over to the machines. Application to approval time have gone from 30 days to 90 minutes. Closings have gone from 1.5 months to 1 week. Flexibility has been pushed to the point even I have a hard time believing it.

If getting a mortgage has become so easy, why do you need to read this book? Because many of the same problems that existed at the time I wrote the first version are still around. And, if you do not know what is happening, you will find yourself running around in circles to get an approval and close. Not to mention paying significantly more for what you thought was a low cost, low rate loan. Many lenders have tried to cut costs by hiring people who are nothing more than order takers. When a loan deviates from it's straight line path, you will find yourself cast adrift in a sea of confusion. Only a knowledgeable loan officer can guide you through to the right loan, and the best loan for your situation. I would estimate that well over two-thirds of all loans will encounter some type of problem. It may be minor, or it may cause the uneducated lender to deny your loan. I have gotten more calls from Realtors and borrowers who are frantically trying to save a purchase another lender had messed up. In one recent instance, a lender that advertises nationally and takes the loan by telephone had denied a borrower's loan unless they could put down three times more cash than the original loan application required. It took me 5 minutes to determine they could get a loan almost identical to the original loan for which they had applied. When the other lender found out what I could do, they contacted

1

the borrowers and told them they could do the same thing. Of course, they never would have known they could do it without my "help." The borrowers decided to stay with me, because of my knowledge and experience.

In the case of mortgage lending I completely agree with the popular "Question Authority" bumper sticker. It is all too easy for the lender to intimidate the borrower because the lender has the power of knowledge. The borrower often meekly follows along, even while wondering, "Why is that? I don't understand. Boy, I sure hope that when I get through all this, they approve my loan." This book will change that. By knowing what the lender is doing, and why, you will find the process made immeasurably smoother. This knowledge can, in many cases, also save you hundreds or even thousands of dollars.

The borrower should keep in mind that nothing stays the same. As I noted earlier, change has come exponentially to the mortgage lending industry since 1995. Or, as the saying goes, "the only constant is change." When I was a Realtor in the 1970s to the early 1980s, my job changed to the point where it entailed more information management than sales; getting the borrower through the loan process to closing began to take more and more of my skill and time. The once short, simple application became a nightmare of paperwork. The paperwork and time-consuming process has all but disappeared. However, borrowers must have a knowledgeable and experienced loan officer to insure a smooth process from application to closing, especially if there is a need for a quick approval and/or closing. Loan application anxiety will always be with us. Much of this anxiety is caused by a lack of knowledge on the part of the borrowers and Realtors.

As a result, I began to find myself spending twice as much time taking the loan applications in order to explain each part of the process as I asked the required questions and had the borrowers sign all the required forms. Then I spent more time educating the Realtors so that they could become more professional and knowledgeable sources of information for both buyer and seller. In this book, I have combined all that I have taught, and been asked, along with a great deal more. The book will therefore be of use to both borrowers and Realtors.

By reading this book before applying for a loan, or even during the process, you will gain the knowledge necessary to get the right loan, at the right price, from the right lender. You will head off many potential problems and expensive mistakes. The book is organized such that each section is built on the previous one. It is important that you read it from the beginning to have a clear understanding of why lenders do the things they do, and why certain loans may be better for you in your particular situation than others. In some sections you will probably have the urge to skip ahead to the parts you think contain all you really need to know. If you do that, however, you will miss valuable information that could clarify whatever it is that you are trying to learn. Many things in mortgage lending do not stand alone, but arise from other things. At some point, a light bulb may metaphorically appear, accompanied by a statement like, "Hey! That's why they made me do that!" I hope the discovery will be a pleasant one. That is not always the case.

There are several rules that one would be wise to consider when dealing with a lender. The first one is that famous Golden Rule of Lending: "He who has the gold, makes the rules." Usually, the one with the gold will be the lender. But it is possible for the borrower, or the Realtor if one is involved, to hold enough power to help move or change things when the process gets slow or unreasonable. Just remember that the lender wants to make the loan. It has a product it wants to sell, and if it doesn't sell that product, it will go out of business. Mortgage lending is also a service industry, so the lender is dependent on the reputation and goodwill that it creates for itself to continue receiving business. If a lender does not provide professional and courteous service, the competition will take its market share very quickly.

The next rule is to "assume nothing." Do not assume that you know the lender is doing something wrong, or that you are doing everything correctly. Ask questions. Check on the progress of the loan. See if there is anything that you, borrower or Realtor, can do to help speed the process. A good lender will often tell you without being asked if something can be done in that regard. But as I have already noted, don't count on getting a good one.

The last, and by far the most important, rule is to know your lender. Before making final loan application and paying any money, take the time to find out about the company with which you will be dealing. Is it established and well known? Is it financially sound? What is its reputation in the community? Do not base your decision solely on the recommendation of a friend, or on the single fact that the lender has the lowest interest rates. The saying that "you get what you pay for" sometimes applies to mortgage borrowing. Internet lending is an area of special concern, and often does not have satisfactory answers for most, if not all, of the preceding questions. Know with whom you are dealing.

Because buying a home is such a large investment and creates such a large debt, you would think that all buyers would take the necessary time to study the subject—especially when they will be spending thousands of dollars, in application and closing costs, just to get the loan. Because they don't always take the time, they often pay too much for what they get in return.

This book is dedicated to the idea that anyone who is buying or refinancing residential real estate should know the process for obtaining mortgage financing, and why it works the way it does. The book is not intended to make you an authority on all aspects of real estate finance; what it will do is clear up many of the unknown aspects that keep borrowers from being able to make intelligent, money-saving decisions.

You can avoid the problems and costs that ignorance creates. Let other people tell you about the problems they had to overcome when they applied for a loan; you can tell them how you avoided those problems and saved a large amount of money by doing so.

MY FATHER SAID HE NEVER HAD TO GO THROUGH THIS!

My father said . . . ; my neighbor said . . . ; my Realtor said . . . ; my attorney said. . . . Most people think they know something about real estate financing and where to get the best rates. They are not shy about telling you their experiences, every one of which will probably be different. And all of their stories may be true. Each person's slightly different situation can alter the type of loan the lender recommends and how it is processed. Most loans, however, are approved or denied, based on some very fundamental rules. Over the years, these rules have become the standards by which the industry functions, but they have not always been in effect. Today, most of the accumulated industry guidelines have been squeezed, mashed, stretched, added to, chopped apart, and put back together inside a computer program. Many loans can go from application to approval within an hour. That is why your father, and anyone else who hasn't received a loan since the late 1970s, can't tell you what it's like today.

A good example is my first loan, which I got in the early 1970s. There were basically two lenders in town: a mortgage subsidiary of a bank and a savings and loan (S&L). The S&L was run by an old man who knew just about everyone. I walked into his office one day and said, "I'm buying a house, and I need a loan." He said, "Just let me know about two weeks before you need to close. Who is going to be your attorney?" He wouldn't give you the loan if he didn't like your attorney. That was the entire application and approval. He did not even ask me how much I needed to buy the house. That may be a little easier than even what your father had to do for his loan, but it illustrates the fact that lenders of that time really did make loans the old-fashioned way: They used their own money, or **portfolioed** the loan. Remember the term *portfolioed;* we will talk about it later.

Several years after I bought that house, I did what every normal American does: I bought a larger house and went deeper into debt. This time I went to the mortgage banker, the one that was a subsidiary of a bank that made mortgage loans. He also knew me. Unfortunately, he felt it was necessary to get a little information and keep me waiting for several weeks before I got loan approval. He made references to "verifying" my application. Didn't he trust me? No, he thought that I was just fine. It was **Fannie Mae** who didn't know me from Adam. This made it sound as if we were dealing with someone from James Dickey's *Deliverance.* Fannie Mae might be fat, ugly, mean. Wore one of those sack dresses with small flower prints all over it. Looked at you with a kind of sour squint. Now, why would someone like that be looking at my loan?

As most people today are painfully aware, Fannie is not some mountain blossom, but an acronym for the **Federal National Mortgage Association, or FNMA.** Being a child of the federal government, Fannie Mae herself gave birth to some more mountain folk, **Freddie Mac** and **Ginnie Mae,** known to the more refined as the **Federal Home Loan Mortgage Corp. (FHLMC)** and the **Government National Mortgage Association (GNMA).** Fannie and kin are the ultimate authorities of mortgage lending. In most instances, you do what they say.

If you give these stories a little thought, it may seem logical to go to the S&L. For a long time, most people did exactly that. Actually, to an extent, the same is true today. But things have changed drastically since the late 1970s. How did things change so much? Let's take a look.

WHY DO THEY DO THE THINGS THEY DO?

Once upon a time in the old days (until the late 1970s), savings and loans, or thrifts, were the predominant lenders of mortgage loans. Their charters actually require that the majority of their loans be home mortgages. That is why S&Ls came into existence. The most important thing to know about thrifts is the source of their money. They got it from savers. At some time or another you may have had a passbook savings account, one in which you put $10 or $20 a month at 5% interest. That was, of course, back when inflation was 2% to 3% a year. The thrifts would lend that money out at 7% or 8%, thus making a profit. Obviously, people were constantly putting in and taking out their money, which you might think would wreak havoc when that money was supposed to be tied up in a 30-year fixed rate loan. We know that this didn't happen, so how exactly did they make those loans when the money was coming and going? They borrowed it from the government. Actually, they would normally have sufficient assets on a day-to-day basis to cover most of their loans, but when they were a little shy of cash, they would go to the Federal Home Loan Bank and borrow short-term. The rates would be low enough that those 7% and 8% loans were still moneymakers. The more deposits they took in, and the more income they earned, the more loans they could make. It was a very neat arrangement that provided money for homes and a profit for the thrift.

Are you ready for a quick lesson in math? If Johnny borrows money and pays 12%, and then lends that money out at 8%, how much money will Johnny make on the deal? (Anyone who doesn't think that Johnny is coming out on the short end, please give me a call. I would like to ask you for a loan.) In the mid-1970s what happened to Johnny is exactly what happened to the thrifts.

Inflation and interest rates went into double digits, which meant that the cost of money for everyone, from lenders to homebuyers to the federal government, became very high. The big problem for the thrifts was that they had already lent money out at low long-term rates on the assumption that they would always be able to obtain money cheaply enough to cover those loans, plus overhead and profit. But when you have to pay 12% to cover loans that are already on your books at 8%, you have a substantial deficit on millions of dollars of loans, which is not healthy for the bottom line. To add to the thrifts' problems, people were taking their money out of their savings accounts at the thrifts and putting it into high-yield investments. This phenomenon is called *disintermediation* the movement of funds from one place to another that is caused by a wide disparity in interest rates.

All of a sudden, those friendly folks down at the local savings and loan were not only losing money, but also rapidly running out of money to lend. During this period, when I was a Realtor, I sold some houses and took my clients to the S&L to make their loan applications. To our surprise, it was not making loans. It was taking deposits, but no loan applications. This was the same thrift where I had received my one minute loan application years before. We went to a local bank and got a short-term note that would be paid in full when the purchase could be refinanced, that is, when the thrift again had money to lend.

Where did that situation leave us? It left us with houses to sell, people who wanted to buy them, high interest rates, and, most importantly, very little money available to make the loans on those houses. How did we fix this mess? By using Fannie Mae, Freddie Mac, and all the other investors in the secondary market.

2

THE SECONDARY MARKET

The secondary market consists of Fannie Mae (Federal National Mortgage Association—FNMA), Freddie Mac (Federal Home Loan Mortgage Corporation—FHLMC), Ginnie Mae (Government National Mortgage Association—GNMA), and a wide assortment of other investors. I'm not going to bore you with the history of these folks. What is important is why they were created and what that means to the borrower, the poor soul they try to torture in various ingenious and subtle ways. To understand how real estate financing works, you the borrower must understand how all the little things in the secondary market affect your ability to get a mortgage. Looking at the specifics of getting a loan will make things much clearer.

As the name suggests, the secondary market is the second market for mortgage loans. The **primary market** is the lender itself, to which the borrower applies for the loan. After the loan is approved and closed, the lender, or **originator** of the loan in the primary market, will in most cases sell that loan to an entity, or **investor,** in the secondary market. If the originator does not sell the loan, it is portfolioed, or put on the shelf, as it is known in the trade. We will discuss portfolio lenders in detail later. Right now the question is, "Why do they sell the loan, and how does that affect me as the borrower?" The answers are, of course, money. The sale will not affect the borrower, except minimally, once the loan is closed. Notice that I said "minimally" and specified "once the loan is closed."

First, let's discuss the mechanics of the secondary market in general terms. As we have already noted, Fannie Mae, Freddie Mac, and Ginnie Mae are members of this shadowy group. There are many other members, or investors, in the secondary market.

Insurance companies invest large amounts of their premium income in mortgages. Pension funds and banks also buy loans. Banks buy loans directly, or they have a mortgage subsidiary to purchase loans from other lenders.

When lenders buy loans from other lenders, they do it through what is called the *wholesale division* of that purchasing lender. Actually, hundreds of lenders have very large and aggressive wholesale divisions looking to buy mortgage loans originated by other lenders. That is why many loans made by a lender today will end up with another lender after they close. Why would lenders want to make a loan and then get rid of it? Don't they want to make money? Isn't that why they charge those usurious interest rates? The answers are, to make money, yes, and yes. If you don't understand, you are not alone. But to understand why, you first have to know what drives the secondary market, or what makes it profitable.

As we all know, lenders originate loans to make money. Now, if we set aside any consideration of interest income, exactly how do lenders make money? Let us look at a loan from the initial application all the way through to its final sale to the secondary market to see where all the money goes.

FEES, POINTS, AND OTHER GARBAGE

When the application is submitted, the lender will typically collect money for appraisal and credit report fees because the lender will be billed for them whether or not the borrower closes on the loan. Another fee now being collected at application is an Underwriting fee to pay for Desktop Underwriting. The lender is charged a fee by the institution that owns this proprietary system. The cost is nominal, usually around $20. We will look at Desktop, or computer, underwriting later. These fees will vary from area to area and lender to lender, depending on many things, such as size and location of the property, the borrower's employment (self-employed, commission income, and so on), what the various appraisers and credit bureaus charge, and whether the lender tries to add a little something to those fees for itself. The amounts added to the appraisal and credit fees will create some fee income for the lender beyond the normal charges. Some lenders will also try to collect "Processing Fees," "Application Fees," or "Rate Lock-In Fees." These are part of what are called **Garbage** or **Junk**

Fees. Garbage fees are in addition to the normal points and costs of closing the loan. In some states the lender cannot collect more than the actual cost of the appraisal and credit report fees, but they can collect an application fee. So, the lender will collect an application fee that just happens to pay for the appraisal and credit report in addition to the additional fee income, often non-refundable. We will get into this in more detail later.

Points are the fees that really get your attention. They are part of the standard cost of closing a loan, and normally there are two different types of points, the **origination fee** and the **discount points.** These are expressed as a percentage of the loan amount; that is, one point is 1% of the loan, two points is 2% of the loan, and so forth. **Points can be quoted in increments of one-eighth of one percent (0.125%).** So you can be given lender quotes like 2.375 points or 1.875 points—sort of like a blue-light special for $19.95.

The origination fee goes to the lender for originating the loan. Usually 1% of the loan amount, it is most often collected at time of closing. Sometimes the lender will collect it at application, refundable only if it cannot do the loan. Refinances are often handled in this manner; the borrower is not under the same sense of urgency, and is much more likely to jerk the loan than a purchaser. One of the great fears for originating lenders is that borrowers will pull their loan applications after the lender has put in time and effort, leaving the lender nothing to show for it. Another more common time for the lender to collect the origination fee is at the time the loan commitment is issued. Once the lender has done its work and has approved the loan, the borrower must start paying the piper in order to get it. So, the origination fee is one of the primary income fees that the lender will collect, and it is normally 1% of the loan amount.

The other big fee is known as **the discount point(s).** When a lender is asked for its interest rates, the quotation will include the rate and points, such as 10%, 1 + 2. The *one* is the origination fee, and the discount will usually be the bigger number, in this example *two.* Some lenders will quote the discount rate first, that is, 2 + 1; and others will just combine them, as in 3 points. When you are quoted points as one amount, make sure you ask the lender if that includes both the origination and discount points. You may think you have found the best deal, only to discover that you were only quoted the discount.

The important thing to remember about discount points is

that **the lower you want your interest rate, the higher the discount points will be.** In other words, the discount points buy down the interest rate, as interest up-front. Or, they *discount* the interest rate. For example, say that 10.25% is 1 discount point, or 1% of the loan amount, then 10% might be 2 discount points, or 2%; 9.75%, 3 points; and so on. The number of discount points for a particular rate can differ significantly from lender to lender. This number is an important thing to look for if you are shopping for rates. People joke about getting a 3% interest rate. They can get it, but the discount points needed to buy that rate would support a small army.

Not that these points aren't expensive enough just to cover what is required to get the normal interest rate, but the lender can (and will) add onto them for its own profit. If the required discount points for 10% interest are 2, the lender might quote you 2.5 or 3. The extra is an **overage to the lender** that is taken as additional fee income, just like the garbage fees. If you don't fully understand discount points right now, don't worry. Just remember that they are a cost, and a potential source of fee income to the lender. You will get a short course on rate pricing later, when we cover rates, points, and lock-ins.

So, the lender gets 1% to originate the loan and in all probability some type of overage on the discount, usually from 0.25% to 2% or more. On a $50,000 loan a 1% origination fee and a 0.25% overage on the discount equal $625. If the lender gets a 1% overage on the discount, then it gets $1,000. If one loan office averages 15 to 30 loan closings per month, that activity can bring in $10,000 to $30,000 in fee income. Even after expenses, we can be talking about a lot of money. And the average loan today is well over the $50,000 we used as an example. But we're not through yet.

Remember the *garbage* fees? Our friend, the lender, is still devising ways to add to income. Now, let me add that some of these garbage fees are legitimate and necessary. One of the more common fees is called the *tax service fee.* This one-time fee pays a specialized servicing company to ensure that the taxes and insurance on each loan are paid each year when they come due. If you do not want your taxes and/or insurance escrowed, it is possible to have the escrow waived. The loan cannot be over a certain LTV, and you will have to pay .125 to .50 in extra points. But, you will still have to pay the tax service fee because most lender's contracts with these companies specify the company will get a fee for all loans closed. Some lenders may charge for next-day delivery (e.g., Federal Express™) of documents in connection with the loan. This is often a small price to pay for expediting your loan. Today, more lenders and closing agents are using the Internet, and actually e-mailing the closing packages. This will be covered when we talk about the Internet as a tool for obtaining a mortgage. However, no one has ever accused mortgage lenders of not being profit-oriented. Some of these fees can strain the imagination.

The lender is offering a service for which it collects a fee of at least 1%, and usually more. Then, after you have applied for this loan, or service, the lender begins to hit you with things like application, processing, underwriting, commitment, document preparation, and closing fees. Any or all of these fees can range from $50 to $500. Added to the origination fees of those 15 to 30 loans per month, you can see that the temptation is often too great for the lender to resist. Wouldn't it be simpler just to add them into the discount points? Yes, and some do. But, look at it from a marketing perspective: Doesn't 10% with 1% discount sound like a much better deal than 1.5% or 2% discount points? It's easier for the lender to set the hook and then reel you in slowly. Always ask about the lender's fees, why they are charged and if they are non-refundable, and compare them with other lenders' fees before making final loan application, and paying any money.

In the real estate market where I worked there was a lender who used to take a loan application, process it completely, and then—when it was ready to be submitted to the underwriter—call the buyers and tell them that they would have to pay the 1% origination fee before submission as a commitment fee. Nonrefundable. Even if the loan was denied. As if this weren't bad enough, the lender made a practice of never disclosing this requirement to the borrower at application. How many people would complete the application if they knew it would cost them 1% just to find out if they can get the loan? The lender was using an unethical method (not disclosing the collection of the fee at time of application) to collect a normal fee. To understand the lender's perspective on this maneuver, let's look at their rationale.

The Cost of Doing Business

The borrower makes application and pays for the appraisal and credit report (for which the lender will be billed). Then the lender begins to process the loan. A file is set up, all of the verifications are mailed out, telephone calls are made, documents are received and checked for accuracy, all disclosure requirements must be checked, and, when all the necessary information is received, the loan is sent to the underwriter for approval or rejection. All of this work requires a large number of hours from personnel who expect to be paid as well as the expense of forms, office space, mail, and telephone—not to mention the cost of underwriters and the central office. If the borrower decides not to buy the house, or for whatever reason does not close the loan, what has the lender got to show for it? Probably no more than the cash to pay the appraisal and credit report bills. If the lender added some additional fee income into the costs, their loss would be less.

Even if the patient dies, the doctor gets paid. Why not the lender? I am not suggesting that anyone should have to die in the transaction, although that thought has certainly crossed the minds of many disgruntled participants. The reason very few lenders collect fees before closing is that most loans will close, and the lender will collect its fee, and more. And, the competition won't allow it. Our local lender who tried to collect the origination fee at submission without prior disclosure came under intense criticism. Realtors stopped sending business to this lender, who had to stop collecting its commitment fee because none of the other lenders in the area did. It's whatever the market will bear.

If a lender has an extremely low rate, or a special loan that everyone wants, then it may be able to add a premium to the cost. Back when 30-year fixed rates were 13%, the mortgage company where I worked had an adjustable rate mortgage that started at 9.75% with 1 + 2.75 points. People were eager to get it. A rate with 3.75% in points didn't slow them down one bit. Today that may be different.

For an average loan amount of $70,000 with a 1% origination fee, a 1.5% discount (with 0.5% being an overage to the lender), and $150 in garbage fees, what is the gross income per month to a lender that closes 20 loans? That would be an average of $1,400,000 in loans per month. That value times 1.5% in fee income (1% + 0.5%), not counting the minimum required discount, equals $21,000, plus $3,000 in garbage fees equals $24,000. Take a mortgage lender with five offices and you can see why there is competition for loans.

Selling And Servicing Your Loan   It's Not That We Don't Like You, But . . .

Why do lenders sell loans and how do they make money from them? So far, we have seen that the fee income by time of closing can be significant. After that, the lender is stuck with a thick folder of papers, a note that says the borrower owes it money, and a mortgage that says the property secures that debt. The lender also has its money tied up in a loan that may or may not earn it money, depending on whether the interest rate charged is torpedoed by rising rates over a sustained period of time. Remember what happened to the thrifts that got caught with a portfolio of low-interest loans in a rising market in the early 1980s? So do the lenders of today. Consequently, these lenders have adopted a method not only to solve their immediate problem, but also to make still more money off of the loan. As a result, borrowers are subjected to a big-business approach to mortgage lending.

The lender to whom you make your payments is said to **service the loan.** That is, it takes care of the day-to-day, month-to-month, year-to-year management of the loan. Collecting the payments, crediting the interest and principal, making sure the taxes and insurance are paid, monitoring delinquent accounts, adjusting payments and sending new payment notices on adjustable rate loans and changes in escrow payments, and passing on the principal and interest payments after deducting their servicing fee—all of these are what lenders dream of in their sleep. The questions arise: Where are the principal and interest passed, and What servicing fee? This is where the lender and the secondary market come together.

When a lender quotes an interest rate of, let's say, 10%, that rate is a gross interest rate that includes a **servicing fee** built into it. The actual interest rate yield required by the investors in the secondary market will be less. For example, the required rate may be 9.75% and the lender adds in 0.25% for a **servicing fee.** This fee pays the servicing lender for all the things I just noted. Based on 0.25% of the principal balance and collected out of each month's payment, it doesn't seem to be a lot of money. And by itself it isn't. But remember all of those other loans that the lender is closing, and you can see that after a while the servicing income can become substantial. It is also reliable, as long as borrowers don't pay off their loans too quickly. As a matter of fact, lenders recognize that most loans will be paid off early, and they adjust for that possibility.

Servicing fees are not all the same. They range from as little as 0.25% to 0.625%, and in some instances even higher. Obviously, the higher the fee added to the secondary market's required yield, the higher the final interest rate charged to the borrower, and that rate may not be competitive in the market. But the market does not normally set what the fee will be; it is often set by the secondary market investors. They are the ones who buy the loans.

The lender that has completed and closed the loan has a big hole in its pocketbook. Several $100,000 loans can use up your cash very quickly. Not only that, but also the money tied up in the loan cannot be used again until the loan is paid off. The lender must keep generating sufficient cash, or it will be out of the loan-making business. It has closed the loan and taken all the fee income that can be squeezed out, so the lender gets rid of it. The loan is sold to someone else, the Secondary Market.

Although the originating lender sells the loan, the borrower may continue to make payments to this lender. In this case, it has retained the right to service the loan for the purchasing investor, and to receive the servicing fee income. Often the originating lender will sell not only the loan, but also the servicing. That means, the loan actually has two parts that can be sold, the note and the servicing. The note may be sold to FNMA or securitized by other means. The servicing can be sold multiple times to different lenders while the note never moves. A small caveat here: If your loan servicing is sold, you will receive a "Goodbye" letter from your current lender and a "Hello" letter from the new one. If you receive a "Hello" letter telling you to start sending your payments to a new address without a notice (Goodbye) from your current lender, call your current lender to confirm the sale of the servicing on your loan before making any payments. There are scams out there. The originator will receive a premium price for this **servicing released loan,** which means more profit for the originator. This is why it is not unusual for a borrower to end up making payments to another lender. The originating lender then has that money free again to make more loans that can be sold.

Because of the confusion brought on by the sale of servicing, the federal government now requires that all loan applicants be given a disclosure called, appropriately enough, the *Mortgage Servicing Transfer Disclosure* (see the Appendix for a copy of this form). My state actually has a disclosure telling you the lender must give you the disclosure.

The significance of the secondary market is that it creates a place where lenders can sell and buy mortgage loans on a regional, national, and even international basis. This market helps to move money from areas where there is excess cash to areas where there is little. It also helps to relieve lenders of the burden of carrying portfolios of loans with potentially volatile interest rates, frees up the lender's cash, and, most importantly, provides a vast and reliable source of money for mortgage loans. (Remember my purchasers who could not get a loan at the S&L because there was no money?) Another benefit, for the borrower, is that the more investors there are competing for the pool of loans, the more they will aggressively price their purchases, which can mean lower rates for the borrower. Conversely, if loans are flooding the market, the secondary market investors can be more selective and less aggressive. Supply and demand. Let us consider how the secondary market affects the borrower's ability to qualify for the loan.

THE SECONDARY MARKET UNDERWRITING GUIDELINES
Cash-CREDIT-Income-Value

When a lender sells loans to an investor in the secondary market, those loans must meet certain minimum standards, or guidelines. If they don't, then the investor won't buy them. As a result, the lender is stuck with unsalable loans, which makes the lender very unhappy. To remedy this situation, the lender will process each loan according to the guidelines specified by the investor to which they will be selling the loan in the secondary market.

All secondary market guidelines are based, in one form or another, on those established by Fannie Mae and Freddie Mac, the kingpins of the secondary market. (With Federal Housing Administration—FHA—and Veterans Administration—VA—loans there are some differences, but the underlying concepts are the same.) These guidelines evolve, based on the constantly changing mortgage industry. These changes, in themselves, can cause mortgage lenders to feel as though they were becoming mentally unglued. But, the basic tenets have remained essentially unchanged.

Fannie Mae and Freddie Mac each publish volumes of guidelines covering everything from qualifying to closing to selling the loans. These form the core of what are known as **conforming guidelines,** or those guidelines that conform to conventional Fannie Mae and Freddie Mac rules. Other investors in the secondary market will adapt one or both, or parts of both sets of guidelines. If the guidelines are outside of the standards set by Fannie and Freddie, then they are called **nonconforming** guidelines.

A good example of a conforming vs. nonconforming guideline is the permissible loan amount. Fannie and Freddie set the maximum loan amounts that they will buy; these are adjusted periodically based on increases, or decreases, in the cost of housing. Any loan amount over that limit is considered nonconforming, and they will not buy it. (Remember, these amounts can change yearly. In 1990 the maximum conforming loan was $187,450. As of the year 2000, the maximum was $252,700 for a single family home. In 2001 this way raised to $275,000. See Chapter 15.) This nonconforming, or "jumbo" loan, as it is called because it exceeds the conforming limits, will then be marketed to other investors who specialize in "jumbos." These investors' guidelines will often be similar to the standard secondary market guidelines with the exception of loan amount.

The foundation of all loan guidelines, and hence all loan decisions, are based on four areas of the loan that the lender must consider:

1. Cash
2. Credit
3. Income (read "income and employment")
4. Appraised value of the property

Meet the test of each, and you qualify. Flunk one, and you may be rejected. A loan application may be strong enough in one area to compensate for a deficiency in another. This possibility will vary by lender, depending on the rigidity of the guidelines of the investors to whom they sell their loans. Regardless of the individual lender's quirks, all criteria are based on the Fannie Mae-Freddie Mac guidelines. Let's look at these guidelines and how they relate to the borrower's ability to repay the loan.

Cash   Where Did It Come from, and Prove It's Yours

The borrower must have enough cash to buy the house and close the loan. I don't think anyone would argue with that logic. The lender wants to know several things about this cash. To get this information, the lender will verify the borrower's cash and other liquid assets. Today, something called **Alternate Documentation** is used. Depending on the loan, the lender will request the borrower's one or two most recent monthly statements for the accounts holding the assets. They must have all pages, even if one has nothing on it. A statement with the last page missing will raise concerns that there may be something on that page, such as an undisclosed debt. Otherwise, and sometimes instead of Alternate Documentation, the lender will send an industry-wide standard form called a **Verification of Deposit** or **VOD** (see Appendix) to the bank, credit union, stockbroker, and so on to be filled out by that depository and then returned to the lender. This VOD will tell the lender several things about the borrowers and their money:

1. The kinds of accounts you have—savings, checking . . .
2. The account number
3. The current balance
4. The average balance over the past two months
5. The opening date of the account
6. Any outstanding loans that the borrower has with the bank

The first three are simple to understand; it's the last three that can get you into trouble without your even knowing it. For example, say that you have two accounts, checking and savings. In the checking account you have a current balance of $2,000 and an average balance for the past two months of $1,500. No problem. An increase of $500 is not abnormal. But, let's say that the savings account was opened 30 days ago and $2,000 is the average since the account was opened. Why is this a problem? Lenders take a very dim view of new money. They want to know where the money was before you put it into that account. If you don't tell them, and prove it's your money, they won't count those funds toward the cash needed to close. (Remember the Golden Rule of Lending?) Why?

First, these seemingly paranoid lenders want to make sure that you did not borrow the money to purchase the property, incurring a debt that you have not told them of. If you borrow money, it must be borrowed on a secured basis. That is, you can get it by borrowing against a car, stock, other real estate—but it cannot be borrowed in an unsecured manner such as a personal note, except on certain loans such as VA. In addition, the debt you create will be counted against you in the qualifying process. Money borrowed against a retirement account, such as a 401K, that allows you to pay it back in the form of a loan is allowed, but some loans will count that debt for qualifying and others do not. This seems to change yearly. Check with your lender.

Second, they want to make sure that the money in the bank really is your money and does not belong to someone else. And you have to prove it in writing. One of the cardinal rules of the industry is, "If it's in writing, it's true. If it's not in writing, it does not exist." How do you prove that the money really is yours? It depends on where the money did come from. If you transferred it from another account, just give the lender a copy of the last statement from that account. If you sold some stock, get a copy of the statement of sale and proceeds. Sell a house? Get a copy of the closing statement (HUD 1) to show the net proceeds to you. Borrow it? A copy of the note from the lender showing that it is secured. Had it hidden under your mattress for the past five years because you didn't want your spouse to find it and spend it? Don't laugh; this is more common than people might think.

I have had borrowers who actually did save their money in their mattress, and others who put it in tin cans that they buried in the backyard. They were all honest, hard-working people who just did not trust banks. Proving that the money is yours can be tough. One Realtor had the borrower make photocopies of the money. Never mind that making copies of U.S. currency is absolutely illegal, which, incidentally, is not acceptable to the lender. The best that you can do is open a bank account where the lender can verify the money, and hope that you do not get an underwriter who is having a bad day. FHA loans will accept "cash on hand" as long as the borrower puts it into some type of account where it can be seen and the borrower can show how the money was saved. But $100,000 held by a 30-year-old bricklayer might be a tough sell.

If the borrowers do not have sufficient cash at the time they make application, but will be able to save it prior to closing, a lender will give them an approval subject to verifying the funds and showing how it was saved. Copies of bank statements showing the money going into the account and copies of the source, such as paystubs are the alternate documentation verifications. It must make sense that the borrower can save the money needed in the time prior to closing. A letter to the lender explaining how the money will be saved is a good idea, and some lenders require it.

Lease-purchase is a way of taking possession of the property and then accumulating the cash necessary for the down payment. It has become more common, especially in areas where properties are not selling quickly. It works like this: The potential purchaser offers to lease the property from the seller for a given period of time. The leaseholder has the option to purchase the property at a previously agreed upon price at any time during the rental period. Part of the rent paid to the seller is to be considered as cash toward the down payment. Both the seller and the purchaser benefit. The seller gets rent to cover the mortgage, and the eventual sale of the property, instead of having to continue paying the mortgage while waiting for the house to sell. The purchaser, who does not have enough cash to receive a loan, gets to move into the house and set aside the down payment as part of the rent. This is a very good way for buyers and sellers to get together in a slow market, or when the buyer has little cash but is otherwise qualified. There is just one potential problem that you need to consider.

If part of the rent is to be used as cash to purchase the property, only that portion above the normal market rent can be used. Let us suppose that a monthly rent of $800 has been set. You would like $200 of that to go toward the purchase. If the market rent is $600, there is no problem. If the market rent is $700, then only $100 can be used. How do you find the market rent for the property? You can talk to agents who specialize in renting similar properties, or you can get an appraiser to tell you. The lender will use an appraiser to determine the fair market rent when you make loan application.

To ensure that the portion of the rent set aside for the purchase meets the guidelines, the lender will have the appraiser do a Comparable Rent Schedule, by comparing the rent of the subject property to the rent of other similar properties. Basically, you will have to pay that amount you want to use toward the purchase above what you would normally have paid as rent. So, in our example, if the market rent is $800, you would have to pay $1,000 in order to get $200 per month credited toward the purchase.

The Gift

What if your Uncle Joe gave you some money? This gift may or may not be a problem. First, we have to define the source of this gift. Relatives are the best, and usual, source. Close friends aren't bad if you can show a demonstrated long and close relationship. Realtors and sellers are a no-no (except for certain closing costs that the seller and/or Realtor can pay. We will get to that shortly). Anyone with a financial interest in the transaction is not acceptable as a source for any of the money required for the down payment. Assuming that Uncle Joe really is your uncle, and he really did give you the money, what's next?

He will need to give the lender a **gift letter** (see Appendix) that states why he is giving you the money, how much he is giving you, and, most importantly, that no repayment is expected or implied. All the money may not be intended for the purchase. Part of it may be to pay off debts or to buy furniture. That's fine. He just needs to say that in the letter. And (Uncle Joe will love this) Fannie Mae and most investors will require that he show that he has **the resources to give you the gift.** This is done by a copy of the canceled gift check and a copy of the borrower's bank statement showing the funds in their account. The bank can print out the statement if there is not enough time to wait for it. If it is funds to be given at closing, it is best to have it in certified funds (some states require all funds to be cash or certified). A copy of the check with the borrower's and donor's names must be in the closing file. FHA has become stricter about gifts because of fraud. They require the donor to show where the funds originated. If the donor borrowed the funds, that person must provide a copy of the note proving they are the borrower and not *our* borrower.

Uncle Joe says that he wouldn't be caught dead giving them that information. Then Fannie Mae, or any other secondary market investor, says that she doesn't care—if he won't give the information, she won't buy the loan. She has hundreds of thousands of other borrowers who want to do loans, why worry about one? And you will have to accept this attitude. This type of confrontation drives loan officers to distraction. They are stuck in the middle between an intransigent Uncle Joe, who just wants to help his relative buy a house, and Fannie Mae, the monolithic corporation that lives by the rules. One would hope there must be a good reason for all this fuss. And, in most instances, there is.

When you get the money, **the lender wants to make sure that it is not a loan, but a true gift.** If it were a loan, then the debt might keep you from qualifying, aside from the fact that the loan would probably be unsecured. If the transaction were stated as a gift when in fact it was a loan, and you ultimately defaulted on the mortgage because of excess debt, you would be in big trouble not only with the lender and the investor, but also because you would have committed fraud to obtain the loan. Obviously, if no one ever finds out, then you have no problem. But, by reprocessing the loan after it closes, as a quality control measure, lenders can find out. They will do this to a certain percentage of the loans that are bought by the secondary market not only to ensure that borrowers are not giving false information, but also to ensure that the lender is giving reliable documentation. (All investors require the lender to have a quality control program.) It is a sign of the times when lenders who are fighting for their share of the market will make loans by altering the documentation to make a loan fit the guidelines. Imagine the secondary market investors' surprise when they find a debt that wasn't supposed to be there, and your written word stating that there is no such debt. It is not a good idea to lie on a loan application. Big Brother is watching.

Because the lender wants to make sure that the gift donor has the ability to give you the money, the lender requires the documentation we discussed earlier. While the system may not be perfect, showing that the donor has the money will at least make it more plausible that he will in fact give you the gift. Verifications are a picture of the borrower and the property at a given time. Lenders understand that things can change, but they also know that most borrowers recognize they must have the cash to close, and will be less likely to spend it before closing.

Now that we have been through all this, you are probably wondering, "Is a gift worth the trouble?" The answer is, absolutely. The process just sounds complicated. A good lender will walk you through it without a hitch. And, the more money you have available, the easier it will be to get the loan and buy more house. As a matter of fact, more loans are made with gifts than you might imagine.

Playing Games—Trying to Beat the Rules

Whenever people are using someone else's money, they quickly figure out ways to get around the rules. People discovered that if you get the money two or three months before you apply for the loan, then the account statement or VOD will show an average balance in line with the current balance with no unexplainable large deposits, and suddenly you no longer need gift letters—or angry uncles. This action is called *seasoning the money* and it can work, in some instances. Anticipating this ploy, some lenders, and some types of loans may require that borrowers submit copies of their bank statements as far back as three to six months. Or, if there is an unusually large amount of money that would not normally be associated with the borrower's income, then the borrower may be asked to show how it was accumulated. It's part of the game, a bit like roulette. You pay your money and you take your chance. The longer you have held the money, the better the chance you will win the game.

While we are on the subject of your money, you should always give the lender the number of your check for the earnest money on a purchase contract. When the lender gets a copy of your bank statement showing the check clearing the lender will know to add it to the cash needed for closing. Otherwise, the borrower may not get credit for that cash.

Is It Enough?

Once it is established that the borrower has money in the bank and that it was not stolen, the question arises of just how much money is actually needed. On Fannie, Freddie, or any conventional loans, **the borrower must have enough verified cash** to do the following:

1. Pay the down payment on the loan.
2. Pay all required closing costs associated with the purchase of the property and the loan closing.
3. Cover the equivalent of two months' house payments above and beyond the down payment and closing costs. This requirement is unrelated to how much the borrower has for the down payment. This is called the *reserve,* and it is required because everyone will need money for miscellaneous expenses when they move into a new house, like moving costs, drapes, utility deposits, food, and the first month's house payment. With computer underwriting, strong borrowers may not be required to show reserves or to show the liquidation of any assets, such as stocks, being used for funds to close. This is discussed in the credit section.
4. When the cash down payment is less than 20% of the total purchase, 5% of the cash must come from the bor-

rower's own resources. That is, the borrower cannot get that 5% in a gift. If the cash down is 20% or more, then the 5% rule does not apply (at least, not at the time this was written). There will be some exceptions to this rule, depending on the secondary market investor and the loan type, such as F.H.A. and V.A.

And remember, all of this must be verified in writing before the lender will approve the loan. Government loans have slightly different requirements, which we will cover when we discuss FHA and VA. Fannie and Freddie now have programs to help the cash challenged, who otherwise meet all the requirements, which only require 3% with no reserves and all the money can be a gift. We will cover it when we discuss loan types.

Let the Seller Pay It

Sometimes, or more often than sometimes, the borrower does not have enough money to pay the down payment plus the closing costs and show two months' worth of payments. And the buyer can't get a gift. If it is so close that it's just a matter of not having enough to cover all the closing costs, there is another source. Let the seller pay it. As in everything else, there are certain rules, but in this case Fannie and Freddie and almost all investors have identical, unequivocal guidelines. These, like everything else in mortgage lending, are subject to change at any time. What these rules say is that there are certain costs that the seller, or Realtor, or lender, can pay. And there are certain costs that only the borrower can pay. The rules also specify how much can be paid.

Prepaid items cannot be paid by the seller on some loans, and they can on others. This is another area that can change back and forth. Check with your lender to find out what is allowed. We will cover these in detail later, but they are:

1. Prepaid interest (the house payment for the month in which you close)
2. Homeowner's insurance (first year's premium and escrows)
3. Real estate tax escrows
4. Mortgage insurance escrows (if the loan requires them)

Everything else is fair game—with one exception. Depending on the Loan-to-Value (LTV) ratio, or how much cash the borrower puts down, **only a certain percentage of the value of the property can be paid as closing costs by someone other than the borrower.** On conventional loans, the maximums are:

1.   95% LTV (or less than 10% down) = maximum of 5% of value. Fannie and Freddie's rule says 3%, but they will allow some lenders to go to 5% if that lender has proven it takes good loans.

2.   90% LTV (10% or more down) = maximum of 6% of value

3.   75% LTV = some loans will allow up to 9% of the value

Value is the lesser of the sales price or the appraised value. When we get to FHA and VA, you will find that these percentages are quite different.

It is not unusual in many markets to ask the sellers to pay some points, and with the increasing cost of housing it is becoming more acceptable to ask them to pay some of the other costs as well. Depending on what the sellers' bottom line is, they may be more than willing to pay in order to make the deal work.

For example, the sellers are asking $100,000, but will take $97,000. If you offer them full price and ask them to pay $3,000 in closing costs, they will get what they wanted, and the house sells. If the house sells and everybody is happy, then it is a win-win situation. All you have to do is convince the sellers that they are winning by paying $3,000 of the borrower's closing costs. Here a good Realtor and lender are invaluable. They can provide the information and the negotiating expertise that make the difference between dead contracts and live ones.

Employer paid costs, usually associated with relocation, are not normally subject to the 3%/6% rule. The only time there may be a problem is when the employer advances the employee/borrower the equity in her present home and makes it subject to repayment. This creates a debt. Also, if the employer agrees to take over the payments on the house, the employer must state that the borrower will not be liable in the future.

Some lenders will offer **a higher interest rate with no points** called **Premium Pricing.** Because the borrower is paying a rate higher than the market rate, not only do they not pay any points, the lender actually pays them points which are used to pay closing costs. The higher the rate, the higher the "points" available to pay closing costs. These will vary day-to-day depending on the market. The company can do this because of the large premium that the secondary market will pay for this above-market interest rate.

The last question on the verification of deposit form asks if the borrower has any outstanding loans with that depository. In most instances, borrowers will tell the lender about all of their debts, but some borrowers actually believe that if the lender doesn't know about them, it won't find out about them. Not only will the bank tell the lender about these debts, but it will also tell the credit bureau, and the debts will show up on the credit report—which leads nicely into our next area of qualification.

CREDIT   The Single Most Important Part of the Loan Application

Credit is *now the single most important part of a loan application.* This cannot be repeated too many times. Income and assets, while important, can diminish in importance when the borrower's credit is excellent. If the credit is poor, income and assets may not be able to compensate. And, if they do make a difference, it is often to qualify for an alternate type of loan, such as a "subprime" loan. I will discuss subprime in the sections on loans and lenders. The mortgage industry now uses a system of computer-based programs that assign every borrower a **CREDIT SCORE.** These scores are the benchmarks upon which the loan process now revolves. I cannot stress strongly enough how important it is to maintain good credit, and good credit scores. That said, let's jump into the rapidly evolving world of consumer credit.

Credit reports are called *"tri-merged" reports* because they are pulled from three separate credit repositories. The main repositories are Equifax, TransUnion, and Experion. You will normally receive three credit scores, one from each repository. Because creditors do not always report to all three, and to make sure the lender gets all available credit, they use the tri-merged report. An *"in-file" report* is pulled from a single repository and a large amount of a borrower's credit can be missing, giving an inaccurate picture.

These repositories each assign a credit score based on many factors. Until recently, the borrower was not told the actual reasons for the scores. But, because of mounting criticism, this is changing. Fannie and Freddie have announced they are developing their own credit scoring software, meaning much of the criteria will be refined over the next several years. However, most lenders know the basic reasons for good to bad credit. Some of the things that influence credit are.

1. **Too much open credit.** A large number of credit cards, even if you make the payments on time or pay them off in full each month, has the ability to increase your debt quickly if their balances are run up. What I always recommend to my borrowers is that they only need one or two cards. These should be used for emergencies and purchases where a card is needed, such as catalog ordering. Close all other accounts by calling and following up with a written request. Request the creditor to send you written confirmation that the account is closed. If you have been a good customer, they do not want to lose you, so sometimes they will ignore your request and keep the account open, assuming that down the road when you discover it is still open you will decide to keep it. Closing the account with a balance does not mean you have to pay it off in full at that time. You will continue to receive monthly bills until you pay off the balance. **Pay your debts on time,** and try not to keep large balances.

2. **Too much debt.** Even if you can handle all the payments, the computer will look at the total of payments and balances and think "these people have too much debt." Only borrow what is necessary and pay it off as quickly as possible. A past history of paying off debts does help your credit.

3. **Late payments.** Late payments are reported as 30, 60, or 90+ days late. They normally will show on the right side of the report under one of three columns representing the above. They can also be expressed as $30 = I \times 2$, $60 = I \times 3$, $90 = I \times 4$, Over 90 as $I \times 5$ (up to 9). The "I" means it is an "Installment" debt. If it is a revolving debt (credit card, line of credit) it would have an "R" instead of an "I." The more late payments, the worse the credit score. Recent lates will lower the score quickly, and by leaps. Old lates will cause less damage as they recede into the past. Derogatory credit can remain on your report, depending on the creditor and the type of bad credit, from

three to 10 years. (The guidelines in the past required a written explanation for any late payments showing on the report. This is no longer strictly true. Computer underwriting will say if a written explanation is needed. Usually only marginal credit cases or something such as bankruptcy will require an explanation.) The longer the late payment, such as 90 days, the faster the score will come down. And, it does not make a difference if it is a mistake, if a late payment shows on the report the score will come down until it is removed. My advice is very simple: **Never borrow what you do not need. Never borrow more than you need. Never make a late payment.**

4. **A large number of recent (past three to twelve months) applications for credit.** These will show up as **"Inquiries"** on your report. If you are shopping for a car, every time you go into a dealer they will try to get your name so they can run a report. Amazingly, they do not need your consent to do this. I have seen reports with over 10 inquiries, all coming from car dealers. The assumption is that if you have applied for credit, then you must have increased your debt, or are attempting to increase it. Because inquiries will stay on your report for six to 12 months (Fannie now wants all inquiries to remain on your report for 12 months), try to avoid applying for too much credit, or just having your credit checked, in any 12 month period, especially if you know you will be applying for a mortgage. When you are talking to a lender about a loan, do not let them pull your credit report unless you are reasonably certain you are going to use them. Having a couple lenders pull your report within a short time of each other will not lower your score as long as you make application within a few weeks. If you are talking to more than three lenders, just don't let all of them pull reports. One report will tell you what you need to know. And, just because that lender pulled your report does not mean you have to use them.

5. **Collections and/or Judgments.** Pretty self-explanatory. If you do not make your payments, the creditor will use all legal means to make you pay. And you will pay with more than just your money. These things will devastate credit. I have had any number of borrowers with

collections or judgments placed against them because they refused to pay "out of principle." The computer does not know, or care, if you were right or wrong. If you are heading towards this type of credit problem, get with the creditor to try and work out an acceptable repayment plan that does not involve reporting derogatory credit.

6. **Bankruptcy.** You will have low credit scores for at least two years after date of discharge. DO NOT make any late payments after being discharged. Obtain a couple sources of low-to-moderate credit and pay them on time. Further into this chapter I will discuss bankruptcy and exactly how it affects your ability to obtain a mortgage.

These are some of the more common causes of low credit scores. Things that can raise scores include avoiding all the above. I had a borrower who is a doctor with excellent credit. There were no lates or any other derogatory credit showing at any time. But, their credit scores were just average when I had expected them to be very high. The reason was that between the doctor and his wife they had about 10 credit cards, and most of those did not have balances. Watch your credit. It takes work to keep it good, and it is very easy to make it bad.

One more cause of low credit scores has nothing to do with the borrower, but with the system. A case in point. I had a borrower who told me he had excellent credit, never made a late payment and only had two current debts, one being a credit card he paid off each month. His report was an entirely different matter, or shall we say an entirely different person. It showed eight debts, including two judgments and three collections. The credit scores were almost nonexistent. Someone else had used his name and social security number to run up large debts, and then walked away. My borrower did not know about them because the other "him" had used a different address in another state, so the bills and notices went to the fictitious address. I could not use computer underwriting because of the low scores. It is the borrower's responsibility to make sure the credit reporting agencies and repositories know it is wrong and to have them correct it. And, this is important, until he gets the credit corrected, and then usually 30 to 90 days after that, the scores will not change. Creditors can be very slow to change incorrect information and send it to the repositories. This borrower was persistent and supplied the creditors, and repositories, with the information necessary to have all the fraudulent information removed. It was fixed in three weeks. The credit scores did not change for 45 days afterward. To protect yourself, you can request a "fraud alert" to be put into your credit file. This will cause the credit reporting agencies to confirm with you any attempt to use your name and social security number to obtain credit before the credit will be approved. I hope that the credit agencies will change the way they do business and speed up the process. With the huge change in how we now approach credit, I cannot imagine this not being corrected in the not-too-distant future.

Consumer credit counseling agencies are available to help people who have gotten too far into debt, or feel they need help before they go over the edge. These agencies will negotiate with your creditors for payments and/or lower rates you can afford to pay. Then, you must make one payment to the agency each month and they pay the creditors. This is an excellent way to correct your credit problems, but there are several things that you must keep in mind.

When the agency negotiates a lower-than-required payment with the creditors, the creditors may agree, but they may also show the payment as late until it becomes current (based on the original higher payment). This, obviously, does nothing to help your credit. Ask the agency how each creditor will report the negotiated payment.

If you are still in the program when you apply for a mortgage, there are various rules depending on the type of loan for which you are applying. Some loans, such as F.H.A. and V.A., will look favorably on it as long as your credit is good. They will require that you have been in the counseling for a minimum period of time. If you had bad credit going into counseling, the time period could be up to a year or longer. If you did it as a preventative measure, Fannie and Freddie will normally require that you be out of counseling for at least a year. A letter from the agency will be required detailing to whom payments are being (or were being) made and your payment history to the agency. Other loans consider being in consumer counseling as a kissing cousin of bankruptcy. These loans will not consider you until you have been out of counseling a minimum of two years or longer.

I dealt with one couple who exemplified what not to do in making mortgage payments. They owned a home on which they had been making payments for over three years. They were transferred, and contracted to buy a new home. The mortgage payment verification showed that out of their past 12 payments, 11 were received 16 to 30 days late. Always giving the borrower the benefit of the doubt, I asked them to explain. It was very simple, really. They believed in using "other people's" money (their words). So they waited until the last minute to give it to them. This is not a good answer. The loan was denied, even though they could easily have made their payments on time each month. Lenders do not want to make loans to people who habitually make late payments. These particular borrowers told me that the lender was getting a late fee, so the lender was making more money out of the loan anyway. This is not usually true.

The lender may want to sell the loan to an investor in the secondary market, which expects to receive its interest and principal payment on a certain date every month. If the originating lender retains the servicing rights to the loan, it is responsible for getting the payments to the investor on time, and will take money from its own account to make sure that these payments are made, even if they have not been received from the borrower. In combination with using its own money and then having to send notices and keep track of the delinquency, the servicing lender will use up the late fee. On top of that, lenders who originate and service loans do not want a high rate of defaults (a loan is technically in default the minute the payment is past due) and foreclosures. When the lender deals with an investor in the secondary market, one of the most important things that the investor considers, before buying the originating lender's loans, is the ratio of loans in default and foreclosure on the lender's books. If the ratio is higher than the average, the investor might infer that the lender does not use due care in underwriting and servicing its loans. They may decline to buy loans from that lender, or not pay competitive prices. This means that the lender either has one less source to which it can sell loans, or may not be able to give as low an interest rate. Either of these, obviously, can affect the interest rate that borrowers are able to get for their mortgage. Interest rates aren't as simple as you thought, are they?

Many people have late payments that they never knew existed. They find out only when they apply for a mortgage that a payment to Visa™ three years ago was reported late. The standard answer is that they do not know why it was late, but it must have been delayed in the mail. If there is derogatory credit showing on your report, you may be required to give a written explanation. Computer underwriting will specify if it is necessary. If the loan is not underwritten by computer, then you will have to provide an acceptable explanation. Human underwriters are not programmed to waive guideline requirements.

Regardless of the reason for the late payment and how embarrassing it is to the borrower, it does help to tell the truth, even when it is painful. All information given to a lender is confidential, and sometimes a hopeless case can turn out differently from what it would seem.

Even a Lender Has a Heart—When Bad Credit Can Be Forgiven

A woman applied to refinance her residence. She also had a rental property on which she had a mortgage. Her mortgage verifications on both properties showed 22 late payments in the past 24 months. An inexperienced lender would assume that her application had no chance whatsoever. In this case, a few additional questions made all the difference.

When asked to explain, she told a story that truly made the underwriter cry. Her husband and three children had been in a car wreck in which the husband was killed and the children were seriously injured. The children were in the hospital for a long time, and then required extensive rehabilitation. They literally had to learn to walk and talk again. The borrower's medical insurance had run out long before all the hospital and therapy bills were paid. Knowing that she could not make all her payments every month, she made arrangements with her creditors to pay medical bills one month and mortgages the next. Her lender at that time accepted this plan as long as none of the payments was more than 30 days late, and a letter to this effect was put in her file. By the time she came to me for refinancing, she had paid off all the medical bills and had begun to make her mortgage payments on time. We made the loan to her.

This was an extraordinary event over which the borrower had little or no control, and it was unlikely to re-occur. The borrower did all the right things to help maintain her credit. She contacted her creditors before her problem got out of hand and worked out a plan to ensure the payments were made. No reputable lenders want to foreclose on a mortgage. They will go to great lengths to help the borrower if the borrower works with them.

This example would normally not qualify for computer

underwriting because the credit scores would be too low and, in fact, it was done in the days when humans made the decision. To be approved today, without computer underwriting, that borrower would need to fit within all qualifying standards. Such as not exceeding qualifying ratios and having sufficient cash reserves. Even then, some underwriters and mortgage companies may not want to approve her. This is why the loan officer should know everything before taking the loan application. If there is a doubt about the loan being approved, the loan officer can run it by the underwriter first. At least, that is what the loan officer should do.

CREDIT SCORES

Now that I have sufficiently forewarned you about how credit scores can be influenced, let's look at the scores themselves. Fannie and Freddie have set a benchmark score that is considered the base, or lowest acceptable score. It is **620.** Don't ask why this particular number. I assume it has something to do with the scoring program itself. As I noted earlier, you should receive three separate scores from each of the credit repositories. I have rarely seen two of them with the same number. The computer programs used by each repository are different (Beacon, Empirica, and FICO). Also, as mentioned earlier, each repository does not always receive information on all of your credit. When one of the repositories does not have enough information on you, it may not issue a score. When you have *three scores,* the middle one is used. If you only have *two scores,* the lowest one is used. If you have *no scores,* I will discuss that in a minute. The higher above 620 the easier it is to get a computer approval. If the scores are over 700, it is very easy. From 750 to over 800, having a pulse would just about be the only requirement. The farther your scores are below 620, the harder it will be to get a computer approval and to exceed any of the guidelines. But, there are loans (FHA, VA, some sub-prime loans) that do not have a given base score. So, there is always an alternative. On the opposite end, there are certain loans that require higher base scores, such as the Flexible Alternative loan. I will discuss these later.

Let me give some examples of how scores affect approval. A self-employed borrower would normally be required to submit the past two years federal tax returns and a year-to-date profit and loss statement. If they are incorporated, the corporate returns would be required. A score in the mid- to upper-600s will usually require only the most recent year personal returns, and maybe the most recent corporate returns. Scores in the 700s will only ask for the most recent personal return. If the score is over 750, combined with assets and LTV, the computer may not ask for anything except for the lender to call and make sure the person is still in business. Pretty much like a no income loan. If the borrower is liquidating stocks for cash to close, normally they need to show verification of the liquidation. Higher scores will not require this verification. The appraiser normally goes inside the house when doing the appraisal. Higher credit scores can change that to an outside inspection only, which may only be a true inspection and not an appraisal. This appraisal is cheaper and is passed on to the borrower as lower closing costs. The more liquid assets remaining after closing, the lower the loan-to-value, and the more stable the borrower's employment, combined with high credit scores, all can cause the computer to approve a loan with less verifications, or with much higher qualifying ratios. I will discuss how much higher in the section on qualifying and being approved, but you can have ratios that are almost off the chart.

Because of the variances between the repositories, you could have scores of 750, 600, 680. This kind of wide range usually indicates one of several things: The borrower has bad credit with none reported to one, all reported to the other, and some reported to the third. And, sometimes bad credit is not the factor. As I mentioned earlier, too much credit and/or debt can reduce credit scores, remember? In this example, 680 is the score used.

Sometimes a borrower will have little or no credit, or possibly none that is reported to the repositories. Then, only the repositories with sufficient credit reported will give a score. If only one score or no scores are shown, we have to use a "traditional" or alternative means of obtaining credit information. This means the old fashioned way, sending verification forms to the landlord(s), utility companies, insurance companies, or any other creditor to whom the borrower may have a history of making payments. Most loans will require a minimum of four credit lines, although some will allow three. When we use this type of credit reporting, the loan cannot be computer underwritten. Borrowing only to establish credit is not always necessary. After all, little or no debt may show frugality and the ability to save. The lender only wants to make sure that the borrower can make the mortgage payment and all other monthly obligations. If you are in the no-debt category, you are indeed in a minority. Americans are creating and maintaining credit debt in record amounts. The lender must ensure that this debt will not put the mortgage loan at high risk of default.

Different Ways of Being in Debt

Some of the more prevalent types of credit include the following:

1. Credit cards
2. Bank notes
3. Car loans
4. Education loans
5. Other mortgage loans
6. Alimony and child support payments

Each debt likely has different terms and characteristics that the lender will have to consider in determining the borrower's actual monthly obligations.

Proving That You Are in Debt

Credit cards and revolving credit are established in several ways. First, the lender will qualify the borrower by using a standard 5% of the current outstanding balance as the monthly payment. When the lender receives the credit report, it will use the reported payment to qualify the borrower. However, the credit report will not always show the payment or the actual current balance. Credit bureaus often give the balance 30 to 60 days ago. But (wouldn't you know) the borrower has just paid that $2,000 balance down to $500, or paid it off completely. The payment the lender sees on the report throws the borrower into a ratio that exceeds the qualifying ratios, while the balance of zero would meet the guidelines. The astute lender will tell the borrowers to request a statement from the creditor showing the current balance. If the next statement will arrive prior to closing, the lender can make it a condition of the loan that the borrower provide the statement, showing the lower balance and payment, prior to loan closing.

Car loans and other bank loans are normal in today's society, but the increasing cost of automobiles has begun to put a strain on the borrower's ability to buy a home. My answer to that is, "Get your priorities in order. Buy the house first, then the BMW™." It is not unusual to see a car payment that is as large as a house payment. And this is on a depreciating asset.

When Is a Debt Not a Debt?

When the borrower has a loan that amortizes out in a given amount of time, like a 4-year car loan, that monthly payment is considered in the long term debts for purposes of qualifying until it has *10 months or less left to be paid.* Now, for every rule, there is an exception. If the loan has 10 months or even five or six months remaining but is for a Mercedes at $800 per month, then the lender is less likely to ignore that debt, unless the computer approves the loan carrying the debt. Also, a borrower with a payment of $250 who is right on the edge of qualifying without counting that payment may not be approved if the lender feels she cannot handle the debt load until the $250 is paid off. (The greatest risk of default and foreclosure will be in the first one or two years of the loan.) Debts of short duration also may be counted on some loans of over 90% loan-to-value.

There is a way to avoid being denied because of a high-payment, short-term debt—convince a rich relative to give you the money to pay off the loan. There are several variations on this theme.

You can wait to see if the computer or the underwriter likes you. If the loan is approved with the debt, fine. If not, then you must assure the loan originator that you will be able to pay this off with a gift, if necessary, so that this information can be passed on to the underwriter. That the loan is paid off will then become a condition of loan closing. There must be a gift letter, and the receipt of the funds must be verified. (You didn't think they would let you get away without that, did you?) Or, you may be able to pay the loan down to a low enough remaining balance, like two to four months, that even an underwriter would probably let it slide. If you do this, the loan must be paid down before the debt is verified the first time. Some secondary market investors will not accept a condition of paying down a loan. By the time it is verified, you are stuck with an all-or-nothing proposition. (Again, play the game. Do not try to argue your way through it. You are dealing with people who play God every day.)

Short-Term Notes

Bank notes, or **personal notes,** are the bane of those who live by an irregular payday. Commissioned sales people, such as Realtors, see money like an untuned car, in starts and spurts. To live during the periods when they can't quite seem to get their motors running, they will take out a "90-day note." They get $5,000 at 12% and then scramble to make the sales to pay it back. Then, when it is paid off and they can give a sigh of relief, they realize that the bank just got their last buck. So, the cycle starts again. Much to the delight of banks, this phenomenon is not confined to sales people, but also includes doctors, lawyers, and some people with expensive tastes.

Some loans don't have a regular monthly payment. The lender can't just count the whole debt as a single payment in qualifying a loan application. How does one come up with a reasonable method of setting a qualifying payment? If you have a bank note that is not on a monthly payment schedule, the lender can adjust the payments to reflect an equivalent monthly schedule. If a payment is made quarterly, the lender will divide it by three and use that figure for qualifying. If the payment is interest only, the requirement for qualifying may vary from lender to lender. Usually, the lender will break the interest payment into monthly payments and use that debt according to this criteria:

1.   The debt is not due within a short period of time, and/ or . . .
2.   The creditors state that they will renew the loan when it comes due, and/or . . .
3.   The borrowers could pay off the loan out of remaining assets after they have purchased the house.

Education Loans

Education, or student, loans have more options than a car on order from Detroit. For instance, most are deferred until the borrower is out of school from one month to one year, or further if the borrower goes to graduate school, or teaches, or requests a further deferral. Then payments are set up monthly, quarterly, semiannually, or yearly. And, if the payment is deferred, often neither the borrower nor the creditor knows what the payment will be when it starts.

A good example would be a borrower who recently graduated from school and has several student loans. One of them may be set up to begin payments and can be readily verified. That one is easy. Another may be deferred for another one to three years. Depending on the type of loan, a deferral period of as little as one year will allow the lender to not count the payment for qualifying. Others may require a period of three years or more. Fannie, Freddie, and FHA currently will allow one year, but check with your lender. They used to require three years.

To make matters worse, the borrower too often forgets that he has a student loan, or thinks that it is not a debt because he is not paying on it. Everyone will go blithely along until the credit report is pulled. Suddenly, the loan on which the borrower just barely qualified, and that the Realtor had been assured would be approved, is rejected because of new debts. The Realtor rationalizes that the lender should not count what is not being paid in order to save the sale, the borrower is angry because the lender never asked him if he had any education loans (mind-reading is a prerequisite to be a lender), and the sellers are angry because they had been told by the Realtor that the lender had assured her that the borrowers qualified. My experience with student loans is that they are often very poorly managed by the creditor or agency responsible for notifying the borrower. Many times I have seen late payments because the borrower did not receive the monthly bill for several months. While they may know they have the debt, most borrowers will rely on the receipt of the bill to remind them to pay it.

The Borrower with More Than One Mortgaged Property—
Multi-Mortgage Mania

There are also guidelines for **borrowers who have other existing mortgages.** When a borrower has another property on which there is a recorded lien (mortgage), that payment is included in the total debt. However, that property usually will be rented. The secondary market allows you to take **75% of the gross rents** and subtract that from the mortgage payment (PITI) on the rental property. If the number is positive, you can add it to income for qualifying. If it is negative, then that amount is added to the total debts. If you have one or two years tax returns showing the property on the schedule E, then the lender can use those figures, adding back the depreciation into the bottom line. Depending on the loan and how it is underwritten, the borrower may have to provide copies of the current leases.

An example would be a property with a mortgage payment of $700 and a lease payment of $800. Most borrowers will say that they have a positive cash flow of $100 per month. But that is not what they report on Schedule E of their federal income tax returns. Secondary market lenders recognize that there are expenses and vacancies, so they use the conservative figure of 25% of the gross rent to cover these costs. If you can show by your past two years' tax returns that this figure is high, then the lender will give you the actual cost. Using the 75% factor, the borrower would have a net of $600 (75% of $800), or a minus $100 that would be added to the debts for qualifying.

In the past, Fannie and Freddie have only allowed a borrower to have a maximum of four properties with recorded liens, one of which is the borrower's primary residence. They now have no restrictions on the number of properties a borrower may own. If a property has no recorded financing on it, then it is not counted. Fannie and Freddie put the four-property maximum in place when they had a large number of multiple defaults from individual borrowers. They must feel their underwriting and quality control is now sophisticated enough to insure lower ratios of default. Any multiple-unit property up to a four-unit dwelling (quadraplex) is considered as a single property. Properties with five or more units are considered commercial property and are not eligible for normal Fannie and Freddie financing. (They have a separate "multi-family" financing division for commercial, or apartment, properties.)

If a borrower owns a property with another person, the lender will consider the borrower to have 100% of the debt, not just 50%, because they are jointly and severally responsible for that debt. If one borrower disappears, the other will be obligated for the full loan. Borrowers will argue that they are not responsible for the payment, or only for their corresponding percentage of ownership in the property. You need to read the fine print on those mortgage documents that you sign at closing. You are committed body and soul, you don't get to choose.

D-i-v-o-r-c-e

In our society, divorce has become all too familiar. One of the standard questions that a lender must ask a borrower, male or female, is, "Are you obligated to pay alimony, child support, or separate maintenance?" A surprising number will answer "Yes." This obligation is a debt. The lender will require that the borrower provide **a complete, executed copy of the separation agreement and the divorce agreement** before the loan can be approved.

The lender is not interested in why the separation and/or divorce occurred, but in what the borrower's obligation is, and for how long. To determine these, the entire document must be provided. I have had many a borrower who tried to get by with giving me just the page outlining the payments, and then argued with me that the rest is irrelevant. Fannie and Freddie (and everyone else) won't buy the loan without the full documentation. If you fit the description, be prepared to provide the paperwork.

Notice that I said "executed" copies. That means copies of documents that have been agreed upon and signed. Occasionally, a borrower will try to buy a house before the separation is down on paper. This is another instance where the lender can play God. The borrower must have an executed agreement detailing if there will be any obligation to pay, and if so, what the terms will be, before the loan can be approved. On the other hand, some people will have lived apart for years without any formal written agreement. They may have to draw up a separation agreement and sign it before a lender will make the loan. Sometimes desktop underwriting may not require as much documentation. And if the borrower can show he has been making regular, agreed-upon payments to his estranged spouse and has high credit scores, plenty of reserve assets, and a low LTV, then the lender may approve the loan without a signed agreement. Just know that the chances are good a signed agreement will be required.

One borrower who applied for a loan tried to browbeat me into accepting just a statement from his attorney. When I demonstrated that I could not be intimidated, I then found out why he was so reluctant. His support payment was over $5,000 per month! The amazing thing is that he made so much money that he still qualified for the loan.

There will always be the occasional borrower who tries to sneak a prior divorce and alimony obligation by the lender without telling. Sometimes it will work, but what usually happens is the credit report may show previous joint credit or, if tax returns are required, the alimony deduction will be on the 1040 form.

*Judgments and Collections—Pay Me Now Or Later, But You
Will Pay*

Why do people get judgments or collections? Usually they are
filed against a borrower for two different reasons. The first is that
the person didn't pay the debt, and the second is that the person
didn't think the debt should have to be paid. The latter is usually
a dispute over some type of goods the person received, or did not
receive, and refused to pay. I've seen judgments where the goods
had been returned, and the creditor never gave credit for the return. The borrower then moved away and the judgment notice is
sent to his last known address. The person later discovers this un-
pleasant fact when trying to convince a lender to let them borrow
a large sum of money. If you have had any adverse credit in the
past two years, it will show up. More than likely, anything in the
past seven to 10 years will be shown. Applying for a mortgage is
one of the best ways to find out exactly what is on your credit.

Judgments and collections have been for as little as $5. The
borrower refused to pay, out of principle. He's right, and the other
guy is wrong. The mortgage lender may be sympathetic, but the
secondary market is not. In almost all instances, judgments will
be required to be paid prior to closing.

Before you conclude that all you have to do to get the loan is
make sure that you pay off, understand that these things are part
of your credit history. One judgment for an understandable reason, such as a dispute, may not cause denial. But, if you have con-
sistently poor credit, or the judgments were recently filed for bad
credit, or the judgments were filed for nonpayment of rent, then
you have a problem. Slow payment of rent is considered with the
same prejudice as slow mortgage payments. Only a couple of late
payments in the past 12 months can be the kiss of death. Remember that credit scores are determined by computers. A judgment
or a collection will cause a significant reduction in the score.

Any recent poor payment history can lead the lender to conclude that you are currently not a good credit risk—even if you
had the ability to have made the payments. If you know you have
judgments that will show up on your credit report, even if they are
paid, tell the mortgage lender about them right at loan application. That way, there will be more time to solve any potential
problem, or to save the cost of application if it is apparent that
they will cause the loan to be denied.

Bankruptcy—Spin the Wheel Again

Many people (too many) have used bankruptcy to solve their credit problems. In a nutshell, bankruptcy is a way for a borrower who has more debts than income and assets either to rearrange his or her credit so that the debts can be paid, or, in extreme cases, to allow all or most of the debts to be written off so that the borrower can start a new credit life. Some people who declare bankruptcy do so because they have been advised by someone who may not be considering factors that can come into play several years down the road.

Let's say that our borrower has a good job and the family has a good credit history. Naturally, every bank and credit lender would love to have people paying them 18%. So, they send them unsolicited applications for credit, or they just send the credit card with an invitation to use it. Our borrower yields to the temptation of that snappy new sports car, and the rest of the family buys all new furniture because the original stuff looked "used." In general, they were only trying to keep up with the proverbial Joneses. Suddenly, where they once could pay bills and have money left to go out occasionally, they are now having to borrow from the bank to meet their obligations. This doesn't sound good, does it? Like faltering governments that try to renegotiate their debts, so should our borrowers—right after they destroy all their credit cards and cancel all their credit accounts. Cold turkey. Most creditors will work with a hard-pressed borrower because this way they may be able to get their money. If they don't, there is an option available to the borrower, through which the creditors may get zero.

When all else fails and the borrower can no longer make his or her debt payments, bankruptcy may be the only alternative. The best approach is Chapter 13 bankruptcy, if at all possible. This gives the borrower time to renegotiate his debt, in order to repay it and have money on which to live. The creditors may not get all their money back, or it may take much longer, but at least the borrower is attempting to meet these obligations. For people who are incorporated, Chapter 11 works the same way. Chapter 7 bankruptcy allows the borrower to void all debts and start over with a clean slate.

If the borrower exhibited poor judgment in using credit, future lenders will look at them very carefully to see that the same mistakes are not repeated. Sometimes, though, bankruptcy may be the only solution. If people lose their job, or have major medical expenses that are not covered by insurance, the debt may be so overwhelming that nothing short of a clean break will allow the borrowers to live within their means.

Bankruptcy would seem to be a way to keep a borrower from ever getting a mortgage again. This conclusion is not true. What it does keep the borrower from doing is getting a mortgage within the next two to 10 years from the date that the bankruptcy is **discharged,** that is, from the time the court says that the borrower is no longer in bankruptcy. Each investors, each lender, and even each loan type may require a different time period. Depending on the type of loan, and the circumstances of the bankruptcy, the borrower will have to have one to 10 years before applying for a mortgage.

What Fannie and Freddie say is that they will consider buying a loan when the borrower makes loan application after having been **discharged for a minimum of four years.** They will consider a shorter period of time, but not less than two years if the Chapter 13 bankruptcy was satisfactorily repaid or the bankruptcy, foreclosure, or deed in lieu of foreclosure resulted from a documented extenuating circumstance. For example, if the borrowers are **forced into bankruptcy by something beyond their control,** such as medical bills, a lender may make the loan in less than the two-year period. Both FHA and VA have a minimum of two years, with as little as one year for circumstances beyond their control. But some investors do not want to consider anyone who has declared bankruptcy for any reason until it no longer shows on the credit report. And that is seven to 10 years. There are loans that will give a mortgage to borrowers who have been discharged less than one year, but they are in the sub-prime category. I will discuss these in the chapters on lenders and loans.

If the borrower has declared bankruptcy in the past, he or she needs to disclose that to the lender before writing any contracts of purchase. If the lender feels that it can make the loan, the borrower will have to provide the following:

1. A full executed copy of the Bankruptcy petition
2. A copy of the discharge papers
3. A complete written explanation as to why it became necessary to declare bankruptcy

People who have gone through bankruptcy are given the chance literally to start over. This means that they should learn from their mistakes or misfortune and maintain a good credit history in their second life. If there are late payments on their credit reports after the bankruptcy is discharged, the lender will assume the borrower may not have learned their lesson. One or two lates that are old may not be a problem. Recent late payments can be very detrimental.

Foreclosure, Or Deed in Lieu of Foreclosure

Another credit problem, although it is not so prevalent as bankruptcy, is foreclosure or giving a deed in lieu of foreclosure. If you have been foreclosed on, you can usually count on not getting any normal mortgage for the next two to 10 years, except in certain economic circumstances. (FHA and VA can be more lenient.)

When borrowers give a deed in lieu of foreclosure, they simply turn over the deed, and ownership, of the property to the note holder without going through the foreclosure process. This saves everyone involved a large amount of time and expense. It is used primarily in instances where the borrowers, through no fault of their own, can no longer afford to make the loan payments and cannot sell or rent the property to cover the loan. The situation in the Texas-Oklahoma oil patch during the 1980s' recession that put large numbers of people out of work is a classic example. Homeowners were without jobs and sufficient income to meet the mortgage payments. They couldn't rent their property because the market was glutted with houses to rent, and there certainly weren't many people looking to buy. Under the circumstances, most lenders agreed to take the deed in lieu of foreclosing on the property.

Good Credit—Once You Have It, Keep It

In maintaining good credit, remember these:

1. Do not borrow unless you need to.
2. Make sure that you can pay back what you borrow.
3. Plastic money is expensive.
4. Make your payments on time, especially your rent or mortgage payments.

5. If you can't make a payment on time, see the creditor to work out a plan that will keep your credit in good standing.

6. Credit can be destroyed easier than it can be built.

7. The only interest that is still deductible is mortgage interest and margin account interest (unless Congress changes its mind).

What Is Long-Term Credit?

You also need to know when debt is considered long-term and must be counted against you when qualifying for the loan, and when is it of such short duration that it does not need to be counted. We discussed this distinction earlier. Here are the rules:

1. Any **revolving debt,** such as credit cards, will be counted if there is an outstanding balance. The lender will use 5% of that balance as the qualifying payment unless the credit report shows a different payment or the borrower provides a statement of the account, showing a lower payment and/or balance, that is more recent than the credit report figures. Borrowers who have a bunch of credit cards will be considered as a higher risk because they could increase their debt rapidly.

2. On **installment loans** with a regular payment, such as car loans, the payment will not be counted in qualifying by most lenders, if the loan has 10 months or less left to pay. If the monthly payment is excessive and will adversely affect the ability of the borrower to make the mortgage payments in the first year, then the payment may be considered. If the borrower's income cannot easily support it, then it could be counted, although consideration will be given to its short-term nature.

3. If a **borrower has co-signed a debt** with another person, that debt will be considered as the borrower's debt, unless it can be shown that the other person is making the payments. Most loans will allow the debt not to be counted if the borrower can show six to 12 months of canceled checks showing the other borrower is making the payments, then the debt will not be counted against our borrower, as long as the other person maintains a

good credit history. Our borrower could ultimately be responsible for the debt. If the loan has had late payments, these will appear on the borrower's credit report, even though the friend is the one who is at fault.

4. Your **total house payment (principal, interest, taxes, insurance, and mortgage insurance and homeowner's dues if required) and monthly debt payments** should not exceed about **36%** of your gross monthly income. F.H.A. and V.A. allow up to 41%. Computer underwriting can take that well beyond the norm if the credit scores are high. I have seen total debt ratios of 65% to 90%. I have heard of loans approved with ratios even higher. FHA and VA loans which are computer underwritten, will usually not allow debt ratios beyond 50%–55%.

Income   (It's Never Enough)

We now know there are certain minimum requirements for cash and credit to qualify for a mortgage. Normally, the borrower must have sufficient income to satisfy the lender they can pay their debts, including the mortgage. As I have noted earlier, excellent credit can make income less of an issue, and lower credit scores will make income much more important. Again, the decision can vary from lender to lender, investor to investor, and loan type to loan type. Certain minimum guidelines set by the secondary market form the basis for all lenders' decisions. If you satisfy these rules, then you qualify for the majority of conventional loans.

Past And Present Employment—How Many Jobs Have You Had in the Past Two Years? Prove It

A mortgage loan application will always include **a two year history of the borrower's employment.** It must cover a full 24-month period from the date of the application. If you have been in your job for two or more years, the process will be easy. But, if you have changed jobs within the past two years, every employer during that period must be on the application. On occasion I have sent five or more Verifications of Employment (VOEs) out on one borrower. With alternate documentation, the borrower will need to provide one to two years of W-2s for all jobs and a copy of their most recent paystubs covering a 30-day period. This is followed with a verbal verification of employment no later than 30 days prior to closing. Computer underwriting can require all of the above or as little as a verbal verification, based on credit and assets. If necessary, or required by the loan not using computer underwriting, a **VOE** (see appendix) may need to be faxed or mailed to the employer.

The Verification of Employment has two sections, one for the current employer and one for previous employers. On the current employment section the employer is asked these questions.

1. Present position of employee
2. Date that employee began employment
3. Probability of continued employment
4. If the employee receives overtime or bonus income, and if so, whether its continuance is likely
5. What the employee's current base pay is and how often the employee is paid (for example, monthly)
6. The employee's earnings for the year-to-date (YTD) and for the past year
7. Overtime and bonus income YTD and for the past year
8. Commissions YTD and past year
9. A remarks section where the employer can say what a nice person you are, or nothing at all

The question regarding present position shows the lender that the borrower is employed in the job stated on the application and that there is some relationship to other positions that the borrower has held within the past two years. The lender is looking for evidence of continuity of skills. Someone who was a computer salesman and becomes a computer operator demonstrates this, while a person who went from being a Realtor to being a computer salesman would not.

Under the section on date of employment the lender is interested in knowing how long the borrower has been in her present position. If it is a full two years (24 months) from the date of application, that job is normally all that needs to be verified. If it is less than two years, then the lender will verify any previous employment back to the full 24 months. If there is any **gap in the borrower's employment,** normally anything over two weeks, then the borrower must explain this period of unemployment in writing. There is nothing wrong with having a gap in your employment. It is not that unusual. Many people changing jobs and/or moving will take time between jobs. Others may take time that they had not intended to take, in the form of unemployment. As long as the explanation shows that the borrower was willing to work, that the gaps are not normal, and they have a low probability of recurring, the borrower should not worry.

It is not unusual for someone to have changed jobs. Many people applying for a mortgage have taken a new job and are transferring into the area. Changing jobs for advancement or an increase in income is normal. That **the borrower has changed jobs without any additional benefit** may raise questions.

If the change occurred because the person was fired for incompetence, or has changed jobs frequently because of incompatability with management, then there may be a problem. These reasons suggest **employment instability.** To strengthen the case the lender may want to document more than two years of employment and income.

Amazingly, some people cannot remember where they were for the past two years. Borrowers have been known to give information at loan application, only to find out that they left out a job or had the dates of employment wrong by 6 months or more. How productive do you think someone was if he or she couldn't remember the job one year later? The biggest problem with questions resulting from queries concerning employment history is that the loan process is slowed down and approval is delayed. The lender may have all the verifications and information to approve the loan, only to be held up by a last-minute VOE that should have been sent at application.

For the question of the borrower's **probability of continued employment,** the usual answer is "good" or "excellent." Depending on the mood of the employer, there have been some other very interesting answers. More than one employer has put "subject to the economy." I have seen "on probation" or "on a 6-months trial basis." These don't indicate the employer has a lot of confidence that the employee will be around for very long. In the worst I have had the employer inform us that the borrower was being laid off at the end of the week. This was bad enough, but when I asked the borrower about it, I found out that he had not yet been told. I did the employer's dirty work. The moral is "Never apply for a loan unless you are certain you have good job stability."

When the VOE is being filled in by **a previous employer,** the company only needs to give a few answers. The lender wants to know what the employee's last position was with the employer, what the person's income was at that time, the dates of employment, and reason for leaving. The problem with previous employers is getting them to return the VOE in a reasonable amount of time. In almost all instances today, only W-2s for the past one or two years are now required for previous employment. Rarely is a VOE sent.

Current income should be in line with the borrower's type of employment and past years' income. A ditch digger would not be making $50,000 per year, but an accountant would be expected to earn that much or more. A borrower can be expected to get **raises and promotions.** When income goes from $20,000 to $50,000 it may need to be explained. Even a $5,000 increase may be questioned, depending on the lender. When the borrower's income goes from $50,000 to $20,000, the lenders will certainly want more information. As long as the changes are reasonable and can be explained satisfactorily, there should be no problem. When there is any doubt, the borrower or the borrower's employer may be required to give substantial evidence to back up the unusual change in income. Employers have been known to lie to help an employee get a loan. As a matter of fact, **if you work for a relative,** such as a parent, you will have to provide tax returns to substantiate income. Historically, too many relatives have lied to help get loans.

Just recently, one of my loan officers had a borrower whose supervisor lied about his employment by stating, in writing, that the borrower had worked there one year longer than was true and that the borrower was a permanent part-time employee. The truth came out when the paystubs did not fit and my processor called the home office to get clarification. It seems the borrower was a temporary employee who had been working there less than two months. Result: The loan was denied and both men were fired.

Overtime And Bonuses—Unless the Economy Slows Down

If overtime and bonus income need to be used in qualifying, the lender wants to be certain that it will continue to be earned if it has been received in the past. If there is this assurance, then the lender will ask the employer how much has been earned year-to-date and in the past year. Most lenders will require that two full years be verified. Because this income can fluctuate, the lender will in most cases **average it.** If you made $2,340 last year in overtime and have made $700 for the first six months of this year, then the lender would divide the total of $3,040 by 18 months for an average of $169 per month. Computer underwriting may vary the requirements for counting overtime, or the loan may allow using overtime within six months to one year if it is reasonably certain to continue on a regular basis. Bonuses usually need to have been paid a minimum of one year just to be considered.

The best way to use overtime and bonuses is not to use them. Qualifying for the loan on base income alone puts you in a much stronger position, not only because the lender will know there is additional income that was not used, but also because overtime and bonuses have a habit of disappearing just when you need them the most.

Commission Income

As more of us strive for financial success, commission income has become a means to attain higher earnings. In theory, the harder you work, the more you earn. In reality, the results often do not work out that way.

Because you have good days and bad days, the lender will look at commission income in the same way as overtime. Normally, you should have been in that job for **a minimum of two years** (some institutions will allow one to one and a half years). Your income will then be averaged over the number of months that it represents. (Doing so smooths out all the peaks and valleys that occur. After 10 years as a Realtor, I can attest to the fact that it truly is a roller coaster ride.)

If you are on a **draw against commissions,** the draw can be used if it is not subject to repayment. Some lenders will require that you have been in the job for six months to a year, to demonstrate staying power, before the draw can be counted. Ideally, your commissions for that period will meet or exceed the draw. The best idea is to wait until you have established a reliable earning pattern. This is what lenders really want.

Other Income—Stocks, Bonds, Alimony, Grandfather's Money, and the Self-employed

Now that we have covered the mundane aspects of income and employment, let's look at some of the unusual and exotic ways of earning money.

Interest and dividend income.   Interest and dividend income is one of the more common sources of "additional income." Usually borrowers will have cash and/or assets on which they are earning some return. To use this income to qualify, they will have to show **1099 forms** (the equivalent of W-2 forms for interest and dividend income) from their past two years' tax returns (some lenders may allow the past two years' year-end statements in lieu of 1099s) and their most recent statements showing balances and year-to-date income. If it fluctuates, it will be averaged. If it comes from bonds or other securities earning a constant continuing income then that income is used.

The key is whether the income and the underlying assets will continue to be available in the future. When the borrowers show they have held the assets for two or more years without reducing them substantially or the assets have increased, it is more likely that the borrowers will continue to hold them. If a borrower has just deposited a large sum (the origin of which can be verified) into an interest-bearing account, the lender must determine whether this income will be reliable in the future. A new five-year bond or three-year certificate of deposit would tend to have more staying power than a money market account. Dividends are normally counted as reliable income because most people buy stock for income or long-term growth.

The problems in using this income to qualify are usually with the borrowers themselves. I have seen them go through the entire loan application process using the interest and dividend income to qualify. Then when they are asked what they intend to use for the down payment and closing costs, I discover they are going to liquidate their investments to buy the house—which, of course, means that they no longer have the interest and dividends to use as income with which to qualify.

Trust income.   Trusts make a very reliable source of income in most cases. A verification from the administrator of the trust and/or the past two years' tax returns will show the trust's ability to provide continued income.

One borrower that I remember was attending a university and living on his trust income. Unfortunately, he forgot that the trust was not just paying out interest. It was paying interest and part of the principal. At the end of two years, just as he finished school, the trust would be completely depleted. If it had paid out in a three- to five-year period, or continued to provide income into the foreseeable future, then most lenders would not have balked.

Luckily for our student, he had made the point of telling me that the existing loan on the property was assumable at 12.5%, a rate he was not interested in paying. When he found out that he could not qualify for the loan, which was currently a 9% rate, 12.5% started to look pretty good. It looked even better when I told him he could assume that particular loan and then refinance it at a lower rate without having to qualify for the payment. As a result, he was able to buy the property without qualifying and get the lower, current rate of 9%. Unfortunately, those loans (FHA) are no longer offered as assumable without qualifying.

Tax-free income.   Tax-free income has gained popularity as the government keeps tinkering with our deductions. Income from tax-free bonds and certain nontaxable military payments is not only usable income, but also represents more than the face value. Because lenders use gross income to qualify the borrower, the qualifying ratios, or percentages of the gross income that can be used for house payment and debts, take into account that the usable portion of a person's income will be significantly less after withholding. (VA loans are handled differently because of their method of qualifying.) When tax-free income is used, lenders can "gross up" this income to compensate for the withholding adjustments built into the ratios. *Grossing Up* means that the lender can add onto the tax-free income what the normal withholding tax would have been. The minimum amount the income can be grossed up is 115%. If you received $1,000 a month tax free, it could be grossed up to $1,150.

Alimony and child support income.   Alimony and child support are probably the most widely available sources of alternate income. For many divorced women, and a few men, alimony and child support mean the difference between purchasing a home or renting.

The law states that a lender may not ask if the borrower is receiving alimony or child support; further, if the borrower does volunteer this information, the borrower can refuse to let it be used to qualify. Obviously, if the borrower can qualify without it, so much the better. Why? Because most divorces end on a less than amicable note. The lender wants reassurance that the income is reliable.

A copied set of the borrower's bank statements from the last six to 12 months, showing the payments being deposited, is the usual method of verification. The biggest problem with this is that the former spouse seldom deposits the check either by itself or in its entirety.

As an example, say the lender is looking for monthly deposits of $500 around the first of each month. What the lender finds are deposits of amounts like $623.45 (alimony plus the proceeds of yard sale) or $254.13 (what was left after paying the dentist bill) or $0.00 (the alimony was taken as cash). Along with a letter of explanation from the borrower, most lenders will accept these variations as long as there is evidence that this income, plus or minus, appears each month.

There is an easier way to verify receipt of the alimony income. If the former spouse is under court order to pay alimony directly to the court, most lenders will accept a copy of that order as verification.

If the divorce was amicable (I've seen two), then the alimony recipient can ask the former spouse for copies of the last 12 canceled alimony checks. Sometimes the former spouse will even provide a copy of the federal income tax return to demonstrate this adjustment to personal income.

The idea is to **show that alimony and child support are reliable sources of usable income.** Once we know that it is being received, we need to ensure that it will continue for one to five years, depending on the type of loan. The age of the child or children will help determine how long the support will continue. If the child is 15 and the decree specifies payments until age 18, we know there will be three more years of that income. A difficulty arises when, as in most cases, the agreement specifies that the support will continue until age 21 if the child goes to college. At 16 no one can say whether the child will continue their education after high school. Normally the lender decides that it will end at 18, and uses it as a compensating factor.

Just as the borrower who pays alimony or child support has to provide **copies of the executed agreements,** the borrower who is receiving it also has to give copies to the lender, if the income is being used to qualify. There are instances of divorce settlements for which the former spouse is not required to make any payments but does as a result of a feeling of obligation. (I've seen one.) If the borrower can show evidence of this, plus a written letter from the former spouse, some lenders will allow it as income.

Most, however, will only use it as a slight compensating factor, since nothing forces the continuance of that income.

Note income.   People will often act as small lenders themselves, taking back a note for property that they sold, for money that they have lent to others, or for goods and services. The income is usable as long as it meets the standard Fannie Mae–Freddie Mac rules. For example, there must be a written agreement. You have to show evidence that it is being received (bank statements, tax returns). It has to continue for at least one to five years, depending on the lender and the secondary market investor. A secured note is much easier for the lender to accept than an unsecured one. Notes give you two advantages. They create income for qualifying, and they are listed as assets on your financial statement.

Gift income.   For the well-heeled, gift income is a good way to distribute assets. By law, you can give up to a certain amount as a gift each year. If the donor has given this income in the past and states in writing an intention to continue it in the future, many lenders will accept this gift. Do not assume that every lender will use it. Some are less trusting than others. I have known underwriters who required copies of the donor's tax returns for the past two years to prove their ability to give the gift. Others may require verification of assets, or whatever the source of this largess may be.

Rental income.   Rental income is something that everyone wishes he or she could claim. You have an appreciating asset (we hope). It creates income. And it can show a paper loss, which means less taxes. Lenders look at rental income several ways.

The normal rental income is from an investment, or non-owner occupied, property. Taking 75% of the gross rents and subtracting that from the PITI payment on the property leaves 25% for vacancy and expenses. If the difference is positive, it is added to your income for qualifying. If it is negative, it is used in the long-term debt total, not the full PITI payment. Here is an example:

Gross Monthly Rent = $800 × 75% = $600

PITI payment = $700

$700 *PITI* = $600 *net rent* = –$100

The negative $100 *would be debt.*

The lender may require **copies of leases.** For purposes of qualifying for a loan the standard is that the lease be for a period of at least a year with three or more months remaining. This will vary by lender. If you don't have a lease and operate on a month-to-month basis, you may have to get, at the very minimum, a one-year lease with a 30-day notice by either party. If the term remaining is less than two to three months, a new lease or a tenants' affidavit, stating that they plan to renew the lease, is acceptable. Other lenders will accept tax returns that show the property has been rented in the past plus a tenants' affidavit that they plan on living there for the foreseeable future.

If the tax returns show less than 25% vacancy and expense, the lender may allow the lower figure. Depreciation is always added back into the income when you are looking at Schedule E—Supplemental Income and Loss (from rents, royalties, partnerships, estates, trusts, REMIC, etc.) on your tax returns. Adding back the depreciation will almost always create a positive cash flow on the Schedule E. Computer underwriting may require varying amounts of documentation. Normally, last year's tax returns or current leases are all it will ask to be provided.

The Self-Employed Borrower.   I have saved the best for last, the Self-Employed Borrower—the entrepreneur who has risked all to make large sums of money on which little or no taxes are due owing to large business expense write-offs. What a great life! That is, until you have to go to a mortgage lender.

Remember, income must be verified. How do you verify a self-employed borrower's income? By getting copies of his or her FULL tax returns, with original signatures, for the past two years. Plus a year-to-date Profit and Loss (P&L) statement, and a year-to-date Balance Sheet, if the borrower is incorporated or a partnership. The Balance Sheet and P&L statement must be done by an accountant or bookkeeper and signed by the preparer. Fannie and Freddie currently are much less demanding, requiring at most the past two years' personal returns and corporate returns. Profit and Loss statements and balance sheets are rarely required, except for loans from other secondary market investors. Computer underwriting can require as little as a verbal verification that the borrower is still in business. This is as close to a no-income loan as Fannie and Freddie are likely to approve. I have had quite a few loans for self-employed borrowers with the computer not requiring any documentation other than the verbal verification. All of these borrowers had credit scores in the mid-700s or higher.

A borrower who is self-employed should have been in that position for at least two years. A shorter period may be acceptable in some situations if the borrower was doing essentially the same thing previously. A one- to one-and-a-half-year period may be acceptable, if you can demonstrate that your income is stable and increasing and can be reasonably expected to continue. If you bought an existing business that has been profitable, the lender may look at you after one year if you show that you are continuing to make a profit.

Now, when I say make a profit, I mean enough money to live on, not just break even. The interesting thing about being self-employed is that it is not hard to lose money for tax purposes. Nevertheless, the bottom line is that the lender will look at your net income, after adjustments for paper loss add-backs such as depreciation. Do not expect the lender to fall for the routine about really making more than the tax returns show.

There are several different ways one can be self-employed. You can be a sole proprietor, a partner, an independent contractor, or incorporated, which has several different categories in itself.

Sole proprietor.   The **sole proprietor** is a self-employed person who simply earns his living by practicing a trade without benefit of being a partnership or corporation. At the end of the year, a sole proprietor files a normal tax return with at least a Schedule C, and usually several additional schedules.

Under the basic guidelines, not using computer underwriting, the lender will look at your **tax returns and all schedules for the last two years, signed by you, and a year-to-date P&L statement** prepared by a third party such as a bookkeeper or accountant. You don't normally need a balance sheet, because all the business assets are personal assets. The lender will take the net income for both years and YTD, add back all paper losses, add the totals, and divide by the number of months represented. The result will be the monthly income used to qualify.

Most people will show a profit. And the add backs can make a considerable difference. Because tax laws change frequently, some things may or may not be usable. Right now, we can talk about the basic ones.

Depreciation is number one. It truly is a paper loss and is added back into the net income. This can account for many thousands of dollars per year.

Depletion is another add-back. Without oil or gas wells, you probably won't need to worry about it.

The write-off for **use of part of your home for your business is usually** added back to the extent the room is used. The house payment is already considered a debt, so there is no need to hit you twice.

Unusual, one-time, nonrecurring expenses can often be added back or prorated over a longer period. An example would be the purchase of a $9,000 copier which you elected to write off under Office Expense. Because it is unlikely that you would spend $9,000 on a copier every year, most lenders will prorate it for three to five years, so that on a five-year schedule, $7,200 would be added back. Of course, the best way to write it off is by depreciating it, instead of the one-time deduction.

On the first page of your federal 1040 form, you can add back most of the items listed under Adjustments to Income. **IRAs and Keoghs** are income that is not taxed. **Alimony** will be counted as a debt, so it can be added to income. **Penalty for early withdrawal** of savings can be added back as long as it is not recurring. As we discussed earlier, income or losses from schedule E can be adjusted usually to show a profit. A **capital loss** can be added back if you do not claim it on a regular basis, just as a **capital gain** is not counted unless it is claimed on a regular basis. People who buy and sell real estate and/or stocks continually would claim some type of capital gain or loss.

On the subject of tax returns, it is important the borrower understand that the lender can find several things that the borrower may not be eager to have known—things such as alimony payments, partnership in a money-losing business venture, or rents from properties that the borrower did not acknowledge owning. I had one couple who wrote off over $9,000 in one year for a show dog that they owned. Tax returns can often show debts or other obligations the borrower would never have considered revealing to the lender.

Another type of sole proprietorship is the **independent contractor.** Realtors are among the most common in this category. They work as an independent contractor for the company, with some of the costs of doing business paid by the company. In return, the agents split their commissions on all sales with the company. The agents are given W-9 forms by the company for tax purposes (instead of a W-2), and they use Schedule C to write off their own expenses.

Sometimes, the borrower cannot to come up with year-to-date figures for expenses. In such cases, some lenders will average expenses claimed on the Schedule C for the past two years and then subtract that adjusted average from the gross income (almost all borrowers know how much they have taken in). This procedure is appropriate as long as the expenses are not abnormally high or low for either of the years.

Let us consider an example for which the gross income of our sole proprietor for the first 10 months of 1999 is $100,000. Expenses (adjusted for depreciation and so on) in 1997 were $22,000 and in 1998 were $31,000. Summing, $22,000 + $31,000 = $53,000 and dividing by 24 months = $2,209 average expense for one month. So, $2,209 \times 10$ months = $22,093 average expense for 10 months. Thus, 1999 YTD net income = $77,907.

Partnerships.   Being a partner in a partnership is midway between being a sole proprietor and being incorporated. The difference is you are in business with other people and together you file a partnership return. In turn, you will have a Form 1065 to fill out on your returns to claim your portion of the income or loss.

For the lender, the key is whether the borrower **owns 25% or more of the partnership.** If it is less than that, only personal tax returns may be required if the borrower is using income from the partnership to qualify, or if there is debt associated with the partnership that must be disclosed. But, if the borrower owns 25% or more, then the borrower's **personal returns for the past two years, two years' complete partnership returns, and YTD P&L** may be required.

Corporations.   The incorporated borrower can be **sole stockholder or own 25% or more** of the corporation. In either case the lender may require **full personal tax returns for two years, full corporate returns for two years, a YTD P&L, and a balance sheet.** If she owns less than 25%, then a simple Verbal Verification or VOE will verify her income. The lender needs to know if the borrower is the corporation, or works for it.

The lender needs to see if the company can indeed afford to pay the borrower the income she claims. In addition, it wants to see how viable the company is, if there are any debts that the borrower may ultimately be liable for, and if the company is being used as a cash cow, to be milked of all its income and assets, leaving a shell. The documents will show the lender if the borrower's employment and income are reliable and recurring.

In summary, the self-employed, partnership, or corporation borrower may need to provide some or all of the following. Remember, computer underwriting may require significantly less documentation.

1. Full federal tax returns for the past two years with all schedules and original signatures.

2. Year-to-date profit & loss statement (within the current quarter) prepared and signed by a third party (account-ant or bookkeeper). Some lenders may require that it be audited in order to use the YTD income. This is required for sole proprietors, partnerships, and corporations.

3. Full federal partnership returns, signed, for the past two years.

4. Full federal corporate returns, signed, for the past two years.

5. Balance sheet (within the current quarter) prepared and signed by a third party. This is required for partnerships and corporations. The two years' and YTD net income are averaged for the number of months that are represented. This is the income used to qualify the borrower.

I have provided a basic *Self-Employed Income Analysis* form in the Appendix for anyone who would like to figure out what their usable income for qualifying might be.

The Low Documentation Loan—The More Cash Down, the More They Trust You

A way to avoid all the paper work shown here is called the *No Doc* or *No Income Verified Loan*. Depending on the lender and the loan, if the borrower puts down as little as 5% to as much as 30%, depending on credit scores and the type of No Doc loan. The income is not verified. These loans are not sold in the normal secondary market.

The *No Doc, Limited Doc, No Income Verified,* and *No Asset Verified* loans have changed tremendously over the years. It used to take a minimum of 20% down. Now, you may be able to find a 100% LTV No Doc loan. The actual requirements will vary based on LTV, what is and is not verified, the type of property (single or multifamily, owner occupied or investment), and credit scores. As you can guess, the pricing on these loans will be significantly higher than your normal Fannie Mae-type loan. Because of the structure of these products, the borrower must be prepared to go through a longer processing period and potential last-minute requirements. However, these loans serve a purpose, and can sometimes be the only way to buy, or refinance, a property.

The Second Job and Other Part-Time Income

As people stretch to make ends meet, a second job may become a necessity. Lenders recognize this income as long as they are assured it will continue. Getting a second job for the extra income just to qualify is not going to help in the short run. Fannie and Freddie will use income from a second job if the lender can determine the likeliness of it continuing for at least a three-year period. Starting a new second job after leaving another one the borrower has held for a good while would be acceptable. Starting a second job for the first time and having been employed there a short period of time would not normally be acceptable. The guidelines on second jobs tend to change periodically, but using common sense to determine the likelihood of continuance by past history is usually how the lender will approach it. The reasoning for this guideline is that the lender does not want the borrower to get a part-time job just to qualify and then later quit.

There are many other potential sources of exotic income, and the use of them for qualifying comes down to a very simple rule. It must be **reliable, recurring, verifiable, and extend into the future for at least three to five years.** Different lenders will interpret the rules to fit their secondary investor's guidelines by expanding or contracting the necessary documentation and time periods.

3

MAKING THE PAYMENTS
Avoiding Deficit Spending

The lender looks at your income and determines what is usable in order to be assured that that income is sufficient to make the mortgage payment, carry all current debt, and have money left for normal living expenses. Any excess income makes the borrower that much more qualified for the loan, and can make the lender more flexible. Here, again, you are faced with the basic guidelines established by Fannie and Freddie, how the computer looks at it, or both.

The two areas in which the borrower must qualify are **Income to Total Housing Expense** and **Income to Total Housing Expense Plus Monthly Debt Payments.** The standard for mortgage loan payments is called the **Total Housing Expense,** and this includes the following:

1. **Principal and interest** payment (PI)
2. **One twelfth of the annual real estate taxes** (T)
3. **One twelfth of the annual homeowner's insurance premium** (I)
4. **Mortgage insurance** escrow, if the loan is over 80% LTV (MI)
5. One twelfth of any **homeowners association or maintenance fee,** if one is charged (HOA)

WHAT THE HOUSE PAYMENT REALLY PAYS (PITI)

The **principal and interest payment** is the payment necessary to amortize, or pay off, the loan amount (principal) and the interest over the specified term, such as 30 years. You can figure this payment by buying a financial calculator or a book of amortization tables, calling your local lender or Realtor, or using the table in the back of this book. Almost all lenders now have websites with many financial tools, including an amortization calculator.

With the **homeowner's insurance,** the lender is only concerned that the dwelling itself is covered by the hazard portion of the insurance policy in the amount of the loan. (Some states now have laws that prohibit the lender from forcing the borrower to insure the dwelling for the loan amount if the value of the dwelling without the land is less than the loan amount.) All homeowners should get full coverage for things like theft and liability, buying enough coverage only to satisfy the lender would be a bad decision. Most insurance companies now have a full replacement cost rider, which is acceptable.

The hazard part of the homeowner's insurance protects not only the owner but also the lender in case the house, the security for the loan, is damaged or destroyed. For that reason, most lenders require that the insurance policy be paid up in full for the first year at the time the loan closes; then the lender escrows one twelfth of that premium in the monthly payment. When the policy renewal date comes around the next year, there will be enough money in escrow to pay it again for another full year. By doing this, the lender is protected against the possibility that the owner will forget to pay the premium and end up owing the lender on a pile of ashes, instead of a house, if it burns down. It is possible to find a lender that does not require the insurance to be escrowed, but the borrower will be required to have a down payment of 20% or more and pay between .125–.375 extra in points. Tax escrows can also be waived in the same manner.

Real estate taxes will be escrowed by just about all lenders because unpaid and past due taxes take a prior lien to any mortgage. If the owner does not pay them, then the local government has the power to sell the property in order to collect the delinquent taxes. If the owner owes $3,000 in taxes and $100,000 on the mortgage, the government is only concerned about the $3,000. When the property is sold for taxes, and someone pays $3,000 for a $200,000 property, the taxes are paid and the lender is left holding the bag. (Tax sales are one of the ways that those syndicated, get-rich-quick real estate seminars recommend as a path to the easy life. In reality, this type of thing does not happen so frequently as they might suggest. The lender will buy the property to protect its interests long before it lets the security disappear.) Tax escrow is a safeguard against the possibility that the mortgage lien position could be jeopardized. And let me add that the borrower will not necessarily be off the hook if there is no longer a house to secure the loan. The lender can, and will, file a deficiency judgment against the borrower for any amount still owed on the original mortgage. Try to borrow money with a large, mortgage-sized judgment against you.

Almost assuredly, the insurance and tax escrows will make your payment rise each year. It is ironic that most homeowners want this increase to happen. If the house goes up in value (which you hope it does), you will need to increase your insurance coverage, and the locality where you live will raise the assessed value and your taxes. The good news, if that is how you want to see it, is that the one twelfth of these increases added to your monthly PI payment should not make much difference in the new total payment. However, sometimes the amount escrowed for the prior year leads to a deficit amount in the escrow balances. When this happens, the lender will adjust the escrows for the next year to compensate. This can raise your payment significantly. Of course, they could also have too much in escrow. Then you will get a refund check.

If you put down less than 20%, and get a mortgage for over 80% LTV, you will be required to have **mortgage insurance.** This insurance covers the lender against the possibility of default and foreclosure on loans of over 80% LTV. If you put down 20% on almost all loans, you don't have to worry about it. I will cover mortgage insurance later.

If you live in a development that has a **mandatory homeowner's association fee or some other type of assessment,** this fee will be considered as part of your housing expense. The lender will not escrow for it, but it will be counted in the qualifying process because it is a mandatory expense. Most association dues or assessments are for maintenance of roads and common areas. Others, mostly in town house and condominium developments, will also cover outside maintenance, trash collection, and cable television subscription. These developments are generally called **Planned Unit Developments, or PUDs.** These costs are not optional, and they can be very expensive. Make sure you understand exactly what they are and what they cost before committing to buy. Some states now require that the purchaser be notified within a few weeks of signing a contract to purchase that there are covenants and restrictions, and that they contain homeowner fees.

4

L-T-V (LOAN-TO-VALUE) MEANS R-E-S-P-E-C-T

Now we know that the house payment can include principal, interest, taxes, insurance, mortgage insurance, and homeowner's association fees (PITIMIHOA). Based on standard secondary market guidelines, this total mortgage payment should not exceed 28% of your total gross monthly income (GMI). As we discussed earlier, the ratio for housing plus debt is 36%. These ratios can expand or contract, depending on several factors, not the least of which is computer underwriting.

You want to show the lender that you are a good risk. The more positive factors you can demonstrate, the easier it is to qualify and the more the qualifying ratios can expand. Or, the more negative factors you demonstrate, the harder it is to qualify and the less flexible the ratios will be. A deciding factor is the amount of cash that you put down and the resultant loan-to-value (LTV) ratio.

While you can figure out the actual LTV by dividing the loan amount by the purchase price—for example, a $90,000 loan divided by a $100,000 sales price equals 90% LTV with 10% down—the lender uses a different point of view. Using a $100,000 sales price and a $92,000 loan, most people would calculate a 92% LTV, and they would be right, and wrong. Lenders will acknowledge that this situation represents 92% of the value and 8% equity (cash down) in the property, but for qualifying purposes they look at loans in multiples of 5%. Take that 92% loan. In the lender's eyes, it is considered a 95% loan, just as an 87% loan would be considered as a 90% loan and a 80.01% loan would be 85% LTV for qualifying. Lenders round up to the next nearest

5%. Any loan with less than a 20% down payment will be considered a higher-risk loan, requiring mortgage insurance. The idea is that the less cash that you put down, the greater the risk. So, if you want a high-risk loan, you have to show that you, as the borrower, can minimize that risk.

If you put down the bare minimum (5% cash, and as little as 3% for some special loans) allowed for conventional loans, some lenders may use the more conservative ratios of **25%** for housing expense and **33%** for housing expense and monthly debt. With computer underwriting, the ratios can be over the 28/36 benchmark, but all other compensating factors will determine how much. Credit scores and reserve assets are the most crucial.

On average, for any home loan on which a borrower defaulted and on which the lender foreclosed, the lender has received about 80% of the property's value. When you put down less than that magic 20%, the lender starts to squirm.

No lender wants to face the possibility of having to foreclose on a $100,000 house with a $90,000 loan and ending up with $80,000 with which to pay off the loan and expenses. That is bad economics. Borrowers argue that they are good credit risks and that the house will appreciate quickly anyway. Therefore, the lender will be covered in a short time by normal inflation. That is true—as long as the property does appreciate, which is certainly not a given. Besides, what will protect the lender from a recession, or a depression, or devaluation (say a copper smelter is built next door), or the borrower being fired, or gambling away the house payment, or declaring bankruptcy? Even if you can prove very persuasively that you are a well-qualified borrower at the time, the lender wants to cover the possibility that you may turn into a pumpkin after the loan is closed.

One way that lenders insure themselves against high-risk loans is to require that the loan have **mortgage insurance.** Remember the mortgage insurance escrow that I said could be included in your monthly payment? If you have sufficient cash to put down 20%, then that will save you the cost of mortgage insurance and allow the lending company to be more liberal in their qualifying. FHA and VA have mortgage insurance and a guarantee fee, respectively, that will be charged regardless of the LTV. However, VA's fee is reduced if you put down 5% or 10%.

You can avoid mortgage insurance in your payment by having what is known as "lender paid" or "no MI" loans. With these loans, you will pay extra points, with the amount depending on the LTV. An 85% loan would add about 1 point, 90% about 1.50 points, and 95% about 2.50 points above the normal interest rate and points quote. These points will vary. High credit scores will often allow fewer points as determined by the computer. The good part about this type of MI is your payment is less and the points are tax deductible. If you are planning to pay down the loan significantly within a few years or the appreciation will lower the loan payment to less than 80% quickly, then you may not want to pay these nonrefundable points.

Mortgage insurance can be removed from your loan payment once the loan meets certain criteria. It is required to be removed automatically once your loan reaches 78% of the original value as it is scheduled by normal amortization. (This can vary by the type of property, such as two- to four-family or investment property.) The borrower can request that it be removed when the LTV actually reaches 80% of the original property value. If you want to use current value, the loan must be at least five years old, or two years old if the LTV is 75%. You also cannot have any 30-day late payments in the past 12 months. Having said all that, many lenders will remove the MI after as little as one year if you can prove the LTV is 80% or less, either by having paid it down, or by appreciation, or both. In the worst case, you can refinance the loan to remove the MI. The appraisal will show the value of the property. (You can go to the website www.PrivateMI.com to find out exactly when the MI can be removed.)

However, what if you only have enough cash for 10% down? You have several choices. You can put down your 10% and get the mortgage insurance. You can "hit up" the proverbial rich relative for the other 10% as a gift. Or you can get an 80% loan, put down the 10% cash, and get a second deed of trust mortgage for the other 10%—if you qualify. This is what is known as an 80–10–10 loan. You can also get 80–15–5 and, with special loans, as high as 80–20 or 75–25. That is a 100% total LTV.

SECOND MORTGAGES
Spreading the Debt

If the lender and the type of loan will allow it—and you qualify—then you can get a first mortgage plus a second mortgage and not have to pay mortgage insurance on the first mortgage. Certain loans will still require some mortgage insurance coverage because of the total risk involved. While the first mortgage lender is in a low risk position in case of foreclosure, it will scrutinize the borrower more closely because of the higher possibility that default could occur. Don't assume that, because the first mortgage is 80% LTV or less, the lender is not as concerned. People who put less of their own cash into a property will always have a higher probability of defaulting. Not only is their payment higher, but they will also have less to lose monetarily if they are foreclosed upon.

Most lenders will allow the borrower to get a second mortgage that, in combination with the first, will equal up to as high as 100% **total loan-to-value (TLTV).** The most common will go as high as 95% TLTV (also called combined loan-to-value, CLTV). The 100% TLTV loans are not from Fannie or Freddie and will require excellent credit and a higher interest rate.

The first mortgage will be first in line, or in the first position. In any situation where the loans are to be paid off (sale of the house, foreclosure, sale for nonpayment of taxes, and so on), the first will always be paid off before any other mortgage. The second mortgage, being in the second position, will be paid off second, that is, if there is any money left to pay it.

Secondary market investors have begun to recognize that second mortgages are putting them more at risk, so Fannie Mae and Freddie Mac set guidelines for the maximum TLTV. The maximum first mortgage LTVs and TLTVs have changed several times. Depending on the number of units and if it is owner-occupied or investment property, the first mortgage will go from 80% down to 70% and the TLTV will ranges from 90% to 95%. There are investors that will be more aggressive than Fannie or Freddie, as noted with the 100% TLTV loans.

Lenders don't mind a second mortgage; just don't ask them to give you a high LTV on the first. After you have the first mortgage, there is currently no prohibition to getting as high a second mortgage as possible.

Second mortgages are higher-risk loans, and as such, will normally carry a higher interest rate and a quicker payoff period. Typically, they will be 1–5% higher in interest rate and will amortize out, or have a payoff period, in 3 to 15 years. It is not unusual to have 30-year seconds, but a 30-year amortization with a balloon of 5 to 15 years is more common. What does a second mortgage have to do with qualifying? The amortization period is short and the payment is higher, adding to the housing expense. The payment on the second mortgage must also be added to the house payment in qualifying. It is part of your Total Housing Expense.

THE QUICKER YOU PAY, THE LESS YOU PAY

If you compare a payment for a 30-year and a 15-year loan, you will notice that the 15-year payment is much higher than the 30-year one (see the comparison in the appendix). For example, on a $50,000 loan at 10%, the monthly payment for a 30-year loan is $438.79, for a 15-year, $537.30.

This difference is due to the fact that the 15-year payment includes a **higher amount of principal** each month, meaning that the loan is paid off quicker, in 15 years. (When we discuss loan types, I will show you a little trick that shortens the amortization on loans.)

Let us consider as an example the purchase of a $100,000 property with $10,000 down (10%), an $80,000 first mortgage (80% LTV) at 10% for 30 years, and a $10,000 second mortgage (10%) at 11.5% for 15 years. The loan payments would look like this:

1st	$ 702.06	P&I (principal and interest)
2nd	116.82	P&I
Total	$ 818.88	P&I

The $818.88 figure will be used, along with escrows and any HOA fees, to qualify. Now we can add yet another possible expense to the list making up the total house payment:

1. Principal and interest payment (PI)
2. One twelfth of homeowner's insurance (I)
3. One twelfth of annual real estate taxes (T)
4. Mortgage insurance escrow, if required (MI)
5. Homeowner's association fees, if required (HOA)
6. Other financing, such as a second mortgage, third mortgage, and so on

THE EQUITY LINE OF CREDIT

The equity line of credit, which has become extremely popular since the mid-1980s, is also a second mortgage, unless there is no other mortgage on the property. Then it will be a first. Unlike a mortgage, however, it is a **revolving line of credit** that allows the homeowner to borrow against it repeatedly. Pay it down, and then borrow again just like a credit card, which it is, with one very important distinction. This credit is secured by your home, and if you don't make the payments the lender can foreclose and you lose your house. This consequence is more severe than the poor credit rating and judgment that the typical bank card can impose. Using an equity line of credit as a second mortgage to purchase a home is a viable idea as long as you can make the higher payments. Most equity lines require monthly payments of 1.5% to 2% of the remaining principal balance. Using a line of credit for other expenses requires more thought. Education expenses, debt consolidation (if you cancel the credit being consolidated), and home improvements are some of the more logical debts. Cruises around the world and stereo sound systems are not. As in all things tax-deductible, congress is considering ways to limit the expenses paid out of a line of credit that can remain tax-deductible.

IN THE END, YOU STILL HAVE TO QUALIFY

Now that you know your usable income, house payment, long-term debt (within a safe approximation), and the ratios discussed earlier, you need to understand that these things combined will determine exactly how much you can borrow. As I have noted, computer underwriting looks at everything and can be very liberal, or the computer can refer you as a high risk who does not meet normal requirements.

There will always be lenders and loans that do not fit the basic secondary market guidelines. For example, I know of one investor who will do ratios of 40%/40%, instead of the 28%/36%. But this loan is very restrictive as to which borrowers and properties it will take. These loans are not typically computer underwritten (although there are some that use a different system than Fannie or Freddie). Because they are specialized loans and usually approved by human beings, the criteria for approval will vary widely expensive. Always ask your lender what the company will allow. Also, FHA and VA criteria are different from conventional qualifying, as you will discover when you read the section on them. Try to qualify under the most conservative scenario, then start adding other factors if they are needed. The cleaner and simpler the loan, the easier it is to approve.

Now that we have gone through the borrower's life with a fine-tooth comb, everything else should be easy. After all, the borrower makes enough money, has great credit, and has the money to buy the house. There should be no need to bug her anymore, right? As much as everyone, the lender included, would like to agree, it just ain't so.

MORTGAGE INSURANCE
For Those Long on Income and Short on Cash

Mortgage insurance can influence not only the borrower's house payment but also his ability to qualify. Earlier we briefly discussed the fact that any loan with less than 20% down will require mortgage insurance. Now we need to understand exactly how it affects our loan and our ability to get it.

Many borrowers confuse mortgage insurance with mortgage life insurance, which pays off the mortgage if the borrower dies. While the lender doesn't want the borrower to die, it is more concerned about the fate of the loan. Historically, when a borrower has gone to foreclosure and the house has been sold, the lender received only about 80% of the value of the property. Also, the first years of a mortgage are the years of greatest risk. These facts mean several things to the borrower:

1. The less cash you put down, the more expensive the mortgage insurance.
2. If the type of loan is a higher risk, such as an ARM or any loan with increasing payments, the mortgage insurance is more expensive.

Mortgage insurance protects the lender against loss if there is a default and foreclosure on the mortgage. Normally mortgage insurance covers the top 25% of the loan, thereby reducing the lender's exposure to 75% of the value.

For example, consider a $100,000 purchase made with 5%

down. That creates a very high risk for the lender. In a foreclosure situation it could lose $15,000 or more. The company is not interested in making a high LTV loan without some protection, so it requires that the borrower purchase mortgage insurance to lower the risk.

There are about eight to ten mortgage insurance companies that lenders use. Most lenders have companies that they prefer to deal with because they have developed a good working relationship. Most of these companies' rates fall within a close competitive range, but they can change periodically. Before submitting the loan to the underwriter for approval, the lender will choose the mortgage insurance company that it feels will give the best service. The borrower is not involved in this part of the process other than to pay the premium.

Today, most mortgage insurance is "delegated." That means the lender is delegated by the mortgage insurance company to approve the loan for them. Sometimes the mortgage insurance company's underwriters will be required to approve the loan. If the loan is computer-approved with MI, the computer will assign the level of coverage, possibly lowering the cost to the borrower. The MI company used is often determined by its relationship with the lender. A lender may work with three to five companies, rotating the loans given to them based on these relationships. Mortgage insurance companies can help lenders get lower interest, more investors, or just plain lower the cost per loan. Depending on the agreement between the lender and the MI company, a certain percentage of the lender's loans requiring MI will be assigned to that company. So, mortgage insurance companies can do more than just provide risk coverage.

The Less Your Down Payment, the More It Costs

The purchase of mortgage insurance will allow less cash down and a higher loan amount, but it will cost you. How much? That depends on the cash down, the loan term, the type of loan, the particular mortgage insurance company, the type of premium that is paid, or if it is computer underwritten.

Normal, private mortgage insurance is now a simple monthly payment determined by the amount of coverage required, the amortization period, type of loan, and the LTV. To list all the types of properties, the LTVs, coverages, and so forth would take a great deal of space, and they do change. Just to give you an idea, here are some standard coverage and costs for an owner-occupied residence with an amortization over 20 years.

LTV	COVERAGE	RATE
97%	35%	.95/1000
95%	30%	.78/1000
90%	25%	.52/1000
85%	12%	.32/1000

The rate is divided by 12 and added to the monthly payment: $100,00 loan, 90%LTV = 1,000 × .52 = 520/12 months = $43.33/month. These numbers only show what the relative cost can be Premiums change with time and companies (see mortgage insurance comparison chart in the Appendix).

LOAN TYPES
The ABCS of FRMs, ARMs, GPMs, GEMs, FHAs, and VAs

Although we have looked at many pitfalls and requirements the borrower must understand, we have not yet considered the most important one—the reason that a borrower comes to a lender in the first place—the loan itself. If you think Baskin-Robbins has a lot of choices, start calling all your local lenders. There are so many variations on the loans offered today that even the lenders themselves can get confused. As a result, many lenders emphasize their basic loans plus whatever the special of the moment might be. The special is often a loan that the home office wants them to market aggressively because it has a lot of money invested in this particular loan program. Sometimes the special is a loan the originator understands and thinks is great. During periods of high interest rate, you will see a tremendous increase in the numbers and types of adjustable rate mortgages (ARMs) and buy-down loans. During periods of low rates, lenders will duel over who can show the lowest rates by raising the discount points. Remember, the lower the rate, the higher the discount points. The borrowers' problem is to decide the following:

1. Which type of loan best suits their situation?
2. What differences in the same basic loan offered by different lenders are worthwhile and are advantageous to the borrower?

3. How much are they willing to pay for the loan?
4. Which lender will give them the best service on the loan they choose?

Some of these questions can be answered only by the borrowers, but a competent lender can give invaluable guidance. To start the process, you must first separate the different types of loans, then compare the advantages and disadvantages.

FIXED RATE MORTGAGES (FRMs)

The plain old stodgy, fixed rate loan is still the best for many people. You know what your payment will be every year. You don't have to worry about interest rate increases. You can budget for it very easily. And, if your loan requires it, your mortgage insurance costs less. When interest rates are low it is hard to go wrong with a fixed rate loan.

These loans can be obtained in just about any amortization period that the borrower could want. The standard periods for mortgage loans are 30, 25, 20, 15, and sometimes 10 years. If a loan has an amortization period of 20 years, it will take 20 years of making the monthly payment to pay it off. The shorter the amortization period, the less interest the borrowers will pay because they will not owe the money for as long a period. A 15-year loan will have almost half the interest payments of a 30-year loan at a comparable rate. If we compare $100,000 loans at 10%, keeping the loans for their complete terms, the interest paid would look like this.

30-year: $215,925.20
15-year: $ 93,429.80

As you can see, 15 years is much cheaper. And, making an even better deal, 15-year interest rates are almost always lower than 30-year rates. The lesson here is that the shorter the amortization period, the less costly the loan. Occasionally someone makes the observation that because mortgage interest is almost the only deductible interest remaining on the federal income tax schedules (at least it was when I wrote this), one shouldn't worry about rates or amortization period. This person also doesn't think the federal deficit is something to worry about either. Everyone is entitled to a personal opinion. That's why there are different loan choices.

One reason someone might choose a 30-year loan over the 15-year is that the payment is much lower. The borrower often can qualify for the 30-year loans but not for the 15-year loan. Let's see what the difference is. Using our $100,000 loan at 10%, the monthly payments (PI) would be:

30-year: $ 877.57
15-year: $1,074.61

The difference is $197.04 per month. The obvious reason for this is that payments on the 15-year loan reduce the principal amount much more quickly. (See the loan amortization comparison Appendix.) Without considering tax and insurance escrows and using the 28% ratio, we find that the qualifying incomes for the two loans would be:

30-year: $3,134.18 gross monthly income
15-year $3,837.89 gross monthly income

Or about a $8,500 difference in annual income. Again, remember that qualifying by computer underwriting can allow the borrower to qualify at a much higher ratio.

Prepayment

There is a way to have your cake and eat it too. Remember that I referred earlier to a way that you could design your own loan? Most loans, and all Fannie-Freddie loans, have no **prepayment penalties.** That means you can pay off any or all of your loan principal at any time without penalty. There are some loans out there that do have a penalty, so make sure you ask your lender. If your loan doesn't, you can get creative.

Say you want the $100,000 loan at 10% and you want the 15-year payout, but you can only qualify for the 30-year loan. Get the 30-year loan and make the corresponding 15-year payment. That is, pay the extra $197.04 per month and you will have paid the loan off in 15 years. You have accelerated the amortization, and there's no penalty!

There are a few shortcomings. As you remember, 15-year loans have lower rates than 30-year ones. You may have to accept a 10% 30-year amortization, which you pay off in 15 years, instead of a 9.75% 15-year rate. That is a small price considering the fact that you are able to get the loan, buy the house, and pay it off in 15 years.

If you can't make the 15-year payment, compromise on $50 or $100 more a month—whatever you can afford. It will still accelerate the amortization and pay the loan off faster. You are only required to make the 30-year payment. Only you can take the initiative and create the motivation to make the higher payment every month.

You can also make payments periodically during the year or even once a year. The latter is done by people who may not be able to make regular extra payments, but who get cash (such as tax refunds) once a year that could be applied. Making extra payments monthly is more effective because they are credited toward the principal at the time they are paid and will lower the interest paid more quickly.

In any case, make sure that the lender understands that you are making a principal prepayment. If the payment coupon shows one amount and the check is for a higher amount, the clerk who credits it may put the extra into escrow until your intention is known (late payment, insufficient escrow of taxes, and so on). Most payment coupons today have a space specifically for principal reduction. If there is not a space, I recommend that you make out your regular check for the normal payment. Then, write a separate check for the additional principal reduction and attach a note stating what it is for. This way there is little chance that it will not be properly credited.

One last advantage to rapid principal reduction is that it is **an enforced savings account.** Every dollar that you put into your home is a dollar that you probably can get out later, along with the appreciation that has occurred. A person's residence is usually the largest single investment that he or she will make, and it will also be the largest part of a person's net worth.

BIWEEKLY MORTGAGES

The biweekly mortgage has gained acceptance from borrowers and from the general secondary market. It is a marketing bonanza for banks and other depository institutions that are set up to service it. It also allows the borrower to pay his loan off in two-thirds the time.

This mortgage is a fixed rate loan in which the normal

monthly payment is split in half and paid every two weeks. Voilà! Biweekly! Because the lender receives part of the principal earlier than with a once-a-month payment, the interest charged is less. Also, over the course of a year the borrower makes 26 payments instead of the normal 24 in a monthly payment. At first the principal reduction is very small. But, if it is carried out to term, a 30-year loan will be paid off around the twentieth year.

The lenders that offer this loan have several requirements. The main one is that you must make your payments by automatic debit draft from your bank account. The reason for this stipulation is that it is just about impossible for an individual to get the payment in on time every two weeks. Any tardiness would play havoc with the bank's ability to service the loan and keep the records straight. It also means that the bank will be assured of a regular deposit account and an obligated depositor. If you are interested, check all your local lenders to see not only if they offer them, but also what is required to get one.

One note of caution: Look at them very carefully. They are not doing so for free. They normally charge an upfront fee, and some may have a fee that is built into the payments. So, you are paying a large cost for the service plus a regular fee in each payment. These extra costs could nullify any advantage you might gain. It may be better just to make extra payments each year that go directly toward reducing your loan payment amortization rather than into someone else's pocket as a fee.

BUY-DOWN LOANS
Pay Your Money and Take Your Choice

Buy-down loans are in 2 different categories: temporary buy-downs and permanent buy-downs. For the money, permanent buy-downs will usually work out to be the better deal.

Permanent Buy-Downs

The permanent buy-down is simple. You pay more discount points to get a lower rate. There is no absolute as to what the cost will be. One rule of thumb says 1 point (1%) for every one-eighth percent (0.125%) drop in the rate. If you check different lenders' rates, you will see that the costs can be much less, depending on how competitive the lenders are at the time. For example, a lender might be quoting the following:

> 10% with 1 + 0 (1% origination fee + zero discount points)
>
> 9.875% with 1 + 0.25
>
> 9.750% with 1 + 1.00
>
> 9.625% with 1 + 1.75
>
> 9.500% with 1 + 2.25

Don't try to figure out why the pricing is this way, just decide whether you are willing to pay 2.25% of the loan amount at closing for 0.5% less interest.

Most lenders set rates based on the following:

1. Market rates. (Rates are actually set in the bond markets. I will cover this in the section on interest rates.)
2. Local competition.
3. Regional competition.
4. How they feel the rates are going to move.
5. How much they need the business.
6. If they are making money or losing money.
7. How lucky they think they can get.

The simplest method of choosing which rate you should buy is deciding **how long you are going to have the loan.** (I am assuming that you have the cash to pay the extra points. Of course, if someone else—like the seller—is paying the points, go for the max.) For example, on a 30-year $100,000 loan with the 2.25 points given above, we can make these calculations.

Rate	Payment (PI)	PI difference	Cost of points	Pay back
10%	$877.57	+$440.64/yr	-0-	-0-
9.5%	$840.85	−$440.64	$2,250.00	5.11 yrs*

* ($2,250 divided by yearly savings = Time it will take the savings to pay back the additional discount points)

In this example, the borrower would have to keep the loan for about five years for the savings from the lower payment to equal the additional discount points. This example also does not take into account any tax deductibility of the points paid, or, as a CPA once noted, the time-use of money.

Of course, if you as borrower have to buy down the loan to 9.5% just to qualify, then the decision has at least in part already been made for you. The house itself should appreciate $2,250 in a year during a normal economy (3% on a $75,000 house). If you wait for interest rates to drop (which they may not), the cost of the house may have increased (which it probably will)—if it is still available.

The permanent buy-down offers the advantages of a set rate and payment for the life of the loan. It allows you to obtain a lower rate as well as a lower payment. The only drawback is the additional cost.

It is not unusual for the seller to pay some of the closing costs. Make her an offer. All she can say is no. If the seller is asking $100,000 but will take $97,000, offer $100,000 and get the seller to pay 3 points. You get the house and the lower rate, and the seller sells her house and gets what she wanted. In this situation it is imperative that you have working with you a professional realtor and a knowledgeable lender who know what they are doing.

Permanent buy-downs can also be done on loans other than fixed rate. By paying more points, you can get a lower initial rate on an adjustable rate or a graduated payment mortgage. We will look at these later.

Temporary Buy-Down

A **temporary buy-down** will give the borrower temporary relief in the form of lower payments for the first few years. This is done by several means. In the traditional type of temporary buy-down loan the borrower simply pays the difference between the actual payments and the initial lower payments in cash at closing in the form of points, normally for either two years (2-1 buy-down) or three years (3-2-1 buy-down).

If you want to lower the payment on our 30-year, $100,000 loan at 10%, this is how it is done.

Payment Rate	PI Payment	Yearly Total	Difference	Total diff
10.000%	$877.57 × 12 =	$10,530.84	-0-	
9.000	$804.62 × 12 =	9,665.44	($865.40)	$865.40
8.000	$733.77 × 12 =	8,805.24	(1,725.20)	2,590.60
7.000	$665.30 × 12 =	7,983.60	(2,547.24)	5,137.84

If you bought the initial payment for the first year down to 8.00% (2-1 buy-down) the sum of one year of payments at 8% plus one year at 9% would be $2,590.78 (difference between two years of monthly payments of 10% PI and 8% and 9%), plus any normal discount points that would be on the 10% rate that was bought down. You then have monthly payments of $733.77 for the first year, $804.62 for the second, and the normal 10% 30-year payment of $877.57 for the third through the 30th. If you really want to pay a lot, consider the 3-2-1 buy-down to an initial payment of $665.30 for a cost of $5,137.84, or 5.13784% of this particular loan amount of $100,000.

These loans are normally done when the seller, usually a builder, offers to pay the buy-down cost to help sell the house. The buyer qualifies at the initial payment. However, nothing is free. The builder has just added the extra cost into the price of the house. For about the cost of that 2-1 buy-down, you can get a permanent buy-down of 0.25% to 0.5% over the life of the loan. For the cost of the 3-2-1 you could get the same permanent buy-down and take a vacation as well. Or, if you were smart you would invest the $2,590 to $5,137.

Another type of temporary buy-down, **the lender funded buy-down,** is initially very cheap. For this, the lender offers a very attractive initial bought-down rate with minimal, or no, points and sometimes pays most of the closing costs. By the time the loan has adjusted back up to its actual rate, the borrower is paying 0.5% to 1% higher than the current market rate. The lender is using Premium Pricing and using the cash to pay the buy-down costs. An example would be a 2-1 buy-down with an initial payment based on a rate of 8% with 1% discount point at closing. The second year the payment is based on 9%, and then it levels out for the remainder at 10%. Not bad as long as you knew when you obtained the loan that the current market rate for a comparable fixed rate loan with similar points was 9.25%. This is not to say it's a bad loan. You just need to know what the market is to make a comparison.

The advantage of a temporary buy-down is that it will get you qualified at a lower payment so you can buy more house than a permanent buy-down at comparable cost. Just remember that you will end up making the higher payments.

THE RISING EQUITY PAYMENT LOAN

Another form of temporary buy-down is a very creative loan that starts out with an interest-only payment. Freddie Mac has offered one called the equal loan. For this fixed rate loan the payments start low, then the PI payment increases 7.5% per year until it reaches a year when the payment levels off. (The year of level payment can be anywhere from the second to the eighth year, depending on how far you want to buy it down.) The payment then stays the same for the remainder of the loan term. The loans are usually offered in either 30- or 15-year amortization periods. The 15-year loan is by far the better buy. The most appealing features of this loan are that it only costs a fraction of a normal buy-down and you qualify at the first year's payment.

The lender needs to show why it feels the borrower will be able to make the higher payments in the later years. Likelihood of increased income, lower debts, increase in assets, completion of an advanced degree would all be factors that could show the borrower's continued ability to make the payments.

Using the $100,000 loan and a 10% rate for both the 15- and 30-year equal loans (the 15-year interest rate will in reality always be lower), here is how they compare. (See p. 76.)

The cost is what you pay to buy the loan down! Compared with the $2,600 to $5,100 on the other buy-downs, $510.00 to buy down the 15-year payment to a starting, and qualifying, payment of $790.79 is cheap indeed.

How do lenders do it? They start the payments at a point where the principal reduction is less than normal. In the first 15-year loan example, the first-year payments are actually less than interest-only payments. The 0.510% cost is the difference between the $790.79 payment and the interest-only payment of $833.34. The payments then increase by 7.5% per year until they reach the level payment year. This payment is sufficient to amortize the loan out over the remaining term.

A normal 15-year 10% loan on $100,000 would have a PI payment of $1,074.61, while the rising equity loan's level payment beginning in Year 8 is $1,261.73. The $187.12 difference is what is necessary to pay the loan out by the 15th year.

Underlying this loan is the idea that borrowers can buy a lot more house with less initial income, as long as their income will increase to meet the higher payments. A borrower getting the normal 10% fixed payment 15-year loan would need at least $3,838 per month income, but only $2,825 for the same rising equity loan requiring initial payments of $790.79. That is a difference of over $12,000 per year. It has been called the ultimate Yuppie loan. It allows you to buy now and pay later.

	RISING EQUITY LOAN		3-2-1 BUY-DOWN		2-1 BUY-DOWN	
	15-year	30-year	15-year	30-year	15-year	30-year
Buy-down cost	$510.00	$1,074.00	$4,261.00	$5,138.00	$2,152.00	$2,591.00
	(.51%)	(1.064%)	(4.261%)	(5.138%)	(2.152%)	(2.591%)
First year Interest Rate	5.0%	8.375%	7.0%	7.0%	8.0%	8.0%
PI Payment:						
1st Year:	$790.79	$760.07	$898.82	$665.30	$955.65	$733.77
2nd Year:	850.10	817.08	955.65	733.77	1,014.27	804.62
3rd Year:	913.86	878.36	1,014.27	804.62	1,074.61	877.57
4th Year:	982.40	889.04	1,074.61	877.57		
5th Year:	1,056.08					
6th Year:	1,135.29					
7th Year:	1,220.44					
8th Year:	1,261.73					
15th year	1,261.73		1,074.61		1,074.61	
30th year		889.04		877.57		877.57

The rising equity loan is considered a nonfixed payment loan for mortgage insurance purposes, meaning you have to use ARM premiums. Its advantages are these:

1. The initial payments for qualifying are low.
2. The borrower can buy more house for less income.
3. It is a fixed rate loan.
4. You know exactly what your payments will be every year.
5. The payments rise slowly enough to avoid payment shock.
6. Its cost structure is perfect for a buyer who will be in the house only three to five years.
7. The buyer whose income will increase in the future can benefit from this earnings potential.
8. It has a low-cost buy-down.

The disadvantages are these:

1. The payments increase.
2. Your income and debts must keep pace with the higher payments.
3. The note rate will be higher than a normal 15-year straight fixed rate.
4. This type of loan comes and goes. When interest rates are low, most lenders will not offer it.

ADJUSTABLE RATE MORTGAGES (ARMs)

Also known in some areas as Renegotiable Rate Mortgages (RRMs), Flexible Rate Mortgages (FRMs), or Variable Rate Mortgages (VRMs), these are all the same animal. They have evolved to the point that they now have many of the same basic characteristics.

In the United States the original ARMs were not designed to protect the borrower. As time passed, the consumer received more protection; but, because of increased competition, the lenders themselves took on more of the risk in the form of lower initial rates with fewer points. After the S&L crisis beginning in the late 1980s and the resultant restructuring of the mortgage industry, ARMs have come to more of a middle ground. The initial rates may not be quite so low as they once were, so that a profit is more likely, and the borrower has better protection in the forms of caps on movement of the rate, and disclosures on how the loan works.

An ARM gives the borrower an **initial low payment** that then will be adjusted at a given interval during the loan (every six months, one year, and so on) based on a given benchmark, usually a government or lending index, with caps on the interest rate rise, or fall for each adjustment period and for the life of the loan. That's not too hard to understand, is it? Of course it is. That is why a lender must by law give each borrower a written disclosure of the loan at application.

There are several common features in the disclosures to all ARMs:

1. Initial rate
2. How often the interest rate, and payment, is subject to change
3. Index on which the interest rate change is calculated
4. Margin that is added to the index to determine the new rate
5. Cap on the amount the interest rate can rise or fall
   a. On each adjustment period
   b. Over the life of the loan

To explain the ARM, I will use a normal one-year ARM as an example.

Initial Rate

The initial rate is the actual interest rate that the borrower will be charged for the first period of the loan. For this example, if the fixed rate at the time is 10% for a 30-year loan, let's say the ARM initial rate is 7.75%. (To keep it simple we will not use any discount points, but an ARM normally has 0 to 3 + points. As with any loan, you can pay more points to buy down the rate—in this case the initial rate. However, there are limits on how far down one can buy the initial rate.) At 7.75% you are starting at a rate 2.25% lower than the market fixed rate. The 7.75% is the interest on which your payment is based for the first period of the loan until the first interest rate, and payment, adjustment.

In our example, **the adjustment** will come on the one-year anniversary date of the loan. If the loan closed on June 1, 1990, the first change date would be June 1, 1991. Well, actually it would become effective on that date, but the rate change is calculated sooner. Normally, the lender sets the new rate about 45 calendar days before the effective change date in order to make the adjustment, notify the borrower, and send out a new payment coupon book. Some loans will be adjusted within certain quarters of each year, depending on when the loan closed. As a result the first adjustment could occur sooner or later than the given adjustment period (one year in our example). So, you might have an ARM for which all loans closing June through August be adjusted in June of the next year. Ask your lender to explain it fully.

The Index

How does the lender determine what the new rate will be? One might say it was based on the average air pressure of the bicycle tires in China, and to many borrowers this answer would not seem too far wrong. In reality, it is based on some **type of index.** The most common is the index of **U.S. Treasury Securities** for the period of the loan adjustment. In our example it would be the One-Year Treasury Securities Index. This is a compilation of the rates on one-year treasury securities adjusted to a constant maturity. There are other indexes such as the Federal Home Loan Bank Board (FHLBB) index and the Cost of Funds Index (COFI) for institutions for all districts or just one district such as the Eleventh District, and even a foreign index, the London Interbank Offered Rate (LIBOR). There may be a Chinese Averaged Bicycle Air Pressure Index (CABAPI) for all I know. In any case, the Treasury Securities Index is the one most widely used, and the one we will use in our example.

Many lenders have the history of the index for the past one to five years. Get them to give you a copy, but don't rely on history to provide a key to what the index will be in the future. An index that has been low every year in May could be the highest in its history the May of the year after you get your loan, thereby giving you the highest possible adjustment.

The index itself changes once a week, and the change is reported by the Federal Reserve. In normal times the index moves in increments of 0.125% to 0.25% in any given week, if it moves at all. Of course, it may move 1% or more when the economy experiences a major event like a stock market crash. The amount of adjustment on an ARM is at the mercy of what the index is on the week the lender makes the change. One week it could be 7.5%, and the next it could be 6.8%. I have seen ARMs that were adjusted within one to two weeks of each other with new rates that differed by over 0.5%.

For our example we will say that our 7.75% initial rate comes up for adjustment on June 1 and that the index used is determined 45 days before that date, or April 15. In the week of April 15 the index is 8.375%. Before you congratulate yourself on getting such a great loan that you will only be paying 8.375% in the second year, we need to add to the index rate the margin.

The Margin

The margin is a percentage that is added to the index to determine what the new interest rate will be for the next period (one year in our example). Most ARM margins will be in the range of 2.00% to 3.00%. For our example let us use a margin of 2.50%.

Using the 7.75% initial rate with the One-Year Treasury Securities Index, which we have said is 8.375%, and a margin of 2.50%, the new interest rate will be 10.875%. You don't think that is a very good deal? Just because your rate went up 3.125% in one year and your payment increased over 22%? Luckily, "Let the consumer beware" is not the government credo when it comes to lending. To protect the borrower against huge interest increases and **payment shock,** lenders have been forced to cap the maximum that the interest rate can increase, or decrease, in any adjustment period and on the the maximum that the interest rate can increase, or decrease, over the life of the loan.

The Caps

Depending on the different ARMs, caps can be as low as 1% a year and 3% lifetime or as high as 2% a year and 6% lifetime, or any combination. A loan with a 1% maximum interest rate increase would keep your payment (PI) from increasing more than about

7.5% a year, while the 2% cap could take it up as much as 15% in a year. The lifetime cap can certainly make a difference if you are looking at 3% over the initial rate (10.75% in our example) as opposed to 6% (13.75% in our example). For our example, we will use caps of 2% per year and 6% lifetime, which are fairly standard in the market. That would mean the second-year interest rate could not exceed 9.75% and the lifetime rate could be no higher than 13.75%.

In reconsidering our index of 8.375% plus the margin of 2.50% that totaled 10.875%, we find the cap of 2% would prevent the rate being any higher than 9.75% for the second year (7.75% + 2%). The rate will be adjusted toward the total of the index plus the margin, within the maximum rate set by the caps. If the index had been 7.00% (a decrease from the initial rate of 7.75%), then the total with the 2.50% margin would have been 9.50%, and that is what the second-year rate would be, less than the maximum set by the caps.

How High Can It Fly?

As you can see from our example, you would get one year at 7.75%, one year at 9.75% (maximum), and, worst of all, the third year could be 11.75%, for an average of 9.75%. Not bad when you could have had 10% fixed. And, the rate can go down. But, just to rain on your parade, it can also go up and stay up if the index doesn't drop. An ARM will move toward the market rate and, once it is near it, will trade up and down toward it within the caps. It is good for people who know they are going to be in the house only three to five years. But it can be a very good loan for the long term if interest rates stay low with only an occasional jump for a year or two.

With each interest rate adjustment, the payment is adjusted to pay out on the remaining principal balance at that time, over the remaining amortization period left on the loan, based on the new interest rate to which the loan is adjusted (in our example, 7.75% for 30 years, 9.75% for 29 years, and so forth). This schedule will fully amortize the loan over the payment period. Now, if you want to get more sophisticated, you can take the **prepayment** idea that we discussed for fixed rate loans and apply it to the ARM (as long as there is no prepayment penalty). If you prepaid on the mortgage each month or once a year, the balance would be less at the time the rate, and payment, are adjusted. Thus, the payment would be less than it would have been if you just made the regular monthly payments.

Now that we have been through a typical one-year ARM with 2%/6% caps and a margin of 2.50%, let's take a look at some of the other ARMs that are available.

Shopping at the ARM Store
The Six-Month ARM

This works on the same principal as our one-year ARM except that it adjusts every six months. This is not for the fainthearted, but it will have a cap of no more than 0.5% to 1% per six-month adjustment. These are the equivalent, with a normal one-year ARM, of a 1% or a 2% per year cap. The big difference is that you can get the lower, or higher, rate every six months instead of once a year. Is this a good loan? It depends on what the market is doing at each adjustment period, and your luck.

The Three-Year ARM (3/3 ARM)

This resembles the 1-year ARM, except that the interest rate and payment change only once every 3 years. The index normally used for this loan is the 3-year Treasury Securities Index, with caps that are usually 2% per change date (three years) and 5% to 6% lifetime, with a margin of 2.5% to 2.75%.

The initial rate on a three-year ARM will be higher than for the one-year ARM because the lender is stuck with that rate three times longer. In addition, the three-year index is always higher than the one-year index. It is a good loan for anyone who does not need to go beyond the sixth year because even on a worst-case scenario, the rate will be favorable. After the second change, or at the end of the sixth year, it's a gamble.

The Five-Year ARM (5/5 ARM)

This is the same as the three-year ARM, except that it changes once every five years and uses, you guessed it, the five-year index. And, the five-year index will be higher than both the one- and the three-year indexes. If you want a loan for no more than five years, this may be it. Compare it with what is available at the time to see if you will save on closing costs, payments, and qualifying.

3/1, 5/1, 7/1, and 10/1 ARMs

Then there are the hybrid ARMs. You can get a three-year ARM that turns into a one-year ARM after the first three years, commonly called a 3/1 ARM. Or, you can get a 5/1 ARM, for which the rate stays the same for the first five years; the loan then turns into a one-year ARM. Obviously, the 7/1 is fixed for seven years, and the 10/1 is fixed for 10. These loans give you the advantage of a stable payment and rate for an extended period of time, followed by the lower rates and indexes of a one-year ARM.

Overview

To summarize, the intervals for adjustment on ARMs can be any of the following:

1. Six months
2. One year
3. Three years
4. Five years
5. Every one year after an initial three- to ten-year level period

And, ARMs are adjusted based on Indexes such as the following:

1. One-, Three-, or Five-Year U.S. Treasury Securities Index
2. One-, Three-, or Five-Year FHLBB Cost of Funds Index (COFI)
3. One-, Three-, or Five-Year 11th District COFI Index
4. Other, more exotic indexes

A margin, ranging from 1.0% to over 3%, is added to the index to determine the rate toward which the loan will be adjusted. Caps are added to protect the borrower from unacceptably high rate and payment jumps. The caps vary from 0.5% to 2% per year, and 2% to 6% lifetime.

No law governs how low the rates, indexes, margins, and caps can be on any ARM. But, the secondary markets do set certain minimums and maximums that they will allow if they are to buy the loans. Because most lenders today want the loans to be saleable, they will adhere to these guidelines. If you find an ARM with abnormally low characteristics, it may well be a special "in house" portfolioed loan; perhaps it has been purchased by a special investor.

We're not through with ARMs yet. There are still conversions, LTVs, qualifying, and extended lock-ins to cover.

Conversion Feature   Into a Prince or a Toad?

A conversion feature on your ARM allows you to convert it into a fixed rate loan. It is available during the early life of the loan, usually after the first change date, for a period ranging from one year to six years. Some loans charge a one-time fee of $100 to $500 at the time of conversion, and others have no fee at all. Even with a fee, conversion is a much cheaper alternative for getting a fixed rate than completely refinancing the loan and paying all of the closing costs, including points, again. This feature is good to have on your ARM, whether you ever have the opportunity to use it or not. Most ARMs today offer it as a regular feature. Those without it may have a slightly lower initial rate and/or discount points.

ARMs with a conversion option are very common and give the borrower the chance to convert to a fixed rate. This option is also one of the most misunderstood and least disclosed features of an ARM. What most borrowers do not recognize, and often are not told, is that the rate to which the loan is converted is neither the current rate on the ARM nor the current fixed rate being offered in the market. Instead, most conversion rates are based on the Fannie Mae or Freddie Mac 30-day or 60-day mandatory delivery rate, priced at par (that means without any discount points), plus some additional interest, similar to a margin, of 0.25% to 0.75%.

The mandatory delivery rate is usually slightly less than the market interest rate quoted by a lender by 0.25% to 0.125%, but not always. The 30-day delivery rate will usually be cheaper than the 60-day rate. And the Fannie and Freddie rates can differ. In essence, the mandatory rate is the net interest yield required by the investor, before a servicing fee is added, that will be accepted as long as the loan is delivered within the mandatory period—

that is, 60, 30, or 15 days. Almost all lenders can tell you what these rates are, and they can change daily.

The lender will take the mandatory delivery rate and add the additional interest (margin) when you choose to convert your ARM to a fixed rate. Part, or all, of this is for the servicing of the loan. Here is an example:

Current 30-year fixed rate at par (no discount)	10.00%
Current 30-year 60-Day mandatory rate at par	9.77%
Plus 0.625% additional interest added to mandatory rate (rounded up to the nearest 0.125%)	10.50%
Or, plus 0.375% additional interest (normally the lowest)	10.25%

The 10.50% or 10.25% interest rate is the fixed rate to which your ARM will convert, depending on the additional interest.

As you can see, the rate to which the loan is converted would be higher than the current market fixed rate.

The period during which the borrower can convert the loan depends on the loan and the lender. On most one-year ARMs, the conversion period is any time from the thirteenth through the sixtieth month (second through fifth years). Others only allow conversion at a given date once a year from the second through the fifth or sixth year. On three-year and five-year loans conversion is normally allowed starting from the first adjustment date; it is then available for a three- to five-year period, either monthly or once a year.

The borrowers get the conversion by calling the lender servicing the loan (the lender to which they make their payments) during the specified time period. The lender will quote the rate available, and if the borrowers want to convert, the rate is locked in at that time. If there is a fee, it must be sent to the lender within a certain time. The lender will advise the borrowers when their loan will convert, usually within 60 days of the commitment. New documents for the fixed rate must be executed, and the borrowers will receive a new payment book.

In general, a borrower will not benefit from converting the ARM unless the fixed rates have fallen far enough that the new converted rate will be low enough to save money over the remaining period of the loan. This sounds like an oversimplification, but if you have an 8.5% ARM rate and convert at 8% and then the market lowers the ARM to 7.5% or 7.75%, the conversion loses its appeal. But you get the idea. Convert when the rate is low enough that you will be happy with it as a fixed rate.

Qualifying with an ARM

One of the main reasons that people consider ARMs is that they hope to qualify using the lower initial interest rate and payment. Because of changes in the industry, qualifying may not be so easy as it once was. It really depends on several factors: the amount of cash the borrower puts down (LTV), the yearly cap, and/or the length between rate/payment changes.

Under standard secondary market guidelines on a one-year ARM, **the borrower must put down at least 20% cash to qualify at the initial payment.** With less than 20%, the borrower will qualify at the maximum second-year rate. With a 2% per year cap and using a 7.75% initial rate, you would qualify at the payment based on 9.75%. There are ARM loans that will qualify at the initial rate with a higher LTV. These change frequently with the market.

Let's make our computation a little more complicated. If the annual cap is 1% or less, or if it is a three-year, five-year, 3/1, or 5/1 ARM, then you would qualify at the initial rate. The rationale for this is that the payment does not change significantly or for a prolonged period of time.

In qualifying, you would use the standard **28%/36%** ratios. Again, computer-based underwriting can change the qualifying ratios, but the computer will take into account the higher risk associated with an ARM.

When considering an ARM, the most important thing that you can do is to get a copy of the complete **Disclosure Statement** from the lender, which explains the loan. Then, make sure this loan is the best way for you to finance your home. It is not hard to become confused by the multiplicity of products available. And, you have to remember that lenders are trying to sell their products (that is, loans), just like any other business.

The first lender for whom I worked came out with an ARM that no other lender could touch. Fixed rates were running 12.5% to 13%. Our loan had an initial rate of 9.75%, 1 + 2.75 points, 2% yearly cap, and no lifetime cap. A later version even had negative amortization, which we will discuss later. We qualified borrowers based on the initial payment rate, even on 95% LTV, using very liberal standards. Everyone came to us. It was the best deal in

town. The problem was that it was a very high risk loan, and it ultimately created an unusually high incidence of defaults and foreclosures. Also, most of the borrowers eventually refinanced as
soon as better loans came onto the market. And, from the lenders'
perspective, it was a bust because they lost money on that loan
product. In the long run, this loan was not a very good deal for
many of the borrowers, or for the lender. Today, ARMs are designed to benefit both the borrower and the lender.

Long Lock-in ARMs   The Meter Is Running

One more thing that needs to be explained on ARMs is the long
lock-in offered by most lenders. The lender will lock in, or guarantee, the initial interest rate for as long as 9 to 12 months, until
you close on the loan. This is very attractive to people who are
building or cannot close within the normal 60- to 75-day lock period. You do not have to worry about interest rates rising before
you can lock in. What most people do not realize about these extended locks is that the initial rate's adjustment period begins
with the lock-in. That is, if you lock in 7.75% on a one-year ARM,
it will adjust one year from the lock-in date, not the closing date.
If you don't close for nine months after you lock in, you will get
the benefit of the lower rate and payment for only three months,
then it will go to the higher rate and payment. This is not to say
that it isn't worth locking in early. You should just make sure that
you understand the consequences.

GRADUATED PAYMENT MORTGAGES
For the High and Desperate Times

GPMs, or Gipp Em's as they are called in the industry, were originally offered by the Federal Housing Administration (FHA).
They help people qualify by starting out at a lower payment than
would normally be required. They are similar to the rising equity
loan in that the payment starts out very low and increases 7.5%
(usually) per year until it reaches a level payment that is sufficient
to pay the loan off over the remaining term of the loan. The big difference is that it is not a buy-down, but that it is a fixed rate loan.
What this means is that you are making a payment that is less than
the interest being charged on the loan. This is called **negative
amortization.**

To give an example, say that you get a fixed rate loan on $100,000 at 10% for 30 years. The PI payment would be $877.57 and the interest-only payment would be $833.34. But, using a GPM, the first-year payment is $567.80 (the equivalent of a 5.5% interest rate payment), meaning there is negative amortization of $265.54 per month ($833.34 − $567.80). That is, you are paying $265.54 less than you are being charged in interest each month. That unpaid interest is added to the principal amount of the loan. The payments then increase each year (normally 7.5%) until they reach a level payment that will pay off the principal plus the additional unpaid interest within the remainder of the amortization period. GPMs are set up according to formulas that specify the lowest starting payment, the year the payments level off, and the exact amount of negative amortization (or unpaid interest) that will accrue.

If a GPM doesn't sound like a very good deal, it isn't—for most borrowers. But when fixed rates are high, and you don't qualify unless the payment is significantly lower, this may be the loan for you. It isn't pretty, but it will get you into the house. Your biggest concern with a GPM is that the property appreciate enough at least to keep pace with the accrued unpaid interest.

Most GPMs will not allow the total principal and interest to exceed 125% of the original loan balance. If your house appreciates 3% per year, which is minimal, that increase would cover the excess unpaid interest in about six to seven years. If you end up having to sell your home during the negative amortization period, the house must have appreciated sufficiently to cover the increased principal balance to prevent a loss on the sale. With appreciation of 6% to 10% a year, you should be able to sell the house without losing money after three or four years.

With a GPM you know exactly what the total accrued interest will be and, therefore, what the total loan will be with the maximum amount of negative amortization added. You also know when it will begin to amortize positively. There have been negative amortization ARMs whose rates bounced around like a rubber ball. You had no idea if and when the loan would ever completely amortize out. With those ARMs, you could get stuck at the end of 30 years with a balloon payment. Or, along the way you could get hit with very nasty payment increases.

Most negative ARMs have disappeared from the market, at least until rates climb again; the few left are usually paid off by sale of the house or, by refinancing. They also have had more safeguards built into them. My advice is not to get one unless you have explored all the alternatives and it is the only way to purchase the house.

Here is an example of an FHA GPM: On a $100,000 purchase, with an interest rate of 12% for 30 years, the maximum loan amount would be $92,700 plus FHA mortgage insurance premiums financed into the loan, for a total of $96,200. On a normally amortizing (fixed-rate) loan, the PI/MI payment would be $989.53. The GPM would be as follows:

Year	PI/MI Payment	Loan Balance	Negative Amortization
1	$ 761.31	$ 98,745.34	$2,545.34
2	818.40	100,889.36	4,689.36
3	879.78	102,526.82	6,326.82
4	945.76	103,535.14	7,335.14
5	1,016.70	103,771.73	7,571.73
6–30	1,092.95[a]		

[a] The loan will cross the original balance with the 147th payment.

GROWING PAYMENT MORTGAGES OR GROWING EQUITY MORTGAGES
Loans for the Upwardly Mobile

Commonly known as **GEMs,** these loans are designed to force the borrower to pay off the loan quicker than the normal amortization. A GEM works on the same principal as the rising equity loan, however, it does not start at a lower initial payment. If it is a 30-year GEM, it will start at the normal payment and then increase the PI payment 7.5% per year until the payments reach a point that they will pay off the loan in some specified time, such as 20 or 15 years. A GEM will usually have a rate lower than the normal fixed rate. There is nothing wrong with this loan as long as the borrower can make the required higher payments. Neurosurgeons and lawyers who work on a percentage basis would fit this description. Otherwise, get the normal fixed rate and pay it down according to your ability. Also, this loan is not always available. Check with lenders to see who may carry it.

BALLOON LOANS
Exercises in Stress Management

Balloons offer the advantages of **lower rates and lower points.** They also offer the potential for personalized financial panic. A balloon loan is set up like a regular amortizing loan, usually for 30 years, although you can get them for shorter periods. You make the regular monthly payment until a set time, when the balance of the loan comes due, or balloons. The balloon period is usually between three and ten years, five- and seven-year periods being the most common.

As an example let us use a $100,000 loan at 9.0% for 30 years, ballooning in seven years. The monthly PI payment would be $804.62. The balloon balance due at the end of the seventh year would be $93,600.

If you sell the house, refinance, or pay off the loan within the seven years, you have no worries. If you get to the end of the seven years and you can't pay off the loan, then you have to hope the interest rates are favorable and you can qualify for a new refinance loan. Some lenders offer balloons that have a provision allowing for a cheap refinance. Other balloons allow you to continue at the fixed rate available at the due date. Balloon loans are attractive to borrowers who know they will not be in the house until the end of the balloon, know they can pay it off when the time comes, or need the lower rate to qualify.

Fannie Mae and Freddie Mac offer a balloon loan, called the two step or 7/23 loan, which gives you some of the advantages of a lower rate coupled with the security of not being stuck with a large payment due at the end of the balloon. These loans can have a rate that is around 0.375% to 0.75% lower than the current fixed rate with a balloon at the end of either five or seven years. However, you have the option of renewing the loan for the remaining 25 or 23 years for a rate that is similar to an ARM conversion rate. That is, the renewal rate will be about 0.375% to 0.75% higher than the current fixed rate at the time you renew the loan. This type of balloon loan gives you the advantages of a lower initial rate without the uncertain short-term fluctuations of an ARM. It is perfect for anyone who will be selling or refinancing within seven years. There may be a small fee for the conversion.

Another type of balloon loan offered in some parts of the country is **the mortgage bond.** These are usually offered by private individuals or bank trust departments. They are loans of low LTV (usually 70% or less) that are made up of a series of bonds in denominations of $500 or $1,000 multiples. These bonds provide for interest-only payments, usually every six months. At the end of the loan period, typically five years, the principal balance comes due. The advantage of these loans is that you deal directly with the loan maker; there are less rigid guidelines, lower closing costs, and a quicker closing time. All you have to do is make sure that the lenders receive their interest every six months and that you can pay off the principal at the end of the term.

SHARED EQUITY LOANS
Sharing the Wealth

With the higher cost of housing today, many first-time home-buyers do not have the resources to make a down payment on a home. Bringing in someone who will put down part of the money in return for a share of the equity has become an acceptable prac-tice, especially in high-cost areas like California.

These arrangements can become very complicated, but for the most part they are a simple deal whereby the borrower gets money from a person who will in turn get a specified percentage of the net equity in the house when it is sold. Many agreements will state that the investor gets his or her equity by a certain date or when the ap-preciation reaches a set level. Others stipulate that the equity will be divided upon sale of the property, whenever that may occur. In areas of high appreciation, this kind of loan can be advantageous for everyone. It gives the investor a good return and allows the bor-rower to pay relatively little money down in order to get into a house. The borrower hopes to come out with enough money to put down on another home. Not all loans allow shared equity as de-fined here. If it is not allowed, and it cannot qualify as a gift, the funds may need to be on a secured basis other than the property. Nonoccupying coborrowers may or may not be allowed. Check with the lender and let them know how you plan to get the funds.

JUMBO AND NONCONFORMING LOANS
For the Mansion and the Little Grass Shack

These loans exceed the maximum loan limits set by Fannie Mae and Freddie Mac. Or, they may be within the limits, but they do not fit the Fannie-Freddie conforming guidelines for property or borrower qualification, so they are **nonconforming.** Some lenders define nonconforming loans as those for credit-challenged borrowers, but here they are simply loans that do not fit the normal Fannie-Freddie guidelines.

They can be any type of loan, from a fixed rate to an ARM. The big difference is that the many investors who buy them set the guidelines to which they are subject. Most will use Fannie and Freddie guidelines as the basis and then diverge from there. The qualifying can be more liberal, or more conservative. Some of these loans do have the ability to be computer underwritten, but most will still require the human touch.

Most will set the maximum amount that they will loan for any given LTV. This is further restricted by the maximum loan amounts that mortgage insurance companies will insure at specific LTVs over 80%. Many investors will require two or more appraisals for loans over certain amounts.

The differences in jumbo or nonconforming loans are as varied as the number of investors who buy them. If you are in the market for one, do what you would do for any loan—check out all of them, compare them, and ask the lender pertinent questions such as these:

1. How long will the loan process take?
2. Who will be processing the loan—the lender or the investor?
3. Who will underwrite, or approve, the loan—the lender or investor?
4. Exactly what will be required for approval?
5. Is there a prepayment penalty? (Some jumbos do penalize.)

It is very important that the lender be comfortable with the investor and familiar with the way it works. Some jumbos are underwritten by the investor, which can lead to many misunderstandings and problems.

One jumbo that I did was an absolutely perfect loan. The borrower had single-digit qualifying ratios; he was putting down $200,000 on a $500,000 house; and he had enough assets that he could have paid cash. The borrower locked in the rate when it was low. Subsequently, the rates rose. After the loan was approved, and about one week before closing, the borrower decided he wanted to reduce the loan for which he was approved by $30,000. The investors insisted that they must reapprove the borrower, which would take at least five working days. Never mind that the loan package they had approved showed the borrower capable of putting down the extra $30,000 and that the borrower would qualify even more easily. What was obvious was that the lock-in on the low rate was due to expire before the reapproval and closing could occur. The investor refused to extend the lock and would only give the current rate. The borrower was upset; I was outraged; my company was in disbelief; and the borrower's attorney was ready to sue. As it turned out, the attorney's written threat to sue gave the investor a little clearer perspective. The loan closed on time, without reapproval, and with the lower rate. Not all loan stories turn out this way. When you are dealing through a second party (that is, the lender) to get a loan over which the lender has little or no control, there is always the potential for problems. Loans that are underwritten, closed, and serviced by the investor are brokered loans. A lender does not need to be a pure broker to offer these loans. Any lender, and most, can offer brokered loans. I will discuss brokers later.

CONSTRUCTION LOANS

When you are building a house, one of two things will happen: Either the builder pays for the costs until it is finished, or you pay the costs. If the builder pays the costs, you have to be able to pay these costs at the end either by cash in hand or by proceeds from a permanent mortgage that will close after the house is 100% complete. If you have to pay the construction costs while the house is being built, chances are that you will need to borrow on a short-term basis to get that money. This short-term loan, secured by the real estate, is called a construction loan.

The process usually works in this fashion.

1.   The borrower will get a commitment to a permanent mortgage.

2.   The lender will then commit to a construction loan. This lender may or may not be the same one that gives the permanent mortgage. Sometimes a normal mortgage lender will commit to the permanent loan and then a bank will give the construction

loan. Most construction loans will not be granted until there is a permanent loan commitment.

3. The construction loan will be between 70% and 100% of the permanent loan amount (depending on the borrower's needs and the lender's rules). Any equity in the land is counted as cash—that is, it can go toward both the permanent mortgage and the construction loan. If you buy a lot for $25,000 and put $10,000 down, then that $10,000 is part of the money counted as equity. Most lenders take into account the value of the land as a function of how long you have held it. If you have held it for less than one year, they use the purchase price as value, if you have held it for one year or more, they will use the appraised value. Therefore, if the $20,000 lot is appraised for $25,000 after whatever time period the lender requires, then that is the value, and you have $5,000 more in equity.

4. The builder will request **draws** or payments during certain phases of construction. Draws will be for the costs of labor and materials during that phase. A normal draw schedule is after the foundation is done, after the house is under roof, after the mechanical systems (heating, plumbing, electric) are roughed in, after the dry wall is complete and ready for paint, and upon completion. The lender will require that the builder submit both evidence of the work completed and signed **lien waivers** (which protect the borrower and lender against liens that could be placed on the property by any of the builder's subcontractors or suppliers whom the builder did not pay). The lender also will inspect the house before each draw.

5. Upon completion of the house, the lender will close the permanent loan, which will pay off the construction loan balance and any remaining balance due the builder.

A construction loan can take many forms. Interest can be based on the prime rate plus extra interest from 0.5% to 2%. Interest can be at a fixed rate. The lender may or may not, but usually will, charge 1 or 2 points. The lender may charge interest on the entire amount from the beginning of the commitment, although this is very seldom done today. The lender will generally charge interest on the money as it is used. In figuring out exactly how much the house will cost and how much you need to borrow, it is important that you add in the cost of the construction loan. A prime rate of 10% plus an added 1% can run into a significant interest cost after three to six months.

Using our $100,000 loan, let us calculate the costs of the interest expense, based on an 80% LTV (of the permanent loan) with a 1% ($800) upfront fee, a simple draw schedule of four draws a month (equals $20,000 per month at 11% [prime of 10% + 1%]) and completion at the end of the fifth month. Those costs would be $800 + $1,835 approximate interest = $2,635 in additional building costs.

Most construction loans run for six months, up to one year. This is plenty of time to build any normal house. Most are built in six months or less.

The lender who makes the permanent loan will have less risk than the construction lender because the permanent loan will only close when the house is finished, if it was built according to the plans, and if the borrower has sufficient cash to close. The construction lender is a partner with the borrower from the beginning. If the completed house turns out to be trapezoidal instead of rectangular, the construction lender will find itself "holding the bag" without a permanent loan to pay off the remaining construction debt.

Situations like this are why almost all lenders will require the general contractor to have a track record. Contractors must at least show knowledge and a background in building that will assure the lender that they are competent. Borrowers who want to act as their own general contractors will find it very difficult to get a lender to commit on a construction loan, unless it is a low LTV.

The best way to approach building, and the least complicated for the borrower, is to have the builder take care of financing the construction. Financing costs will then be added into the price of the house, but that is not any different from when the borrower has the construction loan. The procedure also allows the borrower to have a set cost for the house, as long as the contractor gives a set price bid. Some builders will build based on cost plus. That means you pay the cost of the house plus a stated percentage as the builder's gross profit. Cost plus 15% to 20% or more is normal.

The **Construction/Permanent One-Closing Loan** is now the most common, and often cheapest, way to finance the construction of your home. The borrower applies for the permanent and gets the construction as part of the package. The rate for the construction loan is usually prime plus a percentage, such as 1%, but it can be fixed or the same rate as the permanent loan, and you pay points once, not for each loan. The biggest difference is that you pay one set of closing costs. At closing, you will then have a construction loan in place to build the house. Upon completion, the construction loan modifies into a permanent loan with regular monthly payments. Depending on the lender offering this combination loan, it is possible to get 15- or 30-year fixed rates, or an ARM. Also, you may be able to lock in your interest rate at application; or, at the very least, you may be offered some type of rate protection such as guaranteeing that your permanent rate will not be more than 0.5% higher than at time of application. Many of the construction/permanent loans will have "float down" features that allow the borrower to float down the interest rate prior to loan modification.

100% LOANS

As I discussed earlier, it is possible to get financing with no cash down with a combination of first and second mortgages totaling 100%. There is also another 100% type of loan that is periodically available. It is a pure 100% LTV loan and is usually a fixed rate. As is the case with any high risk type of loan, the borrower's credit scores will need to be very high. A score of 720 or higher is average.

Along with this type of loan, there is another feature that has been offered by some lenders: the 103% loan. It allows the borrower to finance up to 3% of the value of the property to use for closing costs. The borrower must be very strong. The appeal of this loan will be greatest for borrowers who do not want to invest any of their assets into the property or who will deplete their assets if they are put into the property.

There are some other 100% and 100% + LTV loan programs, such as Farmers Home Administration, Rural Development (part of Farmer's Home), Veteran's Administration loans, and some innovative FHA loans. I will discuss each of these later.

After reading this section, you can see that there are many different loans and variations available because of the competitive and changing nature of real estate financing. As time goes on, other new and innovative products will come along to provide the borrower with even more choices. In making a decision, take it one step at a time. Decide which type is best for your needs, and then look at all the extras. So far we have discussed Fannie, Freddie, and all the mutants created by the conventional market. Now we need to look at government loans.

GOVERNMENT LOANS

What lenders refer to as government loans are those loans that are either insured, guaranteed, held by, or in some way created by the federal government. We will look at FHA (Federal Housing Administration), VA (Veteran's Administration), and Rural Development (Farmers Home) loans.

Federal Housing Administration (FHA)

To get an idea of what you are dealing with in the FHA, you must first know that it is part of and controlled by **HUD (Department of Housing and Urban Development),** one of the largest and most bureaucratic of the federal agencies. This fact doesn't mean that it is a bad loan, it simply means that at times it can become incredibly paper intensive, rule bound, and subject to political grandstanding. Despite the shortcomings, the end product is worth the effort.

FHA was intended as a means by which borrowers, usually moderate income and/or first-time buyers, could get a loan with **less down payment and liberal qualifying.** Because most lenders would be reluctant to make a loan like this, **the federal government insures the loans through FHA.** If your loan is going to be insured, you cannot find a stronger way to do so than by the full faith and credit of the United States government.

The government, through FHA, insures these loans by means of a **mortgage insurance premium (MIP),** just like mortgage insurance companies. FHA does not provide the money, only the insurance. The M.I.P., since July 1, 1991, is **divided into two parts.** The **up-front MIP** is financed into the loan amount. The second part is a **renewal (periodic) premium** that is escrowed into the monthly payment, just like the renewal premium on private mortgage insurance (PMI). (See the FHA MIP Chart on page 100.) The proceeds are held to pay any claims on foreclosed FHA-insured loans.

The FHA sets the guidelines under which these loans are approved, closed, and insured. The rules are similar to the conventional ones, except that they are more liberal and have several significant differences. The loan applications are taken by lenders approved by FHA. Then, the lender can approve the loan and close it. The lender is designated "Direct Endorsement" (D.E.)-approved by FHA. The lender then applies for insurance coverage from the FHA. With that insurance in place, the loan can then be sold to the secondary market as a government-insured loan.

Ginnie Mae, Fannie and Freddie's little sister, was created by the government to purchase and/or guarantee government loans as part of the secondary market system. That is why you hear about buying "government-backed Ginnie Maes" from stockbrokers. For the borrower, knowing about Ginnie Mae's is not really important so far as the borrower is concerned, except to know that Ginnie exists and she does set some guidelines on government loans herself.

The advantage of an FHA loan is that you can put down less cash and qualify under liberal guidelines. There is **no maximum limit on income to qualify** at this time (although Congress has been trying to put a limit on income and it may eventually happen), but there is a **maximum on the loan amount.** Unfortunately, it is not nearly so high as conventional loans. There has been a continuing effort to have FHA loan limits raised to within a certain percentage of the maximum Fannie- Freddie-conforming loan amounts, and to make them uniform nationwide. Mortgage insurance companies and others who would like to see the FHA program disappear entirely have been fighting it. The HUD website www.hud.gov lists all the current information regarding FHA loan limits along with a great deal of other useful information. The FHA sets these limits by region, based on the median sales price and other statistical data. The reason its loan amounts are less is that the FHA is geared toward first-time buyers or borrowers who cannot afford higher-priced homes and the cash down payments they would require. Loan amounts on duplexes, triplexes, and quadraplexes are proportionately higher, just like Fannie and Freddie. To find out what the maximum loan amounts are in your area, call a lender who does FHA loans.

FHA determines the maximum loan that can be obtained on a home using a maximum LTV percentage, depending on the cost of the home. Currently these percentages are **97.75% for properties with values over $50,000 and 98.75% for values $50,000 and under.** There used to be a much more complicated formula for determining the maximum loan amounts, and it is possible that congress will change things again.

The next step is to figure the MIP that will be financed into the loan amount (see the table of factors). Based on the new, revised (read "political") FHA "risk-based premium payments," the up-front premium and the length of time for which the borrower will pay the renewal premium will change, as well as the amortization period of the loan, depending on the LTV.

As of January 1, 2001, all loans closing on or after that date will have the following upfront and renewal premiums for FHA.

Up-Front	LTV Radio	Renewal Premium	Years
	Loans with terms more than 15 years		
1.50%	89.99% & under	.50%	*
1.50%	90.00–95.00%	.50%	*
1.50%	95.01% & over	.50%	*
	Loans with terms of 15 years or less		
1.50%	89.99% & under	None	N/A
1.50%	90.00–95.00%	.25%	**
1.50%	95.01% and over	.25%	**

*Years will be determined when the loan balance equals 78%, provided the borrower has paid the annual renewal premium for at least 5 years.

**Years will be determined when the loan balance equals 78%.

All FHA loans that closed prior to January 1, 2001 are not eligible for mortgage insurance cancellation.

The years are how long the renewal premium will stay on the loan. Most of these loans will be paid off or refinanced before they get that old.

A house valued at $100,000 would have an FHA base loan amount of $97,750. This is the amount used to purchase the property. Then, the **Up-Front Mortgage Insurance Premium,** or **MIP,** is added into the loan. If it is a 30-year loan, the MIP would be 1.50% of the value, or $1,500. The total loan amount would then be $99,260. This is the amount upon which the PI payment is based. Broken down, this is how it would be calculated:

Value:	$100,000
	× 97.75%
Base loan:	$97,750
30 year MIP: $100,000 × 1.50% =	+ 1,500
Total FHA loan with MIP:	$99,250

Most lenders will round down the MIP to the nearest $50, with the difference paid at closing. A value of $120,000 would have a base loan of $117,300 and a total loan of $119,059.50. The loan would be lowered to $119,050 with the $39.50 in MIP paid at closing.

The second part of the FHA mortgage insurance is the **Annual Renewal Premium,** which is added into the monthly payment. Using our $100,000 property with a 30 year loan, the premium is calculated on the base loan amount: $97,750 × 5% = $488.75/12 months = $40.73 added to the monthly payment. At 8.5% interest, the PIMI payment would be $763.15 plus $40.73 = $803.88. Tax and insurance escrows are also added.

As you put more cash down, the advantage of an FHA loan over a conventional loan may disappear. Conventionally financed private mortgage insurance is cheaper than FHA MIP. Also, on FHA loans it does not matter how much cash you put down; there will always be a MIP. The only time you would want to use FHA with more than the minimum cash down is when you need the more liberal qualifying to get a loan.

Now that we have figured out how to get the maximum loan amount, we need to know if it exceeds the **maximum allowable loan limits** for your area. If a house selling for $90,000 was in an area where the maximum loan limit was $86,000, the borrower would not be able to get the $87,950 ($90,000 × 97.75%) loan. The borrower would have to put down an additional $1,950. If the maximum loan limit was exactly $87,950, then the loan would qualify. And, the up-front MIP ($1,319.25 with $1,300 financed) that is financed can be added beyond the amount of the loan limit, for a total of $89,250 in this example.

If you think that you can use a second mortgage (see section on second mortgages in Chapter 4) with an FHA loan to reduce your down payment, you don't understand the system. The FHA will allow second mortgages, but only to the extent that the first and the second combined do not exceed the maximum loan that

FHA would otherwise normally allow. If we consider our $87,950 loan, the first and second cannot total more than $87,950. So, unless the second is a real bargain, there is little incentive. Once you have the mortgage, your FHA lender has no restrictions on obtaining a second mortgage.

Qualifying with FHA

FHA used to qualify by a residual income method that only a statistician could appreciate. Now, they use gross qualifying, just like conventional loans, but with the following higher ratios.

29% of gross monthly income for housing expense (PITI/MIP/HOA).

41% of gross monthly income for housing expense and all monthly debts with over six months to pay off (PITI/MI/HOA/LTD).

FHA now accepts computer underwriting, currently using the Freddie Mac system called Loan Prospector, or LP for short. As with conventional loans, the borrower can qualify for extended ratios with excellent credit, assets, and so on. FHA computer underwriting will also allow lower credit scores. I have had approvals with 590+/− credit scores. With the computer underwriting of FHA loans, the lender can issue an approval within one to two hours from the beginning of application. It used to take as long as 30 to 45 days.

If the loan is not approved by the computer, but is an approvable loan, the lender can above these ratios if there are good compensating factors. What is considered a compensating factor and how high lenders will go vary from region to region (administration of the FHA is divided into regions) and lender to lender. Regional offices will sometimes interpret guidelines differently from what the national office intended. A higher housing expense ratio is more acceptable than a total debt ratio. If you need to go much above 29%/41% you may be beyond your ability to pay anyway.

Using our example of the $90,000 purchase and loan amount of $87,950, let's see what the payment would be and the approximate income to qualify.

$$\$87,950 \times 1.50\% \text{ (up-front MIP)} = \$1,319.25$$

The UFMIP is financed into the loan, so the total is $89,250 (the UFMIP was rounded down and the $28.88 will be paid in cash).

1. Using 8.5% with a 30-year amortization. $89.25 × 7.6891 per 1000 (factor from table on page 236 in Appendix) = $686.25 P & I.

2. $87,950 × 0.5% (renewal premium) = $439.75. This premium, which is calculated on the basic loan before the UFMIP is added, is escrowed into the monthly payment by dividing it by 12 months $439.75/12 = $36.65.

3. $686.25 + $36.65 = $722.90 PIMIP.

4. One twelfth of the yearly taxes and homeowner's insurance is also added for a PITIMIP payment. Because this is just an example, I will use $20 for insurance and $75 for taxes. The insurance figure is probably within a few dollars of what it actually would be, but the taxes can vary considerably. Thus, $722.90 + $20 + $75 = $817.90. $817.90 divided by 29% = $2,820 gross monthly income necessary to qualify. (This computation depends on the borrower's total debts and the flexibility of the lender. It is possible to qualify with less income.)

The 0.5% renewal premium was added effective July 1, 1991. It is being used to keep the MIP insurance fund solvent. Just like the S&L fund, it too suffered huge losses. While adding another 0.5% to your loan is not the best thing to happen, it is better than the alternative, no FHA loans at all.

On FHA-acceptable **energy efficient homes,** lenders will allow the ratios to increase by as much as 2% each. The rationale is that you will save money on your utility bills, so you will have more to spend on your house payment. This compensating factor will apply mainly to newer homes that have been built with more insulation and more efficient heating and cooling systems. The house must be certified as energy efficient, normally by the power company or the builder.

If we use our example one more time, we can see approximately **how much cash will be needed** to get into the home.

Cash down	$2,050
Estimated closing costs(without prepaids)	$1,900
Estimated prepaids (with 15 days' interest)	$870
Total cash needed (give or take $100)	$4,820

That is, around $5,000 to buy a $90,000 house. Not bad when you consider that the total down payment and closing costs will be about 5%.

The FHA is also more lenient toward houses that don't fit the mold of what is common in the market as a whole. They will consider properties such as two-bedroom homes and rural properties, which conventional loans might not be so inclined to finance if the property has a high loan-to-value. If you are considering a house in a rural area, the Farmer's Home Administration guaranteed loan program may fit your needs better. (See section on Special Loans.)

Another thing that FHA has is **different loan types**—Over 30 of them at last count. There are the normal fixed rates, an ARM, the GPM that we discussed earlier, loans for veterans, loans for people who want to fix up a house, loans for people with no money, loans for people with bad credit. You name it and they probably have it (and they designate each one by section numbers. 203b for fixed, 234c for condominiums, and so on). The trick is to find a lender that will do the more exotic ones. Most FHA lenders do the fixed, GPM, ARM, and maybe the rehabilitation loan (203k). They don't get into the others because either they are not familiar with the loan, there is little or no demand in the area, the loans are so time-consuming that there is very little profit in them, or there is no secondary market source that will buy them.

The FHA used to have loans for nonowner-occupied investment property. But, as of December 14, 1989, these loans are no longer offered. What you might find is an investment property with an existing FHA nonowner loan on it that you can assume.

FHA loans have always been **assumable.** However, for loans on or after December 1, 1986 and before December 14, 1989, qualifying restrictions were added. Depending on whether the loan was originally taken as an owner or nonowner-occupied property, the requirements are different. (See the FHA assumption chart on page 200 in the Appendix.)

With the HUD Reform Act of 1989 (December 15, 1989), all FHA loans approved from that point on require that at least one of the assuming borrowers be qualified and have a full credit check.

Any time an FHA loan is assumed, the MIP goes with the loan. The seller cannot request a partial refund. If the buyer who assumes the loan later pays it off, they can request a refund of any remaining MIP.

Something that is disclosed to every borrower in writing, but few borrowers remember, is that if you pay off the loan early, part of the MIP will be refunded to you. (See the Homeowner's Fact Sheet on Mortgage Insurance Premium Refunds and Distributive Shares, on page 198 in the Appendix.) The longer you hold the loan, the less that is refunded.

The ability to assume the FHA loan can make the difference in whether the property will sell or not. Or, it may affect how much the seller can get for the property. Assuming a loan without having to pay much in closing costs will appeal to many potential buyers.

For investors looking for rental property, an assumption can allow them to build up a portfolio. But, there are some restrictions. The FHA will not allow a loan to be assumed if that buyer already owns at least seven properties in any specific neighborhood or development. And, a borrower cannot have more than one high LTV loan (over 75% of value plus closing costs) at a time. The only way that they could have a high LTV would be if it was their personal residence, or they were co-borrowers with someone else (like a child) who is living in the property.

FHA will allow **co-borrowers.** Either the borrower or co-borrower must live in the property. They are qualified based on their joint incomes and debts. The co-borrower must be a relative or someone with a demonstrated close relationship.

One last note on assumability: If the seller has an FHA loan that can be assumed without the buyer qualifying, and if the seller does not request a release of liability, you will remain liable for a period of five years in case of default and/or foreclosure. (See page 197 of Appendix for Notice to Homeowner. Assumption of HUD/FHA Insured Mortgages.) It is better to have the assuming purchaser qualify for the loan and to request the release to protect yourself. And, on assumptions FHA has no restrictions on second mortgages.

In many parts of the country **the seller often pays part of the closing costs.** There are a few limitations on how much cash someone else can contribute and how it is contributed. FHA will allow the seller, realtor, and lender to pay up to 6% of the value of the property toward points, closing costs, and prepaids. However, the borrower is required to contribute a minimum of 3% of the value from his or her own resources. The 3% cannot include discount points or prepaids, which basically means that the 2.25% down payment and closing costs, including any origination fee, equal to .75% of the value. Using our $90,000 purchase, the down payment would be $2,050, leaving $650 of closing cost to meet the 3%. This can come from their own assets and/or a gift. A little note here: FHA will allow the borrower to charge the credit report and appraisal, but if you do charge any costs, they are not counted towards the 3%. If the up-front MIP is being paid rather than financed, all of it must be paid. FHA will not allow part of the MIP to be financed.

If the borrower is receiving gift funds, he or she can pay everything using these funds. The 3%, or any part, can be paid by gift funds. This is currently the rule, and HUD may modify it at any time. But, because you can use gift funds, an innovative way for qualified borrowers with access to little or no cash has become available. Nonprofit organizations and government agencies can give gift funds. One of the best of these nonprofits is an organization called the Nehemiah Program. Nehemiah is a nationwide program. It will give to the borrower a gift of 3% of the value, no strings attached. Note the 3% gift, which covers the FHA 3% requirement. Now, there is a draw-back that must be overcome. Because Nehemiah is a nonprofit, there is not an endless supply of money. It requires the seller to agree to participate in the program and to pay Nehemiah a 4% service fee at closing; 3% replenishes the fund, and less than half of the remaining 1% is used for overhead. The rest goes toward other projects, such as inner city housing. The initial reaction is predictable. No one is going to pay that much money. Not true. I have done a tremendous number of these loans. It all comes down to adjusting the numbers to fit everyone's requirements.

Here's an example. Say we have a seller with a house on the market for $100,000. If the seller is willing to take $96,000, then you just offer full price. What do you do if the seller will not take less? Adjust the price to fit. In this instance, raise the price to $104,000. (You may need to tweak it to adjust for the realtor's commission, if one is involved.) As long as the property will appraise, everyone gets what they want. I have not had one loan that did not close because of underappraising. The realtor should know if the value will cover it. If not, I usually call appraisers and ask them if they feel they can support the value. Now, if the borrower does not have the remaining cash necessary to close, and will not be able to save it prior to closing, there are additional sources of funds. The seller can agree to pay the remaining costs, in addition to the 4% fee. (The price can be adjusted for this, too.) The borrower can get a gift from a family member or friend. Or, the lender can provide Premium Pricing (remember our earlier discussion?).

Or, any combination of these may be used. What do we have? 100% financing! As long as the borrower qualifies for the FHA loan, he or she can use Nehemiah. You can go to Nehemiah's website at www.nehemiahprogram.org. Just as everything else in mortgage lending, the rules and the organizations can change. Check with a lender to see if they participate, or if the program still exists. (Nehemiah can give you the names of participating lenders in your area.)

The FHA 203K Rehabilitation Loan

One of the FHA loans that has had a bad reputation in the past, not without merit, is the **FHA 203K loan.** The 203K is a purchase or refinance *Rehabilitation Loan.* There is no upfront MIP on 203K loans, so you save the 1.50%. The house can be torn down to the foundation and still qualify. What this loan does is to allow a borrower with limited funds to purchase, or refinance, and fix up a property. You can rehab up to a four-unit dwelling, and it actually allows for properties with a small commercial area. (It is for owner-occupied dwellings only.) The improvements can be significant, or just updating a kitchen. There must be at least $5,000 in improvements, and these must fall within certain categories.

There are some required repairs if they are needed: thermal envelope (insulation, etc.), smoke detectors, wood boring pest and moisture damage, septic, well/water, and elimination of health and safety hazards. Other eligible repairs to meet the first $5,000 are modernization and functional changes; reconditioning/replacement of plumbing, heating, A/C and electrical; changes for aesthetic appeal and elimination of obsolescence (such as adding a porch, siding, or additional rooms); roofing/guttering/downspouts; flooring if it is damaged; and energy conservation improvements. Beyond these, you can do just about anything, even repair a pool or get new appliances.

This is how it works. The loan will pay to purchase the property, or pay off an existing loan on a refinance.

1. The first step (after you have been prequalified for the loan by a lender) is to find a HUD-approved *Consultant.* Your lender will normally have certain consultants they use regularly. If not, you can go to the HUD website and find the list of consultants in your area.

2.   Then, you have the consultant do a *Feasibility Study* on the property. The feasibility study is a quick and inexpensive (around $100) estimate of repairs that need to be done (and any additional repairs you want done). This will tell you if the cost is in the range you are willing to pay to fix up the property. (The study is not required, but I always recommend it to avoid any more expense if the costs are too high.)

3.   If the costs are acceptable, then you authorize the consultant to do a *Work Write-up.* This is a full, item-by-item breakdown of each item to be repaired, as well as the estimated cost. The work write-up is expensive and is charged on a sliding scale, going up as the cost of repairs increases. (It is financed into the loan.) You will then go over the work write-up with the lender and consultant to make sure everything you want done is included. You can also add or remove any nonrequired repairs. The termite inspection is normally included in the write-up.

4.   Once you agree to the work write-up, the lender will order an appraisal based on the write-up. The appraisal will give an after-improved value.

5.   You will then solicit bids from builders for the repairs. The consultant should give you a builder bid book, which is the write-up minus the dollar amounts. The bid cannot exceed the cost given in the write-up. (Do not tell the builders the amount in the write-up. You will never get a lower bid if they know the maximum.) If you accept a bid less than the write-up, the loan will still be based off the write-up cost. If there is money left over at the end of the rehab work, it can be applied to the principal or used for additional repairs. The lender will review the bid to make sure it complies with the write-up.

6.   At the same time, the loan is underwritten by a human underwriter. The computer underwriting system may be adjusted to underwrite 203Ks at some point, but because of the nature of the loan, a human being will probably always need to give the final approval. (When you first apply for the loan, the loan officer will run the loan through computer underwriting for an initial approval.)

7. After loan approval, the loan closes. There is an initial payment for the purchase of the property, or to pay off an existing loan on a refinance. The remaining funds are held in escrow by the lender while the work is done.

8. As the work progresses, the builder will request *draws* to pay for the work done to that point. The consultant will do an inspection, and then the lender will issue a check. This continues until the work is complete. At this point, if there is any money left over from a low bid or the required escrow amount that is financed into the loan, any remainder can be applied toward principal or used for additional repairs.

The nice part about a 203K is that many of the loan costs can be financed into the loan, such as permits, work write-ups, supplemental fees, and inspection fees. Two other costs that can be financed are the escrow for contingency costs and up to six months worth of the proposed house payment. FHA will require that you have between 10% and 20% of the cost of repairs financed into the loan for escrows. (The amount depends on factors such as if the utilities were on when the write-up was done or if the borrower is acting as the contractor.) And, if you cannot live in the house while the work is being done, you can finance up to 6 months of the house payments. The maximum length of time allowed for repairs is 6 months, so that is why you can have 6 months of payments financed. The big warning on 203K loans is to use only a lender who is knowledgeable in this loan. They will have to guide you through it, and it is very hands-on. I have actually had loan officers from other companies call me to ask me how to do a 203K. That is not a good endorsement for that lender.

In summary the advantages of FHA loans are these:

1. Liberal qualifying
2. Less down payment required
3. Assumable
4. Can make the resale higher and/or quicker
5. Insured by the full faith and credit of the U.S. government

The disadvantages are these:

1. There is a MIP regardless of the LTV.
2. The MIP is higher than on conventional loans.
3. The loan limits are lower than conventional.

As you may have noticed, FHA loans tend to go through periods of significant changes, especially in connection with the parent agency, the Department of Housing and Urban Development. While the primary role of FHA, to provide low-cost liberal qualifying loans, should remain relatively unchanged, politics has a way of altering how these goals are accomplished. Always check to make sure the rules have not changed. Assume nothing. And *always* use a competent, established FHA lender.

Veterans Administration (VA)

VA loans benefit borrowers who are eligible veterans. The **VA guarantees the loan.** The guarantee, known as the veteran's Entitlement or Eligibility, acts in the same function as the FHA's MIP, except that it is not insurance. A veteran can find out if he or she has this entitlement by calling the local VA office. You will then receive a Form 26-1880 (Request for Determination of Eligibility and Available Loan Guaranty Entitlement) to fill in and return. (You may be out of the service, but you will never escape the government forms.) Many lenders also have this form available.

The basic criteria are that the veteran must have served a minimum number of days in active service, depending on whether the veteran served during World War II, the Korean conflict, the Vietnam war, or other conflicts, such as Desert Storm, during peacetime, or after certain dates. The veteran must also have other than a dishonorable discharge if he or she is no longer on active duty.

VA has also given eligibility to members of the Reserves and National Guard, who would not otherwise be eligible, upon completion of six years in the Selected Reserve or upon discharge prior to six years because of a service-related disability. Unless congress changes the law, the entitlement of these veterans will expire as of September 30, 2007.

There are some other persons who can have eligibility. The spouse of an active duty member who is missing in action or a prisoner of war. The unmarried spouse of a member who died of service-related injuries may also have eligibility. And, certain individuals such as public health service officers, cadets/midshipmen at service academies, officers of NOAA, merchant seamen with WWII service, and others they may decide to add.

VA Entitlement

Enlisted after　September 7, 1980 (enlisted personnel)

October 16, 1981 (officers)

Veteran needs two years' active duty, or the full period for which they were called, but not fewer than 181 days. For Operation Desert Storm, the requirement is 90 days. Prior to 9/7/80 and 10/16/81, the veteran must have served at least 90 days in wartime and 181 days during peacetime. A borrower on active duty must have served at least 181 days before being eligible. The two-year requirement is also reduced to 181 days if the veteran was discharged early for disability or hardship. Spouses of service personnel who are officially listed as missing in action or as a prisoner of war can receive entitlement after 90 days.

The dates for wartime and peacetime are:

WW II	9/16/40 – 7/25/47
Peacetime	7/26/47 – 6/26/50
Korean	6/27/50 – 1/31/55
Peacetime	2/1/55 – 8/4/64
Vietnam	8/5/64 – 5/7/75
Peacetime	5/8/75 – 8/1/91
Operation Desert Storm	8/2/91 – 12/1/00

A qualifying veteran will receive a short green or blue form that is called a Certificate of Eligibility (Form 26-8320). This form will show how much entitlement the veteran has, if the veteran has had VA loans in the past, and if they were paid off.

The Entitlement is different from your everyday mortgage insurance or mortgage insurance premium. It is a given dollar amount that is raised periodically as the cost of housing increases. To find the current entitlement amounts you can check the VA website at www.homeloans.va.gov, or you can call your local VA office or a VA-approved lender to find out what the entitlement is at the time and if you qualify. Using the Veteran's Entitlement, VA says that it will guarantee that portion of the loan up to 50% on $45,000 or less, and up to $22,500 on loans in excess of $45,000, but not over $56,250, and not exceeding the dollar amount of the entitlement. On loans over $56,250 up to $144,000 the lesser of 40% or $46,000 is guaranteed. For loans over $144,000, the guarantee is 25% of the loan. All this means is that $203,000 is the maximum 100% VA loan amount. The $203,000 includes the funding fee we will discuss shortly. (Remember, these numbers do change periodically, so check the VA website or with your lender). This confusing method that VA uses to determine the percentage that it will guarantee is not as important as knowing how much the lender (that is, the secondary market) requires.

The secondary market, and Ginnie Mae specifically, says that it will buy the loan only as long as the entitlement and/or cash covers at least 25% of the loan. That way, Ginnie's risk is limited to 75%, just like mortgage insurance (if the loan goes to foreclosure, the lender only has to get 75% of the loan amount and the VA will pay the remaining amount). A word of warning here: if the veteran defaults and is foreclosed upon with the VA having to pay part of the loss, the veteran will still be liable to the VA for that deficiency.

A VA loan is one of the few loans that will allow the borrower to get a 100% LTV, no cash down loan, although the government is trying hard to change the rules to require around 2% to 5% minimum cash down. As long as there is sufficient entitlement to cover the top 25% and the loan does not exceed the maximum allowable amount, the veteran borrower does not need any down payment. If a veteran has $25,000 in entitlement, then upon qualification he or she could buy a $100,000 house with no cash down. The table below shows what the entitlement has been in the past and how it has risen.

If the maximum entitlement was $46,000, for the purposes of the secondary market this means that a qualifying veteran could get up to a $184,000 loan ($46,000 × 4).

Original (1944)	$ 2,000
December 28, 1945	4,000
April 20, 1950	7,500
May 7, 1968	12,500
December 31, 1974	17,500
October 1, 1978	25,500
October 1, 1980	27,500
January 1, 1988	36,000
December 18, 1989	46,000
As of 2000	50,750

VA loans are for owner-occupied dwellings up to a quadruplex, and the veteran can only have one VA loan at a time. If he sells the house and pays off the loan, his entitlement is restored. If he allows the loan to be assumed, and the loan is **assumable** if the buyer qualifies, that entitlement is tied up until that loan is paid off. If another qualifying veteran who has sufficient entitlement wants to assume the loan, she can substitute entitlement (called **Substitution of Entitlement**), which will free the selling veteran's entitlement by replacing it with the buying veteran's entitlement.

The requirements for assuming a VA loan depend on when the loan commitment was issued. Any VA loan that was committed before March 1, 1988, is assumable by anyone without qualifying. Obviously, any loans from 1988, if they exist, will represent a very small part of the value of the property, making an assumption less likely. If the commitment date was on or after that date, anyone assuming the loan must first qualify. The qualifying requirement carries for the life of the loan. An important part of the assumption process is that if the loan is assumed without qualifying, the original borrower remains on the note and is liable, along with the assuming buyer, if the latter defaults. If the assuming borrower is qualified, the original borrower can request a release of liability. However, the veteran must request this release, or he will continue to be liable, even with the assuming borrower having been qualified. A good lender will make sure that the liability is released. But don't assume that it will happen. Regardless of whether there is a release of liability or not, the assumed loan is not counted against the original borrowing veteran as a debt when she qualifies for another loan.

Partial Entitlement

In the good old days, if you sold your house, let your entitlement go with the loan, and VA subsequently raised the entitlement levels, you got the full amount of all new increases. For example, let us say you bought a house in 1976 when the entitlement was $17,500 and then sold it by assumption of the VA loan; the $17,500 was tied up until that loan was paid off. But, over the period since the entitlement was $17,500, it has been raised to $46,000, $36,000 for loans up to $144,000. That increase meant you had partial entitlement of $28,500 ($46,000 − $17,500) or

$18,500 ($36,000 − $17,500). No more. Using the VA Exhibit A (Worksheet for Computing Guaranty under Public Law 100-198) on page 202 in the Appendix, it could be much less.

An example would be an $80,000 purchase using the above scenario with the original $17,500 entitlement still tied up in the old assumed loan. By following the directions on Exhibit A, you would find the partial entitlement to be only $14,500. That would only buy a $58,000 house with no cash down. Using our example, the maximum usable entitlement up to a $144,000 loan would be $18,500. Not a very good deal either way. To avoid loss of entitlement, I recommend that a veteran allow his or her loan to be assumed without substitution of entitlement only if it is an absolute financial necessity.

If you have only partial entitlement, you can use it plus cash to make up the 25% coverage. If you end up putting down 10% or more, you may need to decide if the VA loan is more advantageous than a conventional loan. However, this decision may be moot if you need VA to qualify or if you want to pay a smaller VA Funding Fee, which we will cover later. In our example above, you would need to put down $5,500 cash. The $14,500 partial entitlement plus the $5,500 equals $20,000, or 25% of the loan amount ($20,000 × 4 = $80,000). That would mean a little less than 7% cash down.

You can use a second mortgage in combination with a VA loan, with two restrictions. The VA will not allow a second to make up the difference between the sales price and a low appraised value. The secondary market will not allow a second to make up a shortfall in entitlement, as in our example above.

The VA is very liberal in its qualifying. It does not use straight gross qualifying ratios (at this time), but a **net residual** qualifying method. This subtracts the following from the gross monthly income.

1. Federal income tax withholding on earned income
2. State income tax withholding
3. Social Security withholding
4. Child care expense, if applicable
5. Long-term monthly debts with over six months to pay off. (Debts with less than six months, but that are large enough to affect the borrower's ability to make the mortgage payments, will normally be counted.)

6. Total proposed housing expense (PITI)

7. Maintenance expense from regional VA charts based on finished square footage

8. Utilities expense from regional VA charts based on type of heat, square footage, and construction

What is left is called the **Residual Income.** This is what the veteran has left with which to buy everything unrelated to the house. The VA sets these minimum residual income amounts by region, based on family size and loan amount (see Table 5.1).

If the veteran has at least the minimum required residual income, half the battle is won. Having excess residual can help overcome other deficiencies.

Likewise, compensating factors can lower this residual income figure. It is up to the individual lender and underwriter to determine if the veteran qualifies. V.A. has agreed to allow computer underwriting; however, they are still requiring the lender's underwriter to give the final approval. This is not actual computer underwriting and allows the computer to assign only the degree of credit risk. VA is very slow to adapt to change, so it will probably be a while before they go to pure underwriting by computer.

Table 5.1   Minimum Residual Income

Family Size	Northeast	Midwest	South	West
Loan Amounts of $79,999 and Less				
1	$390	$382	$382	$425
2	654	641	641	713
3	788	772	772	859
4	888	868	868	967
5[a]	921	902	902	1,004
Loan Amounts of $80,000 and Above				
1	$450	$441	$441	$491
2	755	738	738	823
3	909	889	889	990
4	1,025	1,003	1,003	1,117
5[b]	1,062	1,039	1,039	1,158

(Note: As of 2000. These figures change periodically.)

[a] Add $75 each for additional family members numbers 6 and 7.

[b] Add $80 each for additional family members numbers 6 and 7.

The VA also requires that the veteran's total housing expense (PITI/HOA) and long-term debt payments (over six months) **not exceed 41%,** just like FHA. This 41% ratio can be exceeded with compensating factors. It is up to the individual lender to justify the higher ratio.

On page 201 of the Appendix is a copy of the form used to qualify the veteran. You only need to know the withholding amounts (look on your pay stub or get them from an approved VA lender), and to get the maintenance and utility figures from either a local VA-approved lender or the regional VA office near you. It would be a good idea also to make sure the residual figures are still current.

The VA's guidelines for self-employed and part-time income are similar to those for conventional loans. The VA will tend to be a little more flexible in some respects. At worst, it will allow the income from those sources to be used to offset long-term debt in qualifying. Again, check with your local VA-approved lender to find out what you will be allowed.

The VA Interest Rate

VA at one time set the maximum interest rate a veteran could pay and stipulated that the veteran could not pay the discount points. This is no longer true. The rate and points are set in the secondary market, and the veteran can pay the discount points. I have added this information because there is still some confusion by veterans who have not used their eligibility for a long time.

VA Funding Fee

The VA does not have a mortgage insurance premium as such, what they do have is the VA funding fee. The fees as of 2000 are as follows:

Basic Funding Fees—First Time Use for veterans, not members of Selected Reserve:

2.0% of loan amount with downpayments of 0% to less than 5%.

1.5% of loan amount with at least 5%, but less than 10% downpayment.

1.25% of loan amount with at least 10% downpayment.

Funding Fees for Reservists—First Time Use:

2.75% of loan amount with downpayments of 0% to less than 5%.

2.25% of loan amount with at least 5%, but less than 10% downpayment.

2.0% of loan amount with at least 10% downpayment.

Funding Fees for Subsequent Use:

3.0% of loan amount with downpayments of 0% to less than 5%.

1.5% (veterans) and 2.25% (reservists) with at least 5%, but less than 10% down.

1.25% (veterans) and 2.0% (reservists) with at least 10% downpayment.

In this way the government collects money for one reason and calls it something else. Just like the FHA MIP, you cannot pay part and finance part. Either finance all of it or pay all of it. This fee can be paid in cash at closing, or the borrower can finance it into the loan, just like a MIP. If you buy a $100,000 house with a 100% loan and finance the funding fee, the total loan will be $102,000 (first-time use). The only time you cannot finance the fee is when it will exceed the maximum allowable 100% loan. If $203,000 is the maximum allowable 100% loan amount, that amount must include the financed funding fee. This prohibition arises not because VA won't let you do it, but because Ginnie Mae (that is, the secondary market) won't buy it.

There are a few instances when the veteran does not have to pay the funding fee. Obviously, the seller can pay it. Or, if the veteran has a service-related disability, he or she is exempt from the funding fee. If a veteran dies from a service-related injury or disability, the surviving spouse retains the entitlement and does not have to pay the fee. If you think you may qualify, call your local VA office.

Besides being a no cash down loan, VA has another benefit. The seller, or anyone else, can pay all of the borrower's closing costs—if you can convince the seller. Usually, it will be a very motivated seller. I have done three VA loans for which the borrower put no cash down and got the seller to pay all the closing costs. The borrower literally bought the house with no cash out of pocket. But, in addition to having a motivated seller, the borrower must have strong qualifications. Few lenders are willing to make a loan to someone who has no cash in the property and is not well qualified. VA will also allow the veteran to borrow the cash to close on an unsecured basis. They could actually put it on a credit card. Just remember, the debt is counted in qualifying.

Another inovation is the **VA/Conventional loan.** This allows veterans to borrow up to the maximum Fannie/Freddie loan limits using VA eligibility. They will have to put down approximately 4% to 6% and pay the funding fee based on 100% financing. But, it can be cheaper than normal MI.

The **seller concessions** are divided into *two categories* by VA. The *first* includes costs on which there are no limits, such as closing costs (excluding prepaids) and normal discount points. The *second* is limited to 4% of the value of the property and includes such items as prepaid taxes and insurance, the funding fee, temporary or permanent interest rate buy-down discount points above the normal discount, and any other inducements to buy such as microwave ovens or helping to pay off the buyer's debts in order to qualify easier. I have never had a seller offer to pay off some of the purchaser's debts, but then again, I don't think anyone knew to ask. A word of caution. Just because the VA will allow it doesn't mean that the lender will. Remember that each lender and investor can modify guidelines to make them less flexible.

Land Limits

And, for the gentleman farmer, the VA has no maximum land limits (see Chapter 6 for other loan types). You can buy a farm or build a residence on a large parcel of land. If you are going to use income from the farm to qualify, you must be able to show that you have a background in farming.

The VA Appraisal

VA appraisals are called **Certificates of Reasonable Value (CRVs),** and they are performed by VA-approved appraisers. The normal process has been that the lender requests the appraisal, the appraiser sends the finished appraisal to the VA regional office for VA review, and then the VA mails it back to the lender. This system can add a week to the processing time of the loan. Fortunately, the VA now allows approval lenders (called LAPP) to review and approve the appraisals without going to the VA. If the veteran borrower uses one of these approved lenders, he or she can save time, and, in some instances, avoid possible problems. The VA has been known to lose appraisals.

The advantages of a VA loan are these:

1. Liberal qualifying
2. Little or no cash down
3. Relatively high maximum loan amount
4. The fact that the seller can pay any or all other closing costs, points, prepaid taxes, and insurance
5. No mortgage insurance (other than the funding fee)
6. No maximum land limits

The disadvantages of VA loans are:

1. Relatively high funding fee costs
2. Somewhat bureaucratic
3. A little longer to process

OTHER "SPECIAL" LOAN PROGRAMS FOR MODERATE INCOME AND/OR FIRST-TIME HOMEBUYERS

These loans are meant to help the low- to moderate-income buyer and, in some programs, the first-time homebuyer. The federal government has mandated that lenders must make programs of this type available to meet the Community Reinvestment Act. As a result, many lenders will have at least one of these programs.

Fannie Mae's 3-2 Option Loan

To meet the call for affordable housing, and to help take up the slack created by new FHA requirements, Fannie has developed the Community Home Buyer's Program with either the 3-2 option (CHBP) or the Fannie 97 mortgages. (This program is similar to the Revenue Bond Authority Mortgages discussed below.) This program is for owner-occupied single family residences, with approved condominiums (condos) and planned unit developments (P.U.D.s) eligible. The borrower's income cannot exceed 115% of the area median income; this requirement satisfies the goal of providing financing for moderate- to low-income borrowers. (A participating lender will have the income figures for your area.)

The down payment on the 3/2 mortgage works like this:

1. *The borrowers have to put down at least 3% of their own funds.*

2. *The other 2% (for a total of 5% down) can come from the following.*

    a. A gift from a family member, nonprofit organization, or public authority. Don't forget that you will need a gift letter and full gift verification as required by Fannie Mae (see section on gifts in Chapter 2).

    b. A grant or unsecured loan from a nonprofit organization or public authority. These loans are typically deferred and forgivable; since they have no required monthly payment, they do not count in the qualifying ratios.

3. *A secured second mortgage can be used for additional financing, but it cannot be used as part of the 5% down (3% + 2%). With the second mortgage, the maximum TLTV is 95%. This loan must be counted in the qualifying unless it is fully deferred, forgivable, and has no required monthly payment.*

The cash for closing costs also should come from the borrower's own resources. If the buyer does not have sufficient cash, a gift from a family member or a gift or unsecured loan from a nonprofit organization or public entity can be used. Fannie Mae has also **waived the normal reserve requirement of two months' payments** that their other loans have as part of the total cash needed.

You are probably wondering about **the nonprofit organizations and public authorities** that are giving all this money away. Yes, they really do exist for moderate- to low-income borrowers. Many local governments have set up Housing Authorities or Foundations, in one form or another, that will help supply cash, up to a maximum amount, to a borrower who may not have much cash. These loans, or grants, are usually set up so that there is no required payments. If the house is sold before the first mortgage is paid off, the borrower has to pay back the grant plus moderate interest. If the borrower keeps the house until the first mortgage is completely paid off, then the loan is forgiven. Check with your local government housing agencies to see if there are programs available. They should be usable for any of the moderate-income loans discussed in this chapter as well as FHA and VA loans.

The qualifying ratios go well beyond the standard Fannie Mae ratios. They will allow the housing expense to be **33%** of the stable gross monthly income (GMI) and the total expense ratio to be **38%** of GMI Fannie will allow the total expense (housing and monthly debt) ratio to go up to 40% if the borrowers can show they have previously paid a higher portion of their income toward debts.

When figuring for yourself how to qualify, don't forget that there will be mortgage insurance. Several mortgage insurance companies are participating in this program. Using the highest up-front and renewal premiums in the mortgage insurance comparison chart on page 195 in the Appendix, one should be able to make a close approximation of the actual premiums.

This is a great loan for anyone who falls within the maximum income limits and has only a minimum amount of cash. Many lenders who offer normal Fannie Mae loans will have this program.

Another loan offered by both Fannie and Freddie is the Flex or Alternative 97 loan. It is a 97% LTV with no income limits. The cash can come from a gift. You must have excellent credit (about 680 scores). The loan must be approved by computer underwriting. If it is referred, the only way it can be approved is if there is something wrong with the credit report that causes the scores to go down, and it can be proven. The qualifying ratios on these loans are 33/41 with little flexibility other than what the computer will allow. These programs have been adjusted several times since they were introduced, and I would expect further changes. Fannie and Freddie may also create new, similar loans. Check with your lender or the websites Fannie www.fanniemae.com or Freddie www.freddiemac.com.

Mortgage Revenue Bond Authorities

The federal government has granted state and local authorities the power to issue tax-free mortgage revenue bonds. The proceeds are used to make low-interest mortgages to borrowers who are, with few exceptions, **first-time homebuyers with lower incomes.**

Because the bonds sold are tax-free, they carry **a lower interest rate,** which then allows the authority to offer lower rates on its mortgages. These loans are subject to a multitude of rules, based on the federal law governing them. There are **maximum sales prices,** not loan amounts, that a borrower can pay for a house, and **the borrower cannot make a gross income over certain limits.** The house must be occupied by the borrower. It must be a single-family residence. And, the property cannot be used in any way to earn income, either by rent or by running a business from the property (this restriction includes businesses such as Amway™ and the like). The limits on sales price and gross income will vary from area to area, usually within a Standard Metropolitan Statistical Area (SMSA). Each year, the Internal Revenue Service provides data to set the new limits based on incomes and housing costs in each SMSA.

Each state has its own authority. An example is the Virginia Housing and Development Authority, or VHDA, which approves and funds the loans. The mortgage lender receives the application and processes it. The loan is then submitted to the Authority. The lender will normally get the 1% origination fee and the servicing rights. The Authority gets the discount points. As in a VA loan, the borrower cannot pay the discount points. These bond authorities are also creating loans for borrowers without the first-time or income restrictions. They are similar to the Flex/Alt 97 loans in that they are meant to help people with little cash get into a home. Check with a lender in your area that participates in the bond authority programs to see what types of loans are offered. (Most of these authorities will have websites.)

The borrower must be a first-time homebuyer, or not have owned a residence within three years. There are exceptions to this rule, mostly within certain targeted areas. The personal net assets of the borrower also are limited. The object is to help people with limited cash and income.

In line with that goal, these loans offer **liberal qualifying** based on several different sets of loan types. The basic loan is the conventional loan with a minimum of 5% down and mortgage insurance. (There are now some with as little as 3% or 0% down. Check with your lender.) The ratios for qualifying are 32% for housing expense and 40% for housing expense plus monthly debts with over six months to pay off. The lender needs to have a mortgage insurance company that recognizes the more liberal standards and will approve higher-risk loans.

Another option is for the borrower to get an authority-issued loan that is FHA insured. In this type of loan, the income and sales price limits are still set by the authority, but the qualifying and cash down are the same as in a normal FHA loan. That is, the borrower can put as little as 3% down and finance the MIP. The maximum loan amount with the MIP financed can never exceed the maximum sales price set by the authority.

Or, the borrower can get a loan that is guaranteed by the VA if he or she has sufficient entitlement. As in the FHA loan, the qualifying and cash down are done according to VA standards, but the authority income and sales price limits must be met. The loan with the funding fee financed cannot exceed the maximum sales price.

The Farmers Home Guarantee program, discussed below, now participates in guaranteeing revenue bond mortgages. A local lender can tell you if it is available in your area.

Because the guidelines between the lender and the insurer overlap, using a lender who is familiar with bond authority loans is important. Some authorities may not offer FHA or VA loans.

The authority given by Congress to issue these bonds has time limits. Each time the authorization nears expiration. Congress must extend it. Otherwise, the revenue bond authorities cannot issue new bonds. There seems to be a yearly struggle between those who hate to see all that interest income go untaxed, and those who recognize that there must be some way for low- to moderate-income borrowers to purchase a home.

The Farmers Home Administration or Rural Development Loans Guaranteed Rural Housing Loan

We are now discussing the Farmers Home Administration (FmHA), not to be confused with the FHA. This program is designed to provide **financing for rural housing for first-time owners** or for those who do not own a "structurally sound or functionally adequate home." The house must be on a publicly maintained road. (The house can be in development with private roads. Check with a participating lender.) *Rural* is defined by the FmHA as outside a standard Metropolitan Statistical Area. To find out which areas qualify, call your lender or the FmHa. **The loan amount can be up to 100%** of the lesser of cost or appraised value and the seller can pay all closing costs (that's right, no cash down).

And, if the property appraises for more than the purchase price, the borrower can finance in closing costs and the guarantee fee. The guarantee fee is 2%, which is much cheaper than the comparable FHA or VA fees. The guarantee fee can be financed as long as the property appraises for at least the amount of the purchase price plus the fee. Above that you can throw in closing costs. An example would be a $100,000 property. With the fee financed, the loan would be $102,000, so the property would need to appraise for at least $102,000. If it appraised for $103,000, then some of the closing cost could be financed. The loan is obtained from an approved lender, which will process and close the loan with FmHa underwriting.

Some of the limitations to this program include **maximum allowable adjusted gross income** (similar to the revenue bond authorities) and **maximum loan amounts** based on the area's current FHA maximum loan limits. The adjustments to the borrower's gross income include

1. A set amount per year for each child under 18 years, or over 18 years if the child is a full-time student
2. Actual child care expenses up to a set amount per year
3. A set amount per year for an elderly family

The amounts in the adjustments above can change, so I did not want to put in numbers that would become outdated quickly. Other deductions may be published by the FmHA in the future.

For the most part, these limitations are not so low as to preclude a large segment of moderate-income borrowers from qualifying. The interest rate is the same as the FHA/VA rate. Also, similar to a revenue bond authority loan, it must be for a single-family owner-occupied home from which no income can be derived.

The biggest obstacle, however, will probably be the requirement that **the borrower must be "unable to secure the credit necessary to finance a home without FmHa assistance"** (all of these quotations come from the FmHA Information for Lenders booklet). That means, of course, that the borrower must be turned down by or be unable to qualify for any other available loan program, such as conventional, FHA, or VA.

This loan is not for those with a spotty credit history. The credit standards are very strict. Consider

1. No more than one payment over 30 days past due in the past 12 months. This includes credit cards.

2. Less than two rent payments 30 days or more past due in the last three years.

3. No unsatisfied judgments within the past 12 months.

4. No collections within the past 12 months.

Just like FHA, qualifying is based on ratios of 29% for housing expense and 41% for housing and debt expense. However, these ratios cannot be exceeded for any reason (as of the time the program was started).

Not being able to qualify for any other loan program, being in a designated rural area, falling within adjusted gross income slots, and meeting the absolute credit and qualifying guidelines are quite a gauntlet to run. The government is counting on these guidelines to weed out most of the problem borrowers. While this is a very laudable idea, it may also weed out many otherwise qualified and deserving borrowers, in effect, denying loans to those it was intended to help.

FmHA also has a subsidized payment program for borrowers who do not have sufficient income to qualify for the standard plan. FmHA uses a formula to determine if the borrower fits. If you do not qualify under the normal program, ask if you can get the subsidized one. This loan, however, still requires that you have good credit.

6

THE APPRAISAL

The appraisal is one of the four main parts of a loan application. Because the property to be financed will be the security for the loan, the lender must be certain that it has sufficient value. The loan amount is based on the lesser of the sales price or appraised value, called the **Value.** Otherwise, the lender could make a 95% LTV loan on a $100,000 purchase when the house is really worth $90,000. That would be a loan of over 106% LTV. If that happened, the lender had better hope the property appreciates quickly and that the borrower doesn't default. (Yes, there are 103%–125% LTV loans, but even then it is very important to know the actual value of the property.)

The art of appraising residential property has evolved over time into a very sophisticated yet subjective science. The secondary market has developed guidelines with which it expects the appraiser to comply in order to come up with a fair and reasonably certain value. Also, to cover themselves in case of foreclosure, investors in the secondary market want assurance that it is a marketable property. Lenders always look at the worst case scenario.

Lenders want to know whether the property is in an area that is growing, stable, or declining. Is it in a predominantly residential area? Is the area in transition, for example, from residential to industrial? Is the house in good repair? Does it have the minimum number of bedrooms, bathrooms, and the like to give it marketability in the area? In short, is this a property on which it would be safe for the lender to make a loan.

The appraiser's responsibility is to provide the lender with the necessary information to make this decision. A good appraiser will make an independent judgment, uninfluenced by any of the parties to the transaction. If she feels any or all parts of the property do not meet the minimum guidelines, she is obligated to inform the lender. Although the borrower usually pays for the appraisal, it is done for the lender.

Let us say that an appraiser reports a roof needs to be replaced, or the surrounding properties are declining in value. Then the lender would require that the roof be replaced before closing, or, in the case of declining values (known as economic obsolescence), the lender would probably not make the loan unless the LTV was so low as to present minimal risk. If the house had only one bedroom and was located in an area where most houses had three bedrooms and there was no demonstrated demand for one-bedroom houses, then the lender would probably decline the loan because the property would be functionally obsolete. However, certain lenders and loan types, such as FHA, may be more lenient.

Appraisers use the rooms that are aboveground (that is, not in the basement) in determining the total number of bedrooms and bathrooms—even if the basement is a walk-out. This rule can present some special problems. If the house is a ranch style on a full basement with one bedroom on the main level and two bedrooms in the lower level, the property is considered a one-bedroom house by Fannie and Freddie. If this type of house cannot be shown to be common in the area, then the secondary market may decline to buy the loan. That is, the lender won't make the loan.

The value of the land without the improvements is another key part of the appraisal. Most lenders do not want the land to represent more than about 30% of the total value, unless the appraiser can show it is common in the area for the land to exceed that percentage. There are areas where the land is averaging $150,000 per lot, or 40% to 45% of the value. By showing that other properties in the area have similar land values, an appraiser can convince the lender to make loans on these homes. The FHA will vary from region to region, but generally it will use the same guidelines as Fannie and Freddie, except their rules are more flexible. Tax-exempt bond authorities normally limit their loans to a very small amount of land, two to five acres or less. The VA, as we noted earlier, has no land restrictions. Jumbo and nonconforming loans set their own guidelines for land values. There are lenders who will do special loans for farms and estates. If you have a property that you feel might not meet a lender's normal requirements, call around and find out if it will present a problem. Each lender can be different.

Most important of all, the appraiser must establish the value of the property. In the *Market Value* method of establishing value, the appraiser compares the property in question with three recent comparable sales. A second method of establishing value, the *Cost* approach, calculates the value of reproducing the property. The Market approach is used in the majority of appraisals. The comparables must be within a reasonable distance of the subject property, be similar, and have sold within the last six months, or 12 months at the very latest. The comps (comparable values) are adjusted (value added or subtracted) based on their overall similarity to the subject property. If the subject property has a garage and one of the comps does not, then the comp is adjusted by adding the value of the garage to it, or vice versa. The total of these adjustments on each comp should fall within a certain percentage of the value, or sales price, of that particular comp. If the percentages are too high, that fact indicates either that the appraiser used excessive adjustments to justify the subject property's value or that the comp may not be similar enough to the subject property to use as a comparable. The latter reason is why some recent sales that the borrower or the Realtor thinks are perfect comps will not be used by the appraiser in determining the value of the property. Another point that may confuse the borrower is the lender's rejection of certain comparables because they are too far away from the subject property. In suburban or urban areas, the lender expects the comps to be within blocks of and no more than a mile from the subject, and in a similar neighborhood. In a rural area, depending on the lender, the comps can be 5 to 15 miles away. However, most lenders will want at least one comp to be in close proximity to the subject property. Because of the difficulty in determining an accurate market value on rural properties, and because they tend to take longer to sell, it is possible the lender will limit the LTV to 90% or less.

The majority of loan appraisals will have few problems, and most of those can be cured. However, the appraiser can act much like an underwriter, by approving or rejecting the property as acceptable security for the loan.

An example of an appraisal that did affect the loan occurred when a borrower came to me wanting to refinance his house in a very nice area of the city. He had done some renovation work and wanted to recover the cost by refinancing. Based on the preliminary value of what he originally paid for the house and the cost of the renovations, the LTV would be around 60%. The borrower was well qualified, and the loan, all in all, looked like a sure bet— until the appraisal arrived.

The borrower had hired what is known as a jackleg contractor to do the work, that is, someone who is unskilled or untrained to do independent work. This "contractor" had wired and plumbed the house and added interior partitions. The wiring and plumbing were not done according to the local building code. In fact, a permit had never been obtained and the work had never been inspected. If it had, it would have been rejected. The owner was not aware of these defects. He didn't even know that a permit and inspection were required. He was not completely innocent in this mess, however. He designed the changes, which turned the third bedroom into more of a passageway and created a bathroom with such a low ceiling that anyone taller than 5′2″ had to stoop in it.

The appraiser, seeing that things weren't quite right, checked the city building department, where he found that the permits had never been issued. Being a competent professional, he knew several things. First, the city could require that the work be torn out and redone. Second, the lender would not like a bedroom in a hallway and a bath in which people cannot stand erect. The appraiser literally stated in his report that the property was not good security for a loan. Because the borrower was not willing to make the corrections, the loan was denied. Only a lender willing to take a risk and hold the loan in portfolio would have considered this property.

In arriving at the value, one other thing should be mentioned: personal property such as stoves, refrigerators, blinds, rugs, and lawn mowers that the seller has included in the sale. For purposes of evaluation, most lenders will accept the major appliances if the appraiser states that it is normal for them to be included in the sale, and that no value was given to them in arriving at the final value of the property. Short-lived, readily replaceable things like lawn mowers and Oriental rugs should not be part of the purchase contract. If the purchaser will not buy the house without them, they should be purchased by a separate bill of sale that states the items will convey upon the closing on the real estate.

When I was still selling real estate, a couple that was interested in buying a house that I had listed came to me. There was one problem. They had already contracted to purchase another property, which they ultimately decided they did not want (a case of Buyer's Remorse). The contract stipulated they would apply for a first mortgage. It also stated that the seller was throwing in the lawn mower, two rugs, and a horse. As I told them, all they had to do was apply for the loan and they would be turned down. Mortgage lenders do not make 30-year loans on horses.

Most of the appraisals done today will be acceptable. The majority of borrowers have little to worry about. Too often the borrower gets upset over something the appraiser noted about the property which the borrower takes exception to—as, giving the condition of the property as average, when the proverbial "everyone" knows that it is in mint condition. If the lender does not comment on it, don't take it personally and don't worry about it. Worry about the big stuff like old wiring or leaky basements. And be happy that it was noticed by the appraiser, because appraisers are not usually expected to catch the less obvious structural and mechanical problems.

With the computer age, the science of appraising has changed dramatically. With my company, the appraisers now e-mail the appraisals directly to us. No more waiting for pictures to be developed and then waiting until the appraiser can bring the appraisal to the office, or in the worst case, waiting for the appraisal to arrive in the mail. And, with computer underwriting, the appraisal requirements have undergone the biggest changes. Depending on the LTV, and credit, to a lessor extent, the computer may require only an exterior appraisal, a drive-by appraisal, or no appraisal at all. With no appraisal, the computer (Fannie or Freddie) accepts the purchase price as value and only requires the appraiser to do an exterior inspection, just to make sure the house does exist. The benefits to the borrower are lower appraisal costs and a quicker closing. Something else that is occurring, but is not as widely accepted at this time, is an appraisal done completely by computer. Sales and comparable records are pulled directly from locality tax records with the computer program making all adjustments. Nice, in a perfect world. Unfortunately, my world isn't quite as cut and dried.

7

THE DIFFERENT TYPES OF PROPERTIES

Most borrowers don't consider the property that they are purchasing in terms of how it appeals to the market as a whole, as long as it appeals to them. Sellers usually have a definite emotional attachment, while borrowers are trying to justify the purchase and the price in their own minds. Lenders have a less emotional and a more proprietary interest, in the form of large sums of cash. These business and personal emotions can collide when the relative merits of the property are discussed.

Lenders want to make loans on properties that appeal to as wide a market as possible. Borrowers want to own property with character—property that is different from the rest of the houses on the block. The appraisal will define just how unique this property is, and the lender's guidelines will judge whether it is acceptable for the type of loan for which the borrower has applied. Most properties are broken down into different types and then classified according to whether their features, such as number of bedrooms, are common for the market area.

THE SINGLE-FAMILY DETACHED HOME

The single-family home is what almost every American dreams of owning. Most people think of this as being a single, free-standing structure, a single house by itself, on its own lot. The construction style of the property adds further to its definition. There are the standard ranch, the colonial two-story, the split-level, the tri-level, the contemporary, the log home, the dirt-covered energy-saving home, the dome house, and the ones that look as if someone lost the blueprints. The more offbeat or bizarre the construction, the more difficult it is to obtain regular financing.

THE SINGLE-FAMILY ATTACHED HOME, OR TOWNHOUSE

Attached homes or **townhouses** are becoming more prevalent as the costs of land and materials rise. Each of these houses, joined together at a common wall, sits on its own lot. The only difference between the attached and the detached house is that they are—attached.

Townhouses generally are built as part of a development that has covenants and restrictions to protect the properties as a whole and that provides certain basic services such as trash removal and snowplowing. With this type of property you often are subject to homeowner's association fees (HOA) and Road Maintenance fees (when the roads are not public). These fees add another item that the lender must approve. There are lending guidelines for acceptable HOA and Road Maintenance Agreements. Most builders today work with Realtors or lenders who make sure that the covenants and restrictions are acceptable. Also, most state and local governments will have requirements that meet or exceed lender requirements on homeowner's association agreements. It is always advisable to get a copy of the recorded. Covenants and Restrictions before committing to the purchase of any property governed by them. Some states now require that the purchaser be notified that there are covenants and restrictions on the property and that these Covenants and Restrictions be provided within a given period of time after acceptance of the contract to purchase.

CONDOMINIUMS

Condominium was the buzzword of the 1980s. It has also been a dirty word for much of the market, and lenders in particular. Condos are basically apartments that are owned instead of rented (not to be confused with co-ops). They come in many forms, from detached or attached housing in a complex to multiple units. The main distinguishing feature is that everything except the unit itself is owned in common by the entire complex. There are no individual lots. Most condos consist of a complex much like an apartment building in which the units are owned individually. (Many condos today are actually apartments that have been converted.) This sounds great for those who cannot afford a house or who are not interested in cutting grass.

The problems start when not enough units sell to make the complex viable. Then the developer may either abandon it or declare bankruptcy, which leaves the poor souls who got in on the "ground floor" sitting in a mostly empty complex that is not being maintained or managed. Another problem may be the units are sold as investment properties and become run-down because the tenants trash them. In either case, the properties will decrease in value, if indeed there is a market for them in which you can establish a value.

Condos are not all bad. They have their place in the market as long as they are properly designed, marketed, and managed. The secondary market, and almost every lender, feels the same way. But, they will thoroughly scrutinize the development, its covenants and restrictions, condo fees, homeowner's association budget, and bond coverage before they will make loans there. Fannie and Freddie require that the lender determine if the project meets their guidelines. After the project has been in existence for several years and it has demonstrated market demand, it is often easier to get lenders to make loans there.

When it comes to condos, be very careful! Make sure the one you want meets Fannie or Freddie guidelines so that it will have more potential mortgage money available for purchasers when you decide to sell. If only one or two lenders are making loans on the condos, you may later find yourself trying to sell a property on which purchasers cannot find adequate financing. If the original lenders stop lending there, you may have no available financing. Don't buy where more than 20% to 30% of the total units are nonowner-occupied. (Most secondary market investors will not buy loans when over 30% are nonowner or investment units.) Others will allow up to 49%. Check the covenants and restrictions to make sure there is nothing that could adversely affect your investment. Look at the homeowner's association budget to make sure there are adequate reserves for repairs and maintenance. And, most importantly, check around the area to see if there really is a demand for the condos you are considering. Do not get suckered in by the initial low price and the health spa in the basement. The lender won't.

Computer underwriting can remove the condo's requirement

to meet Fannie or Freddie guidelines. Low LTV and high credit scores can make the loan approval subject to little or no condo review. It does not take much effort to make application and have the lender run it through the underwriting program. Then you know exactly what will be required.

TWO- TO FOUR-FAMILY HOMES

Then there are the two- to four-unit multifamily dwellings: duplex, triplex, and quadruplex. The secondary market, and most lenders, recognize properties from two to four units as multifamily residential properties. These can be financed as either owner- or nonowner-occupied homes. A multifamily property will require a more detailed appraisal and comparables that are also multifamily. And these mean a more expensive appraisal.

Anything over four units is considered a commercial property and will need a loan from a specialized lender, usually a bank, insurance company, or a nonconforming secondary market investor. Mortgage lenders for home loans rarely get involved with commercial lending.

LOCATION, LOCATION, LOCATION

Once you know what you want, where do you want it to be? Is it downtown, in the suburbs, out in the county, in the woods, or up on the mountain? Lenders categorize homes as being urban (in town), suburban (on the edge or close to town and all of the amenities such as schools and shopping), and rural (not close to other developments, schools, shopping, and generally not convenient to much of anything).

As a rule, the more accessible, the more urban, and the nearer to a desirable area your property is, the easier it will be to obtain normal financing. It is no fluke that Realtors always say that location is the primary factor for being able to sell a property and to get top dollar for it.

A rural location presents the most problems because it is harder to establish market value and there may be much less demand for a rural property (as we discussed earlier). Lenders will make certain allowances for rural properties when the appraiser looks for comparable sales. And, as the LTV goes down, the lender's requirements also go down. The comps can be 7 to 15 miles from the subject instead of one block to one mile. But, they do have to be similar, and they still must have sold within the past 6 to 12 months. These can be very hard to carry out when there is little around to compare with. On top of that, much of the rural property has **extra acreage.**

The normal mortgage lenders, in particular those dealing with the conforming secondary market, are interested in financing residential properties, not mini-farms. There are other loans and lenders for that type of property. Nonconforming loans, commercial banks, and the Federal Land Bank are a few lenders who will finance your place in the country.

SECOND HOMES

If you want a place in the country or on the beach or on the river as a getaway, you are talking **Second Home.** There is a very large market for these properties, and most lenders offer some type of second-home financing. The secondary market will buy second home loans as long as they meet the standard guidelines. The normal standards are that the cost of your personal residence should not be more than 28% of your gross monthly income, and the total expenses, including the second-home mortgage payment, should not exceed 36%. No rent income from the property can be used in qualifying. You also have to put down at least 10% in most instances. Check your lenders for their programs.

8

INTEREST RATES, POINTS, AND LOCK-INS

As we discussed earlier, lenders set rates based on what the current market is, or what they think the market will be. They also charge points to buy the rate down and/or to get extra fee income. The borrowers' mission is to find the best loan, the best rate and points, and the best service, and to be assured that they will get all of these at closing.

When you call around to the various lenders, you find that their rates are not the same. Some will be 0.125% to 0.5%, or more, higher or lower than the rest. Why is that?

WHY ARE LENDERS DIFFERENT?

The rates and points of each lender are based on various methods of dealing in the secondary market, plus any additions or subtractions that the lender includes. There are innumerable ways to derive pricing from the secondary market. I will cover the most basic methods, and how they can help or hurt the borrower in his quest for the best rate and lender. While this description may not seem very pertinent to getting the loan, it will help the borrower to understand the different pricings of lenders and to avoid being taken advantage of in certain circumstances. It can also make the borrower's choice of the best, most reliable lender easier.

First, one way lenders can sell loans is by either of two methods, called mandatory or optional deliveries. They are exactly as their names imply. If a delivery is mandatory, the loan, or loans, must be delivered within a given period of time. If the lender cannot fulfill the commitment, the lender is required either to pay a stiff penalty or even to replace the shortfall with cash. Most lenders doing a mandatory delivery will make sure that they can fill it before committing, and they will also be less likely to allow any renegotiating of locked rates if interest goes down (see next section). For an idea of how a typical mandatory delivery works, here is an example.

The lender agrees to deliver $20 million in 30-year fixed rate loans to the investor at a rate of 10% with 1% discount (commitments can also be for a range of loans, say from 9.75% to 10.25% with corresponding points to give the investor the interest rate that was agreed upon, 10% in our example). The lender then has a specified number of days in which to deliver this package of closed loans. We will say 90 days for this example. If the lender provides the package at the agreed time, everyone should make a profit. If the lender does not fill the commitment and ships only $15 million within the 90 days, then it will have to pay a penalty on the $5 million shortfall, or else pay the $5 million in cash. In the latter case the investor still makes money and the lender has a serious cash problem. Or, if the lender thinks that the market will go down even further than the rate agreed upon, it might lock in loans for more money than the amount committed for delivery, say $30 million, or $10 million more than the commitment. If the rates do drop, the lender can negotiate a sale at a premium because it has loans at a rate above the current market, and it will make lots of money. If the rates go up, the lender has $10 million in uncovered loans which it cannot sell, unless the lender wants to lose a bunch of money by selling the loans at a discount to their actual cost. (If the market rose to a point where a 10% interest rate required 2 discount points, the lender would have to sell its 10% and 1% discount point loans at a loss of 1% of the $10 million in uncovered loans, or $100,000.) Faced with this potential loss, the lender has several options. It can portfolio the loans (use its own money to hold the loans) until the rates drop, if it has the assets to do this. It can sell at a loss, if it can afford to do this. Or, it can refuse to honor the locked-in loans that it cannot cover, by either outright refusing to close at the agreed interest rate or delaying the closing until the lock-in expires. Either way is unethical and illegal.

The advantage of mandatory deliveries is that the lender can get lower pricing from the investor because the investor knows he will get the loans and pricing on which they agreed.

Optional delivery is safer for the lender because it is only *optional* that they deliver the loan(s) to the investor. On groups of loans, called pools or packages, the lender will pay an up-front, nonrefundable fee to the investor for the privilege of not having to fill the commitment if the lender cannot fill it or does not want to fill it. On single loans, there usually is no fee, except in certain instances where the investor requires a lock-in fee at the time the borrower decides to lock the rate and points. The lender will get better pricing on a commitment for a package of loans than it will for single loans. Smaller lenders and brokers will normally use the single loan delivery because of its low risk. Optional deliveries will sometimes have features allowing the lender to offer a relock option when interest rates go down. For the borrower, rates for loans with optional delivery will be higher than mandatory rates. Do not expect the lender to divulge how it sells its loans. Most branch offices and loan officers have little idea of how the loan is handled once it is closed. I have included this information to give you an idea of how pricing fluctuates and why a lender may try not to close the loan.

Next, consider how the servicing is handled in these deliveries. In Chapter 2 we talked about how the lender can get more income by selling the servicing; that is, the lender receives a servicing-released premium as additional income. If the servicing is released, this premium, paid to the lender, can be used to offer even lower rates to the borrower. Also, most investors offer premiums on a sliding scale, paying a higher one for higher loan amounts. All lenders price on some type of sliding scale with the points going down as the loan amount increases. Different types of loans will have greater or lessor point adjustments because they are more or less profitable. Government loans (FHA, VA, FmHA) are much more profitable than conventional loans. Fixed rate loans are more profitable than ARMs. A longer amortization is more profitable than a shorter one. Therefore, it is reasonable to assume the borrower can get a better deal on an FHA 30-year fixed rate than on an FHA ARM. Of course, you do not want to get an FHA just for the pricing if you can do a conventional, because the pricing is not going to make up for the higher MIP. And, there is no guarantee that the lender will pass on the lower points. They can charge you points without any adjustment and make more money on the loan. (When I discuss other fees, you will see how a lender can quote lower points than another lender, but it will still cost you just as much or more.) An example would be pricing of 10% with 1 discount point to the investor, and an additional 0.375% servicing-released premium to the lender for selling the servicing to the investor. The lender could choose to pass this on to the borrower and offer the loan at 10% with 0.625% discount to the borrower (1% required discount {nd} 0.375% premium rebate = 0.625% discount). Or, the lender could keep part of the premium, say 0.25%, and pass the remainder on to the borrower (0.125%, or 0.875% discount). Assuming the example above is based on a $75,000 loan, a loan of $125,000 might carry a servicing premium of 625 and $200,000 might carry 1.00. The lender can remove any or all of the premium from the points for the higher amounts. Of course, as we have discussed, the lender can keep the whole thing for itself. If the loan is being sold and the servicing will be transferred at the time the loan is closed (this fact must be disclosed at closing or shortly afterward) the lender often will receive an even higher servicing premium, known in this instance as a Service Released Premium. With this, they can either make more money or offer you a lower rate.

Knowing this, in combination with the fact that the lower the interest rate, the higher the points, it is easier to understand how interest rates, and points, are quoted. The higher interest rate will have no (-0-) points, either origination fee or discount points. This is known as the "par" rate. (You know most lenders play golf.) As the rate goes down, the points begin to go up. (Remember the permanent buy-down?) If 8.5% is 0 + 0 (no origination and no discount), 8.375% might be 375 + 0, 8.25%, 75 + 0, 8. 125%, 1 + 375, 7.5%, 1 + 3, and so forth. In reality, rates go down when points go down. Remembering our discussion about the permanent buy-down, the challenge is to decided which rate and points are best for you. In the next section, I will tell you how the points can be even lower.

Now that you are confused by these multiple manipulations of interest rate pricings, let us consider another common way for lenders to sell loans into the secondary market: issuing their own **securities, or bonds,** backed by the loans that they have taken. Without going into great detail (that would require a book unto itself), a lender can package or pool its loans in large amounts, usually millions, and sell securities that are secured by the loans it holds. In this way it can get back the money invested, it still holds the loans and the servicing, and it can often offer an even lower interest rate. The big drawback is that the lender can lose its shirt, and sometimes the whole company, because of the high risk involved in setting its own rates and trying to make sure that it can then sell the bonds into the market before interest rates jump. (Bonds can be sold in a commitment to the secondary market, but the mortgage company's secondary marketing department [often referred to as the marketing department] must know the market. If it misreads the bond market, the company can lose big bucks. You can usually tell when a company is losing money because their rates will go up, they will start downsizing, or both.) Under such circumstances the integrity of the lender is tested. Just as in a mandatory delivery, the lender may be forced to honor interest rates that cost it money.

As you may have noticed, the pricing and marketing of mortgage loans is legalized gambling. How competent and conservative a lender chooses to be can make a tremendous difference in the overall costs to the borrower. The difference between a commitment of a large pool of money and the rates on a per loan basis can be 0.5% or greater on the interest rate. Most lenders will employ some combination of the methods described to devise competitive products and minimize risk. Each lender (and each investor in the secondary market) can have pricing for any particular loan type that will be different from that of the next lender (or borrower) because of how it is buying or selling that loan. Pricing gets much more complicated than this, (remember when I mentioned mortgage insurance companies as a source of better rates?) and there are many variations on how loans are bought and sold, but the explanation gives you an idea of why rates differ. What it means to the borrower is that there are multiple opportunities to get the best rate through this competitive marketing structure.

LOCKED-IN RATES

Lock-Ins reserve the money for the borrower at a given rate and points for a set number of days. Most lock periods are determined by the lender and are for 10, 30, 60, 90, 120, and sometimes 180 days. The most common period is 60 days. The shorter the lock-in period, the lower the discount points, and vice versa. A lender may, or may not, choose to pass this savings on to the borrower. If you are locking in 45 days or less before closing, ask if the lender will give you lower points. Here is a simple example.

The investor is offering to buy 30-year loans at the adjusted full market rate 10%, with 1 discount point, for delivery in 90 days. The lender then offers to make a loan at 10%, with 1 discount point, or even more if it wants additional fee income. The borrower wants to close 50 days from now and wants to lock in the rate. The lender will lock it in for 60 days, knowing that 60 days will provide enough time to process, approve, and close the loan; after that, the lender will have at least 30 days to get the completed documents together, straighten out any problems that might have come up (like attorney mistakes), and then deliver the loan to the investor. (Remember, while this example uses a 90-day delivery, others may have much shorter periods.) If everything goes according to plan, the borrower gets the rate, the lender gets the loan closed, and the investor buys the loan. But, as we know, "The best laid schemes o' mice and men" will often come undone.

What happens if the borrower doesn't qualify or backs out of the contract? If the commitment to deliver the loan to the investor was an optional one, the lender has no problem. If it was a mandatory delivery, then the lender has two choices: Find another loan that can close and be delivered on time to replace it, or pay a stiff penalty. Pay enough penalties, and you can go out of business. To protect themselves, many lenders will hedge, or cover part of the loans in their pipeline with a commitment, and leave the others uncovered based on the normal percentage of loans that do not close. You begin to see the balancing act the lender has to accomplish to be competitive and profitable.

It is not required that borrowers lock in a rate at application. They can wait for as long as several days prior to closing before locking in a rate. By waiting, they are obviously taking a chance, much like playing the stock market. There will always be borrowers who think they can wait until the market is at its lowest and get the best rate. Chances are better that they will wait so long that the market will have gone back up. Don't worry about whether you are getting the absolute lowest rate possible, or you will go crazy trying to outguess the market.

On the other hand, borrowers who lock in a rate may then see the market go even lower. Although they have been guaranteed a rate, and the lender has made commitments to ensure that that rate is available, the borrowers will insist that they get the lower rate. As you saw from what we discussed before, the lender may not be able to give the lower rate without taking a loss. If you, the borrower, are concerned about the possibility of getting the lower rate after locking, ask the lender if it offers that option. Some lenders have programs that will allow the borrower to lock in a rate, and then relock at a lower rate if interest rates go down. Typically, the rate must go down at least 0.25% to 0.50%, and the borrower may have to pay an extra 0.25% to 1.0% in points to get the lower rate. If the lender does offer this feature, make sure it is in writing as part of the lock-in agreement you sign. (Many states require that lenders disclose their lock-in procedures, in writing, at the time of loan application.) Another option many lenders offer is the "Capped Rate Float-Down" feature. It will vary slightly from lender to lender, but, in general, it works like this. The borrower can cap the rate, which means that if rates rise, the borrower will not get a rate any higher than the cap. The cap is usually anywhere from 25 to 75% higher than the current rate, depending on how long a period the borrower wants this option to run before closing. Then, when the borrower is within 30 days of closing, she can lock in the rate if rates have gone down. Most lenders will collect a fee up to 1% of the loan amount for this option. The fee is usually credited at closing and is not an additional cost. If the borrower does close the loan, the fee is forfeited.

Some lenders will not allow the borrower to lock in the rate until after the loan has been approved. This way the lender limits its risk in committing to an investor and then having the loan not close because the borrower did not qualify. A few will not give a rate until the day of closing, but this alternative is not prevalent.

As you probably recognize by now, rates and lock-in periods may not be the determining factor when choosing a lender. Instead, look for one that is established and known in the community, one that has a reputation for honesty and fair dealing. Avoid any lender that has been known not to honor a lock-in or has allowed too many loan lock-ins to expire before closing. A good lender will stand behind a commitment, even if it means taking a loss. You often do get what you pay for.

DISCOUNT POINTS
Money Talks

In Chapter 2 we discussed discount points and how they are used to buy down the interest rate. Points are interest in advance. There is a book published that gives equivalent yields resulting from paying additional discount points to get a lower rate, but not all lenders use these formulas. There is no absolute formula that can be applied to all lenders to determine what they will charge.

(The basic theory is that 1 discount point, 1.0%, will lower the rate one-eighth percent, 0.125%. But, as I have noted, not all lenders are reading from the same page.) They will often undercut the market or set prices over it because they are anticipating changes, they are trying to earn extra fee income, or their particular method of selling loans fixes the price that much higher or lower.

For example, if a 10% loan is at par, with no discount points, different lenders may charge 0.50% to 2.50% discount points for a 9.75% rate. The actual market may require 1.00% or more.

Some borrowers reading this might conclude that they can negotiate points with the lender to get something lower than what is being quoted. They are right, so long as the lender has excess points built in and the lender is willing to forgo this income to get the loan. It has become common for lenders to adjust points to get a loan. They may also do it as a favor to the Realtor in order to ingratiate themselves for future business. Or, if business is slow they may have a limited-time "special" to help bring in business. One company I worked for had regular weekend specials for contracts to purchase written from Friday afternoon to Monday morning.

THE ORIGINATION FEE
Loan Originators Have to Eat, Too

The origination fee is fee income to the lender that helps to pay the cost of originating, processing, closing, and shipping the loan. Unfortunately for the lender, it often will not pay for all of these things. But, as the loan amount gets higher, it begins to cover more of the expenses. While 1% of a $40,000 loan ($400) does not come close to paying costs, 1% of $180,000 ($1,800) takes care of all, or at least a significant part, of them.

Part of this fee goes to the loan originator, either in the form of salary or commission income. Most loan officers are paid a commission. It can be a set percentage, 0.5% of the loan amount being fairly typical. Or, they can be paid on a sliding scale depending on the value of the loans they close in a month. An example would be 0.40% for $500,000, 0.50% for $750,000, 0.55% for $1,000,000, and 0.65% for $1,500,000. On commission income, the originator can get rich (I have seen loan officers make six-figure annual incomes easily), or she can just barely survive.

It depends on whether the lender is competitive, provides good service, and has a good reputation in the community. And, of course, whether the loan officer is competent.

What do these observations have to do with the borrower, other than the fact that someone, most likely the borrower, will have to pay the origination fee? Usually nothing—unless the lender or the originator fouls up to the detriment of the borrower. If a rate was not locked as requested, if the lender did not process the loan correctly, if the originator failed to disclose certain important and costly facts about the loan, or if the originator disclosed facts that later proved to be incorrect, the borrower could be left holding a very expensive bag. If any of these should happen, borrowers can consider several things.

They can threaten to sue, which might yield some money and satisfaction, but it does not get the loan closed. They can pull the loan application, but that would only give them satisfaction. Or, they can negotiate with the lender and/or originator. A lender or the originating loan officer would probably be happy to give up some fee income in order to keep things from getting more embarrassing, and giving them a bad name in the community. Cutting the origination fee to compensate for the mistake is always an option.

I am not suggesting that borrowers insist that lenders cut their fee for every little problem that comes up. Many glitches are not directly the fault of the lender, and borrowers cannot expect to be compensated because they feel things did not go smoothly. I am suggesting that if the lender did make a mistake to the borrower's detriment, the origination fee is one source from which restitution can be made. Using a good, experienced lender will help to avoid this potential problem. Computer underwriting has helped to remove many of the old processing problems, but mistakes are still made.

9

THE TYPES OF LENDERS

The point should be clear that there are all types of lenders. What we will look at now is exactly how different ones operate, and how these differences can affect the borrower.

THE BANKER

The normal, everyday retail bank is what most people think of when they need money. You go to the bank to put in money, and when you don't have any to put in, you go to get a loan to take some out. Banks make loans on cars, computers, horses, people— and on real estate. Unless you are dealing with a bank that has a mortgage department or subsidiary (see below), you will find mortgages are done a little differently by the retail, or commercial, end of banking.

Retail banks use their own money to make loans, which they do not sell. They set their own guidelines and rates. These guidelines can be less demanding than those of the secondary market, but their rates are often significantly higher. They also are less interested than other institutions (which we shall discuss shortly) in making long-term loans. Most bank mortgage loans will balloon or, at best, not go beyond a 10- or 15-year amortization. Every bank will be different. Each has its own rules. Banks often have a separate mortgage lending division which is completely separate from the retail operation. They are mortgage bankers who deal in the secondary market and are discussed next.

The terms of the loan, and whether the bank will do it or not, will often be based on the relationship the borrower has, or will have, with the bank. If you keep large deposits with the bank, you stand a good chance of being approved, and quickly. If you already have significant debt with the bank, it may not be so interested in adding to that obligation, unless all of the debt is renegotiated so that more of it is secured by the real estate.

The advantages of dealing with a retail, or commercial, banker are that the bank may ask for less documentation and may be more flexible. The disadvantages are that the rate will often be higher, the loan term will be short, and the LTV is usually lower.

THE MORTGAGE BANKER
Dedicated to the Secondary Market

A mortgage banker can be a freestanding company, unaffiliated with any other entity, or it can be part of a bank or other depository institution. To be accepted by the investors in the secondary market it needs to have substantial capital enough to sell, buy, and service loans. For that reason, there usually is some connection with another capital-rich source, such as banks, insurance companies, credit unions, or any large company like General Motors and Sears.

Mortgage bankers work closely with the secondary market, using its guidelines and selling the resulting loans or securities backed by the loans. They can fund and close their own loans, and hold them if necessary until the loans are sold. They will also buy loans from other sources to be pooled with their own loans for sale in the secondary market.

Buying loans from other lenders, which is done by a Wholesale Division, allows the lender to acquire loans at an acceptable price without the cost of paying for an originating branch office. The loans they buy can come from other mortgage bankers or mortgage brokers.

THE MORTGAGE BROKER
The Independent Loan Source

Mortgage brokers do what the name implies, they broker loans for other lenders directly to the borrower. Brokers will normally have access to many different wholesale lenders. The broker gives the borrower the wholesaler's price to which they have added their fees in the form of the origination fee, additional discount points, and other miscellaneous fees. Because the wholesaler does not have the overhead of the broker's office, it can discount the price to the broker so that the broker can add a fee and still be competitive. Brokers can offer a wide range of products, including commercial loans.

There are many stories about borrowers going to a broker who promised a loan that did not exist and who collected an application fee that was nonrefundable. Or, more commonly, these tales recount dealings with a broker who did not know enough about mortgage lending to process the loan correctly. The results have been disastrous. A few brokers have been known to take a loan application without knowing whether they will be able to place it or not. The problem is that this fact is not disclosed to the borrower, at least not until the last minute, when the broker has run out of options. Check out the broker carefully before making application. The best ones can be a cornucopia of loan products, and the worst ones can cause you misery. Most of the good ones now have access to computer underwriting. This helps to remove many of the past problems. But, if they do not enter the loan correctly into the computer, big problems can occur.

THE THRIFT
Created to Finance Your Home

The majority of mortgage loans used to be done by the thrift industry. They were the Savings and Loans (S&Ls) or Savings Banks. They originally made loans with their own money and held them, just as a commercial banker does today. They were depository institutions that were in business principally to make mortgage loans. Many of the thrifts have now changed into savings banks or just plain banks. This is more a function of how they are licensed by the state or federal government and it can change how they do business.

They function much the same as a mortgage banker, and in fact, are mortgage bankers. They price, process, fund the closings, and then sell the loans to the secondary market. Like banks and other mortgage bankers, they can also portfolio some of their loans.

For a time during the 1980s, changes in federal regulations allowed thrifts to stray from their main business of making home loans into the domain of the commercial banker. Too many thrifts made loans on high-risk ventures and other projects for which they had little background or capital. The resultant massive failure of many thrifts led to a taxpayer bailout costing hundreds of billions of dollars. The liquidation and absorption of these failed thrifts has caused a shift back into the business of mortgage lending, but with only half the original players.

THE CREDIT UNION
Using Your Money

Similar to commercial banks, except with the very important difference that they are nonprofit, credit unions have checking and saving accounts, make consumer and auto loans, and make mortgage loans. Credit unions have historically used the money of the members to make loans. This means they have a lower cost of doing business and can usually offer rates lower than some other mortgage lenders.

Within recent years credit unions have begun dealing in the secondary market, meaning that they are taking on the same role as a thrift. Many of them offer secondary market mortgages through programs offered by the Credit Union National Association (CUNA), along with other traditional secondary market investors. Access to the secondary market offers the credit union member a wider selection of mortgages. If you belong to a credit union, check out its rates.

LIFE INSURANCE COMPANIES
You Bet Your Life

Life insurance companies have made mortgage loans for a long time, either as investment instruments for their cash or as loans against an individual policy's cash value. Because of their huge amounts of available premium deposits, life insurance companies can be one of the prime sources of mortgage money, often at very attractive rates.

Many life insurance companies target jumbo loans and commercial projects. They can also set guidelines that may not be found in the standard Fannie or Freddie loan. Most of these loans are done through mortgage bankers or brokers, but some insurance companies, such as Prudential, have opened their own lending subsidiaries.

If you have a whole life policy that has accumulated significant cash value, you can borrow against it at a very low interest rate. The loan is cheap, simple—and it is your money. This is one of the few times you get the money before you die.

Call some of the local insurance agencies to find out if their parent companies offer mortgage products. These are sometimes available, even if you do not have a policy with them.

MORTGAGE LENDERS OF LAST RESORT
If it Sounds Like a Good Deal, it Isn't

Some lenders prey on people who, for whatever reason, do not have good credit or enough income to qualify for a normal mortgage. The predatory lender will make a loan with little or no cash down, or refinance the borrower's house and finance the cost of the loan into the mortgage amount. The cost often is equivalent to a large number of points. I have seen instances of 10 to 15 points being added to the loan amount. On top of this, most of the interest rates on these loans are in the range of 18% and higher. The 125% loan for refinancing is one of the more well-known loan product.

Another ploy of these lenders is to lure the borrower in to make application and pay some type of nonrefundable application fee, knowing that they cannot make a loan. The borrowers are then out some money they usually cannot afford, and the lender has picked up some quick income.

The saddest part is that most of these borrowers cannot afford any additional debt, much less a mortgage with stratospheric rates. What happens is that the borrower will ultimately default and this "lender" will all too gladly foreclose on the property. Because the loan amount is usually low, the lender can then resell the property at a profit. It is loan sharking with a legal, and highly unethical, face. The federal government has now started to regulate this predatory lending.

However, there are loan companies that are very aboveboard in their practices. Many of the finance companies will offer mortgages. Because they deal with higher risk borrowers, their rates will be higher. These loans are known as "subprime" loans for the simple reason that they are not the best loans. But, they will not consciously try to overcharge the borrower. If you are thinking of using one, check them all for the best rates. Also, some of their loans will have prepayment penalties. That is, if you pay off the loan early, you will still have to pay a portion of the interest that you would otherwise have paid if you kept the loan to maturity.

SECOND CHANCE OR NEW START LOANS
For the Borrower With a Bad Credit History

Fannie and Freddie offer loans, called A Minus loans, to borrowers whose credit normally would not allow them to get a mortgage. Called Timely Payment Rewards mortgages, Affordable Merit mortgages, and other similar names, these loans have some common features. They start out at a higher interest rate than the normal rate. If the borrower makes all of the payments on time for the first 24 months, the interest rate is lowered. The guidelines are certain to change as more of these loans are on the books and Fannie and Freddie can see how they are performing. If you have had bad credit and the lender says you do not qualify for the standard loans, ask them about these loans. A note here. Most mortgage lenders offer some form of subprime loans. Make sure they understand you are talking about this particular Fannie or Freddie loan. Some lenders may not offer this type of loan. It may be that a subprime loan is the only way to buy a house. If that is the case, you need to decided if the cost is worth it. Houses do appreciate, and you can clean up your credit. You can always refinance once you are back on track.

10

CLOSING COSTS
The Bottom Line

"What will this cost me?" This question always comes right after "What are your rates and points?" Nothing in life is free, least of all mortgages. However, some loans and/or lenders are more expensive than others.

At loan application, or within three working days afterward, the lender must give to the borrowers a **Good Faith Estimate of Closing Costs** (see page 191 of the Appendix) on the loan for which they have applied. While closing cost forms may look slightly different, each has the same itemized costs that must be disclosed. A good lender will disclose this information at application and explain each line. The U.S. Department of Housing and Urban Development (HUD) has helped to make this explanation easier by requiring the lender to give the borrower a booklet called *A HUD Guide to Closing Costs.*

At closing, the borrower and the seller will get a detailed closing cost statement, which is generally put on **HUD-1 Form,** or settlement statement (see pages 205–206 of the Appendix). It will have the actual costs that must be paid, and it will seldom be exactly what was disclosed at time of loan application. This discrepancy arises because the lender cannot know what the final fees will be for all of the items. But, the Good Faith Estimate should not be off by more than several hundred dollars at most, assuming the rate, points, and loan amount do not change. What the borrower should get from the lender is a worst-case estimate. You would much rather be told up-front that the cost will be $40,000 and find out it will actually be only $3,000, than the other way around.

A borrower who is shopping for the best rate will do well to check each lender's closing costs. All of them will charge the basic costs, such as appraisal, credit report, points, and so forth. What the borrower needs to be aware of are the ubiquitous **"garbage" or "junk" fees.** A lender may also add onto the cost of an appraisal or other standard cost so as to collect more fee income. These additions are made part of an **Application Fee** that is nonrefundable. Fees that are specific to the use of the funds, such as the appraisal, cannot be over charged. Only if they are put into an Application Fee, which does not specify the exact amount being paid for each service, can the lender charge more than the actual cost and keep the difference. If an appraiser charges $250 for the appraisal, the lender might collect $300 or more from the borrower, keeping the extra. These fees can more than make up the difference between one lender's lower rate and another's higher rate when the higher rate does not include the additional cost. My advice is this: At time of application do not pay any application or other fee that is not directly, and solely, a cost of processing the loan (such as the appraisal), unless it is refundable and unless you are shown very clearly that you qualify for the loan for which you have applied. There are still dishonest lenders who will take your money and run.

In this chapter we will look at the basic closing costs and some of the more prevalent garbage fees. Because costs in different regions can be significantly higher or lower, my example will only be a representation of these fees. In addition, some government loans set maximum allowable fees for costs such as the appraisal and do not allow lenders to charge garbage fees to the borrower. (The lender can charge the cost of computer underwriting the loan, normally around $20.)

For each item that I cover, there is a number that does not seem to bear a relationship to anything. These numbers correspond to numbers on the HUD-1 Form and are referred to in *A HUD Guide to Closing Costs.* Now, let's see just where all this money goes.

1. *The loan origination fee* (801). The lender charges this fee for processing the loan. It can be fee income above the cost of processing, such as in the use of premium pricing without giving any cost back to the borrower as credit towards closing costs. It is usually 1% of the loan amount, but it can be more, or less. On FHA loans, it is based on the loan amount before the MIP is financed. On VA loans, it is based on the total with the funding fee financed, if it is financed.

2. *The loan discount points* (802). This fee is charged to yield the given rate of interest. The base rate, or par rate, will have no discount points. The lower the interest rate below the par rate, the higher the discount points. Points go to buy down the interest rate and are considered as interest in advance. They can be as high or low as the borrower is willing to pay. They are also a tax-deductible expense. (The IRS says points, including the origination fee, are deductible if it is normal to charge them. Check with your tax advisor.) On a purchase, the points are completely deductible in the year they are paid. For refinances, they must be amortized over the life of the loan ($1,000 in points on a 15-year loan would be $67 deductible per year). If the refinanced loan is paid off early, the remaining undeducted points can then be claimed in the year it is paid off.

3. *The appraisal fee* (803). The lender will always require that an appraisal (see copy of the Uniform Residential Appraisal report on pages 209–211 in the Appendix) be done to determine that the value of the property is high enough to secure the loan, unless the computer underwriting conditions do not require an appraisal. The appraisal fee can vary from $150 to over $400, depending on the type of property, its location, the loan type, or any combination of these. Check lenders in your area to get an idea of the cost. Many lenders will collect this fee with the loan application.

4. *The credit report* (804). Every lender will require that a Standard Residential Mortgage Credit Report be prepared by an approved credit bureau for each borrower. (See the previous section on credit and credit reports.) Married couples' credit will be incorporated into one report. The cost will depend on the type of loan and whether a business credit report will be needed for self-employed or incorporated borrowers. Credit reports range from $15 to over $50. This is another fee that most lenders will collect at application.

5. *Lender's inspection fee* (805). This fee is charged when the lender must inspect the property before closing. It is usually for new construction or renovation work. However, some lenders require that they inspect all properties on which they make loans. The inspections are usually done for the lender by the appraiser who did the appraisal. On FHA and VA loans a separate inspector may be assigned by the FHA or VA.

6.   *Other loan fees* (806–811). Included in this group are assumption fees, mortgage insurance application fees, and space for the lender to list "garbage" fees. Some of the fees listed here are: Application Fee, Processing Fee, Underwriting Fee, Document Review or Preparation Fee, Commitment Fee, and Tax Service Fee. Some of these may also be listed under numbers (1303–1307).

7.   *Prepaid interest* (901). This is the interest that the borrower will pay for the first month of the loan. It is simple interest based on the number of days remaining in the month from the date on which the loan closes. It is the house payment for that month.

As an example, let us consider a $100,000 loan at 10% that closes on June 15. The interest is calculated as $100,000 × 10% =_$10,000, divided by 360 days (365 for government loans) = $27.78 per day (per diem) interest. The per diem interest is then multiplied by the number of days remaining in the month from the date of closing, 16 × $27.28 = $444.48. This is the house payment for the month of June. It is the only time that interest on the loan will be paid in advance. The next mortgage payment on this loan will be due August 1, and will represent the interest that accrued during July plus a principal reduction.

Many borrowers try to close toward the end of the month to lower their closing costs. For estimating purposes, it is always safer to figure on a full 30 days of interest ($833.40 in our example). If you plan on closing on the last day of the month, and for some unforeseen reason, you don't close until the next day, you would be looking at the full $833.40 instead of only one day at $27.78 as shown in our example.

Most lenders also have something called Partial Interest Payment (PIP). This helps borrowers who, for whatever reason, need to close between the first and the twentieth of the month and do not have the funds for per diem interest at that time, but will have funds by the end of the month. Basically, this program allows the borrower to pay the per diem they would normally pay at closing to be paid on the first of the next month. If you close on June 5, there would be 26 days of interest. PIP allows you to pay this on July 1. The normal monthly payment would still begin on August 1.

8. *Mortgage insurance premium* (902). This is the up-front premium or any portion of it that will be paid by cash at closing. If it is being financed, most lenders will show it on the Good Faith Estimate and not add it into the total. This is obviously required only when there is mortgage insurance involved. The cost can be from hundreds to thousands of dollars, depending on the type of loan and the amount. There is a table of premiums on page 195 in the Appendix, or a lender can give you the premiums of different mortgage insurance companies. The FHA MIP up-front premium would be shown here. (See previous section on MI.)

9. *Hazard insurance premium* (903). The lender will require that the first year's hazard (homeowner's) insurance be paid up in full by time of closing. You can find out this cost by calling your insurance agent, or you can use $2.50 per $1,000 of sales price (value) as an estimate. The lender is interested only in the hazard portion of the insurance, but almost every borrower will get full coverage. The $2.50 should approximate the full coverage cost.

10. *Flood insurance premium* (904). If the property which you are purchasing has any improvements that are in a federally designated flood plain, you will be required to purchase this federally funded insurance through your insurance agent. The appraiser will state on the appraisal if this insurance is necessary.

11. *Other prepaid items* (905). These spaces are for items not specifically listed that the lender may require to be paid in advance. The *VA funding fee* is often put in this space.

12. *Hazard insurance reserves (escrows)* (1001). Most lenders will require that the hazard insurance be escrowed into the monthly payment. At closing they will normally escrow two to three months' worth of the yearly premium. From our example above on a $100,000 house the yearly premium would be $2.50 × 100 = $250. The yearly premium of $250 divided by 12 = $20.83 monthly × 2 months = $41.67 to be escrowed at closing. The reason for the two months is that, if you close in June and the first payment is in August, you could be two months behind by the time of the first payment. Then, a year later when the insurance premium renewal comes up, there would not be enough money in escrow to pay it for the next year. The government has something called aggregate accounting which the lender must use to determine the amount of escrows for insurance and taxes.

13. *Mortgage insurance escrow* (1002). On mortgage insurance that has a renewal premium, this cost is handled the same as the hazard insurance. For example, consider a $95,000 loan on a $100,000 property with a renewal premium of $0.49 per $100 of loan amount. The yearly renewal premium would be $0.49 × 950 = $465.50, dividing by 12 yields $38.79 per month × 2 months = $77.58 escrow at closing. On mortgage insurance that does not have a renewal premium, such as the one-time financed mortgage insurance, there would be no escrow. The most prevalent mortgage insurance used today is the monthly premium which does not require any escrows or other up-front cost. Some lenders will collect escrows for mortgage insurance, even when the mortgage insurance company does not require it.

14. *City or county real estate taxes* (1003–1004). Most lenders will also require that the taxes be escrowed into the monthly payment. Since delinquent taxes can be collected by selling the property, and take priority over mortgage liens, lenders protect themselves by escrowing the taxes and paying them directly. A borrower can find out the assessed taxes from the listing Realtor or the government real estate office. Two or more months' taxes will be escrowed. If you are within two months of when the taxes must be paid to the taxing authority, the lender may require that you pay the two months' escrow and the last two months' taxes so that they can be prepaid for the year in advance. Otherwise, the lender will not have enough time to set up the loan and make sure that it receives the tax bill in time to avoid a late penalty. Check with the lender to find out what the requirements are. On the HUD 1 closing statement, the taxes paid under the purchaser's column will show all the taxes due for the current tax period. That is, if you close within one month of when taxes are due and the taxes are collected every six months, the amount shown will be six months plus one to two months escrow. The reason is because taxes are prorated between the buyer and seller, with the seller crediting the buyer at closing for their portion. If the seller owes five months taxes at closing, that amount will be deducted from what the buyer would be paying to the seller and then added to the buyer's column.

15. *Other escrows* (1005–1008). These items are for other reserves that the lender may require to be escrowed, such as annual assessments for homeowners' associations', road maintenance, and flood insurance.

There are certain fees called *prepaid items* that a few loans will allow only the borrower to pay. They cannot be paid by the seller, Realtor, or lender. These include the following:

1. Prepaid interest
2. Mortgage insurance premium
3. Hazard insurance premium
4. Mortgage insurance escrows
5. Hazard insurance escrows
6. Tax escrows

Check with the lender to find out if your loan will have any restrictions.

16. *Settlement or closing fee* (1101). This fee is paid to the settlement agent. Depending on your area, it may be an attorney or a title insurance company. The fee can vary tremendously, as much as hundreds of dollars. Charged by the lender, this is a "junk" fee.

17. *Abstract or title search* (1102). This is done to ensure that the title to the property is clear and does not contain any potential defects, or "clouds," on it. Liens, claims by relatives, undefined boundaries, and easements are a few of the problems that could appear. This search is normally done by either the attorney or the title insurance company. The cost can be $2.00 to $4.00 or more per $1,000 of loan amount. Check with the lender or attorney for the average cost in your area. This cost is often included in the Title Insurance (#1108).

18. *Title examination* (1103). This is a continuation of the title search to make sure that the final title is clear and acceptable. This fee is usually part of the search or the settlement fee. Most attorneys or title insurance companies will search and examine the title for one fee and put it on either line 1102 or 1103.

19. *Title insurance binder* (1104). This is a commitment by the title insurance company to insure the title. Most commitments are included in the final title insurance policy fee (1108).

20. *Document preparation* (1105). Some attorneys, and some lenders, will charge this fee in addition to the normal fee for closing. You will often see it combined with the settlement agent's fee. Charged by the lender, it is a garbage fee. The cost can range from $25 to over $350.

21. *Notary fees* (1106). Most loan closings will require that certain signatures be notarized. More often this fee is included in the closing agent's fee.

22. *Attorney's or Settlement Agent's fee* (1107). Most lenders require the use of an attorney, and most title insurance companies use a settlement agent, whether it is an attorney or title company. This fee will normally include Items 1101, 1105, and 1106 above. The fee depends on the loan type, property, complexity of the title, and the settlement agent. For a good idea of costs in your area, ask your lender or Realtor for the names of three to five good settlement agents and get their fees. They can go from $150 to over $500. Note: The closing agent represents both the borrower and lender at closing even though the borrower is paying the fee.

23. *Title insurance* (1108). This fee pays to insure the title against defects to the title of the property, or defects that existed but were not found in the normal title search. This insurance is issued after the title search and review. The fee usually includes Items 1102–1104 above. For example, let us say a Native American tribe claims that your house is on top of their ancestral burial grounds, and after adjudication the court tells you to move your house. Title insurance would protect you against this by either paying the Native Americans for the land, or paying off the mortgage.

There are two types of title insurance. One insures the mortgage, or **mortgagee (lender's) insurance,** and the other insures the borrower's equity, or **mortgagor (owner's) insurance.** Title insurance is a one-time premium.

1. Lender's insurance covers the mortgage in case there is some type of defect. For instance, I know of an incident in which the seller was a relocation company that had taken over the property for a transferred employee. The borrower closed the loan and moved in. About a year later the lender sent in the tax escrow to pay the taxes that were coming due. The county sent back the taxes for the current year, stating that it could not accept them until the previous year's taxes were paid. Lo and behold, the employee had not paid his taxes, the relocation company was not aware of this fact, and the closing attorney had not caught it in the title search. The title insurance company paid the back taxes and then went to the attor-

ney to collect them because he was at fault. Without the insurance, the borrower would have had to come up with the money and then sue the attorney.

2. Owner's insurance covers the mortgage and the equity that the borrower has in the property at the time of closing. In the case of the Native Americans, the insurance would pay off the mortgage and return the equity to the borrower. This policy will also cover any losses to the owner that are not covered in the lender's policy.

Policy premiums can vary by area and by insurance company. A rule of thumb rate would be $3.00 per $1,000 of loan amount for lender's coverage and $4.00 per $1,000 for owner's coverage. Check with your lender or attorney for actual costs.

24. *Other title charges* (1111–1113). These may need to be listed separately from the other fees. However, these items are usually incorporated in the other fees. A form required by the secondary market called the ALTA 8.1 Environmental Endorsement is an example.

25. *Government recording fees* (1201). The local government where the property is located will charge a fee to record.

1. The deed (to show ownership)

2. The mortgage (to show a lien on the property)

To find these fees in your area, ask a lender or attorney.

26. *City/county tax/stamps* (1202). Each locality can also charge a tax on the deed and/or mortgage in addition to the recording fees.

27. *State tax/stamps* (1203). The state can also charge a fee on the deed and/or the mortgage.

Note: If there are recording fees plus local and state fees, the lender will sometimes combine them when giving the Good Faith Estimate of Closing Costs. The HUD-1 Form at closing will show them separately. Ask your lender if these fees are not clear.

28. *Other government fees* (1204–1205). These spaces are for any other fees that taxing agencies might want to charge.

29. *Physical survey* (1301). Most lenders will require that a physical survey be done before closing. This survey will show the property boundaries with measurements, the outline of the house and outbuildings from a bird's-eye view, all rights of way and

easements, driveways and roads, and any water located on the property. It will also state if the property is in a flood plain. If the house is in a flood plain, then flood insurance will be required. (It will also show under Items 904 and 1006.) The survey is done to make sure that the property is in compliance with local setbacks and that it is not encroaching on or being encroached upon by another property. I have seen a number of properties where the house or an outbuilding is over the property line by inches or feet. More common is a roof overhang or a fence that goes over the line.

A normal complaint is that the property has been surveyed before and since it has not changed, why do it again? Because the previous owner may have transferred a small piece to a neighbor; he may have added a deck since the last survey; or there may be a mistake that the last survey did not catch. If there is a current accurate survey on the property that is not over 10 years old, most title insurance companies (and lenders) will not require a survey if the seller signs an affidavit to the effect that the survey is accurate and there have been no changes. Not all loans will accept an affidavit. Check with your lender.

Back in my construction/development days we were doing the site preparation for an industrial building. The site was a square area located at the end of a pipestem from the highway to the property (a pipestem is a narrow part from the main road back to the main body of the property, wide enough for the access road). The surveyor had set a bench mark, or point from which all points on the property could be referenced by a transit. I was trying to set the corners of the building by the bench mark, but I could not get the corners to align. I called in the architects, who called in the surveyor, who discovered he had perpetuated a mistake that had been made three surveys ago. The pipestem was not 25 feet wide, but 60 feet wide. I hope that the adjacent property owner had title insurance.

The cost of the survey will depend on the size of the property and where it is located. Your lender can give you an estimate. Some problems found on a survey can be insured by the title insurance so that they will not have to be corrected.

30. *Pest inspection* (1302). Some loans may require that the property be inspected for termites and other property-destroying pests. (FHA and VA do require termite inspections.) In many areas it is customary for the seller to pay this cost. If infestation and/or damage is found, most purchase contracts will specify who is responsible for the cost of treatment, usually the seller. The lender will not close the loan until the property is clear of pests and any damage has been repaired. Costs for the inspection can range from $25 to over $100.

31. *Additional settlement charges* (1303–1307). For a property served by a **septic field,** some loans will require that a person knowledgeable in this type of waste disposal inspect it to make sure it is functioning properly. Likewise, **well water** must be tested to make sure that it meets the minimum safe drinking water standards. (The main feature that is tested is the content of coliform bacteria, which should be less than 1.0 per 100 milliliters.) These septic and water fees can range from $25 to over $60 each. The sales contract should specify who pays for these fees. FHA and VA will require septic inspections and well water tests. Most other loans, such as Fannie and Freddie loans, will only require them (and termite inspections) if the appraiser recommends one or all of them.

32. *Total settlement charges* (1400). Here it is, the bottom-line estimate of what you should be expected to pay to close the loan, in addition to the down payment. (Remember, on some loans the lender may also require that you be able to show liquid assets equivalent to two or more months of house payments in addition to the down payment and closing costs.)

I would always recommend that you ask the lender to give you a **Good Faith Estimate** before committing to the loan and paying any fees. If there are fees that seem to be out of the ordinary, check with other lenders to see what they charge. A difference of $20 or $50 may not be significant, but if one lender is charging $300 or more than another lender, that could be the same as paying 0.25% and more in extra points. I cannot stress too strongly the need to check the lender's charges. You may go through the entire application and never be aware that you are actually paying hundreds more than necessary.

An additional note on escrows. I am often asked if the escrows that the lender holds for taxes and insurance earn interest. The answer is that they will always earn interest, but where the borrower lives will determine whether the borrower or the lender gets that interest. Some states require that the lender pay interest on this money. Where the lender does not have to pay interest to the borrower, it is taken as additional income. I find that the small amount of interest that would be earned by the borrower is more than offset by not having to come up with large sums of money all at one time to pay the taxes and annual insurance premium. Paying one twelfth of it each month is much easier on the budget. If you are adamant about not paying escrows, check with the various lenders to see if they have that option.

Another fee which is now becoming an issue is the *Buyer-broker fee.* In this case the real estate agent represents the purchaser instead of the seller. (Many people do not realize that the usual agency relationship is for the agent to represent the seller.) If you are buying and retain an agent to represent you, know who is paying the commission. In most cases, the Realtor will still be paid by commission from the seller. But, that is not always true. I do recommend using a buyer-broker when you are purchasing real estate. Otherwise, you have no one who can give you the kind of advice necessary to make an informed decision.

11

REFINANCING YOUR MORTGAGE

Anyone who has a mortgage will at some time give thought to refinancing it, for many different reasons. Whether it is a sound idea depends on what the borrowers want to accomplish, and how long they plan on keeping the loan.

LOWER RATES
Get Them While They Are Hot

If the current rates are lower than what you have now, the temptation is to refinance. The basic rule is, if the current rate is at least 2.0% and sometimes as little as 1% lower, it will pay to refinance. Doing so will lower your payment significantly enough to save on your payments and pay back the cost of refinancing (the only cost of a normal refinance that you save over the cost of the original loan is the recording of the deed). Here's an example.

If you currently have a $75,000 loan at 12% for 30 years with a PI payment of $771.46, the new payment at 10% would be $658.18, or a monthly savings of $113.28 ($1,359.36 per year). If it costs you $3,500 to refinance, it will take slightly over 2.5 years for the savings to pay back the cost ($3,500 divided by $1,359.36). So, if you plan on staying in the house for over 2.5 years, it is worthwhile. You can do what is termed a streamlined refinance on most FHA, VA, and Fannie/Freddie loans. These will have a limited amount of required documentation and generally will not require being re-approved. They cannot be cash-out refinances and you must be current with your mortgage payments. Because there are several variations among loan types, check with your lender to find out if you qualify and what is required.

If you have an **ARM,** there is a different problem. When fixed interest rates go down, ARMs will also often adjust downward. The dilemma is, you don't know if the fixed rates—and your ARM rate—will go back up enough to make refinancing now a smart move. And no one can accurately predict where the rates will go. When you refinance an ARM, your immediate response is to hope that rates go higher, so that your decision is quickly justified. If the rates don't rise, either you justify the refinancing by saying that not having to worry about those periodic adjustments was worth the cost, or you spend your time agonizing over what you could have done with the money it cost you to refinance. My advice is, if you are happy with your ARM and how its rates have adjusted, keep it. If you really want a fixed rate and you will have the property long enough to make it worthwhile, refinance. Of course, if you have **a conversion feature,** the change will be much less expensive, which can make the decision easier (see section in Chapter 5 on ARMs).

Some people will want to refinance from a 30-year to a 15-year loan. If the rates are low enough, it may be a good idea. However, remember that if all you want to do is pay the loan off quicker, you can make an additional principal reduction payment each month that will accelerate the amortization and achieve the same result without paying any closing costs or having to go through the loan application process. You can determine the payment for whatever amortization (payoff) period you want by asking your lender to calculate this based on the remaining principal balance. Or, if you have access to a computer, you can compute this yourself with one of the readily available programs for amortizing loans. Almost all lenders now have a mortgage calculator on their website. You should also be able to access your loan through your lender's web site to find out the balance.

REFINANCING FOR CASH OUT
Using Your Equity

Other borrowers want to refinance just to gain access to the equity that has built up over the years. If there is a legitimate need and the interest rate is reasonable, it is there to be used. Just remember that you are borrowing savings, and the loan is secured by your house. It took a while for the equity to build. Inflation may not be so kind in the future.

A second mortgage may be a more practical and much less expensive alternative. We discussed these loans earlier in the context of using them to lower the down payment on a purchase. For the purposes of refinancing lenders will allow you to take the equity, without the larger expense and paperwork of refinancing the original first mortgage. However, second mortgages are usually for shorter periods and at slightly higher interest rates, hence a higher payment.

TO GET RID OF MORTGAGE INSURANCE

If you refinance and the LTV is 80% or less, as supported by an appraisal, there will not be mortgage insurance. Not having to pay for insurance is an attraction byproduct if you are refinancing for the lower rate. The savings on the mortgage insurance alone though, will not make up the closing costs on the refinancing. Depending on the type of loan and how soon after you obtained it, there are some requirements to removing mortgage insurance. You can go to the web sites of www.PrivateMI.com, Fannie (www.fanniemae.com), Freddie (www.freddiemac.com), FHA (www.HUD.gov), or VA (www.homeloans.va.gov) to find the rules. In general, with Fannie and Freddie it is broken into two categories: Earliest date for Automatic Termination and Earliest Date for Borrower Initiated Cancellation Request. These are further divided by loans that closed before July 29, 1999, and those that closed after that date. Then, it is separated depending on personal residence, second home, investment property, and how many units are in the dwelling. Fannie's rules alone in the lender's handbook run to three pages. You will forgive me if I don't list all the different rules for all the different loan types.

If you have an FHA mortgage, you can refinance with a conventional mortgage and have a portion of the MIP refunded to you, depending on how long you have had the loan. Refinancing back into another FHA loan will only replace the old MIP with a new MIP, including the annual premium, and should be done only if the rate is low enough, *and* it is the only way you can qualify.

THE MAXIMUM AMOUNT THAT CAN BE REFINANCED

Depending on the type of loan that you are using to refinance, rules (which are subject to change) limit how much you can borrow. See the chart in Chapter 15 for Fannie and Freddie loans.

FHA

For cash out, the maximum LTV is 85% of the acquisition cost ([value plus allowable closing costs] × 85%). Otherwise, the borrowers can get up to the maximum allowable FHA loan amount for their area. FHA will allow all closing costs to be financed into the refinanced loan amount as long as they do not exceed the maximum allowable loan amount.

A Streamlined Refinance program exists for borrowers who have an FHA loan and just want to get a lower rate and payment. In this loan there is no cash out except to pay closing costs. There is no credit check or appraisal. The mortgage cannot be delinquent at application.

VA

VA loans can be refinanced up to the lesser of appraised value or the remaining principal balance plus closing costs if there is no cash out. If the borrower wants to take cash out, the LTV is limited to 90% of value. The maximum Funding Fee on refinancing is 2% for veteran's cash out; 2.75% for reservist's cash out. No cash out is .5% for both.

Construction Loans

Most lenders recognize that paying off a construction loan with a permanent loan is a refinance transaction. Actually, it can be either a purchase or refinance, depending on which is more advantageous. If the actual cost of the construction and land is over 80% LTV, but the appraised value is 80% or less, you want it to be a refinance. There will not be any mortgage insurance on the permanent loan.

12

WRITTEN DISCLOSURE
TO THE BORROWER

Federal and state laws require the lender to disclose certain information to the borrower at various times during the application process, or even before. Some loans will require more disclosure than others. The increase in paperwork is in direct proportion to the involvement of the government. Conventional loans have basic disclosures, while FHA, VA, and Tax-Exempt Bond Authorities have, on average, twice as much in the form of disclosures.

THE STANDARD CONVENTIONAL LOAN DISCLOSURES

1. *The Equal Credit Opportunity Act Statement—(E.C.O.A.):* This statement discloses that the lender will not discriminate. Most lenders are only interested in the color of your money.

2. *A Good Faith Estimate of Closing Costs:* An example of this form is included in the Appendix on page 191.

3. *A Truth-in-Lending (T-I-L) Statement* of loan costs (see page 207 in the Appendix): This form gives the **Annual Percentage Rate (APR),** the total of all interest and prepaid items for the life of the loan, the amount of the loan minus the prepaids, and the total of all the payments for the life of the loan. It also discloses any prepayment penalties, whether the loan is assumable, the payment schedule, and what the late payment charges will be. The lender must provide this statement within three working days of loan application; and the borrower will invariably call the lender for an explanation, usually because the APR is higher than the rate for which the borrower applied. The APR is made up of the loan interest rate plus the prepaid items, and discount points and is based on the idea that these items increase the actual yield to the investor above the note rate. It breaks down each amount disclosed into the following individual items.

- APR (Annual Percentage Rate).

- Finance Charge. This represents the total of the interest that will be paid over the life of the loan plus the prepaid items. The prepaid items listed on a T-I-L form are (a) origination fees, (b) discount fees, (c) other fees, (d) per diem interest, (e) escrows, and (f) initial premiums.

- Amount Financed. This equals the loan amount minus the prepaids. This is the item that most borrowers do not understand. They applied for a given loan amount and the T-I-L statement shows an amount that is significantly less. Do not worry. You will get the amount that you requested. The federal government just wants you to know that because the prepaids are fees, they can reduce your borrowing power by their total. Also, many lenders will "net out" the prepaids from the loan proceeds so that the settlement agent gets a check for the total loan minus the prepaids. "Netting out" is done so that the settlement agent does not have to write a check to the lender for these fees at closing. Thus, the lender gets its fees quicker. The settlement agent will then add in the fees that the borrower pays at closing to the net check to make the full loan amount. An example would be a $100,000 loan with 1% origination, 1 discount point, $240 in escrows, and $417 in per diem interest, a total of $2,657. The net amount at closing would be $97,343. The $2,657 that the borrower brought to closing to cover those items would then be added to get the $100,000 needed to close.

- Total of Payments. This item represents the total of the loan amount and the interest that will be paid over the life of the loan. It is a real eye-opener. If you made all your monthly payments on a $100,000 loan at 10% for the full 30 years, the total of payments would be over $300,000.

- Number and Amounts of Payments and When They Are Due. On a fixed rate loan, these are simple to understand. On a 30-year loan you will have 359 payments plus the last payment, which will be slightly less. On a 15-year loan it will be 179 plus 1. With ARMs it is different. The T-I-L statement will give a worst-case adjustment for the first two or three periods, and then the remainder is based on the current index plus margin at the time the T-I-L statement is done.

4.   *Loan disclosure form:* If the loan is an ARM, the lender is required to give written disclosure about how the loan works. Some other types of loans also must be disclosed if they are sufficiently complicated.

5.   *A Consumer Handbook on Adjustable Rate Mortgages (C.H.A.R.M.):* You must receive this booklet and a form to be signed stating that you received it. It is only for borrowers getting ARM loans.

6.   *The H.U.D. Handbook on Buying Your Home: Settlement Costs and Helpful Information:* This booklet explains the closing cost as given on the Good Faith Estimate and, as the title says, other helpful information.

7.   *Lock-in and Processing Disclosures:* After the financing frenzy of 1986, many states now require that the lender give written disclosure on locking in the loan and the estimated processing time.

8.   *Mortgage Transfer Disclosure Statement:* This tells the borrower the percentage of loans originated by the lender that are sold service-released. If you remember, service-released loans are the loans on which the lender sells the servicing and you make your payment to another lender. Brokers will show 100%. The company I work for keeps over 95% of all the loans we close. There is comfort in knowing your lender. (See Appendix page 189.)

9.   *The Certification of Authorization form:* This authorizes the lender to check your credit, employment, assets. Basically, it allows the lender to do what is necessary to have the loan approved and ready for closing.

FHA REQUIREMENTS

In addition to those for conventional loans, the FHA requires these disclosures:

1.   *A Homeowner's Fact Sheet on Mortgage Insurance.* This tells the borrower about the MIP and how it can be refunded to the borrower. (See Appendix pages 198–199.)

2. *A Financial Privacy Act Notice.* This informs the borrower that HUD has the right to check the borrower's financial records held by the lender without further notification.

3. *An Interest Rate/Discount Point Disclosure Statement.* This notifies the borrower that neither HUD nor FHA establishes the interest rates and points on FHA loans. These are set by the lender and can affect the borrower's ability to qualify. (See Appendix page 219.)

4. *A Notice to Homeowner on the Assumability of FHA Loans.* This explains the rules for assuming FHA loans and the original borrower's liability after the assumption.

(Numbers 1–4 are now combined in one disclosure called: *Important Notice to Homebuyers.*)

5. *An amendatory statement* that must become part of the Sales contract. This statement tells the borrowers that the property must appraise for the sales price, or they are under no obligation to complete the loan. The borrower does have the option of proceeding with the sale, but the loan will be based on the lower value. Many Realtor contracts already contain this statement.

6. *The Watch Out for Lead-Based Paint Poisoning Notification* (see page 203 in the Appendix). This is required for all houses constructed before 1978. It cautions the borrower against the consumption of lead-based paint; if house does have lead-based paint it must be removed.

VA REQUIREMENTS

VA requires the following, in addition to the conventional disclosures:

1. The *Financial Privacy Act Notice.*
2. The *amendatory statement.*
3. A *Federal Collection Policy Notice,* which lists all the bad things the government can do to you if you default.
4. *A VA-Related Indebtedness Questionnaire,* which asks if you have any debts owed to the U.S. government (they check on this, so it does not help to lie).
5. A *VA Assumability Notice,* which explains how your VA loan can be assumed and what that means to you.

6. A form giving the *Veteran's Nearest Living Relative*. This is required in the event the government needs to contact the original borrower and he or she has moved.

OTHER REQUIREMENTS

Revenue bond authorities require all of the disclosures listed for conventional loans. If the loan is insured or guaranteed by FHA or VA, they also require all of the disclosures for that particular loan. And, they also have about four to six additional disclosures that are just for the bond authority loans.

While these disclosures may seem like a nuisance, they do make it easier for the borrower to understand what is going on as long as you read the forms and ask questions when you do not understand what is being disclosed. Take the time to read what is given to you.

13

THE LOAN
Now That I Have It, What Is It?

A loan made on real estate is **a mortgage,** a lien against the property securing the loan. That is simple enough to understand, except that there is more to it. You can get a loan on real estate, but if it is not secured by that real estate all you have is an unsecured loan as evidenced by a note, the proceeds of which are used to purchase the property. To be a mortgage, the property must be the security for the loan. The lender will make you sign **a note** showing that you are in debt, and then the mortgage instrument (mortgage or deed of trust) to secure the debt with the real estate.

You **default** on the mortgage any time you do not meet any of the terms of the loan. If you are one day late on the payment, you are technically in default. If you do not pay the taxes when they are due, you are in default. When you default on the loan, the lender will give you notice that the default must be cured within a certain time or it can recover its funds by foreclosing on the property. When a lender forecloses, it takes legal action to force the sale of the property. Depending on where you live, the lender can foreclose by either a mortgage or deed of trust mortgage.

States that use a plain mortgage require that the lender go to court in order to be allowed to proceed with foreclosure. This is a time- and money-consuming process. Many states give the lender power of sale, or the right to sell the property after default and with due notice to the borrower. A **Deed of Trust (D/T)** mortgage appoints **a trustee** to act in the lender's behalf to foreclose on the property by power of sale without going to court.

As long as you meet the terms stated on the mortgage (read your mortgage instrument), you need not worry. Lenders do not want to foreclose, and they do not want to own your property. They would rather cure the problem. If the lender feels it is reasonable to expect that the borrower will be able to fix whatever problem has placed them in default, the lender will work with the borrower to correct the default. For example, if you lost your job for a long period of time and you have just started in a new one, the lender will work out some type of plan to catch up any late payments. The key, as in any credit transaction, is to communicate with the lender when you know there is going to be a problem. And the sooner, the better.

Now that I have properly scared you, don't worry about the bad things that can happen with a mortgage, think about all the good things—such as owning your home.

14

QUALIFYING YOURSELF
Everyone Is Different and
Computer Underwriting
Knows It!

Now that you have all the basic information, you can get a very realistic idea of how well you qualify for a loan. But, in case you have forgotten, here is a short course.

INCOME, DEBTS, AND CASH

1. What is your base **gross monthly income?**
2. What other **reliable, recurring, verifiable income** do you have that will continue into the next three to five years, minimum?
3. List each **debt** that you have:

   Who is the creditor?

   What is the approximate balance?

   What is the monthly payment?

   How long does it have left to pay off?

On **credit cards and revolving debt,** use 5% of the balance as the payment unless you have a current statement with a minimum payment that is not −0. Make sure you get ALL of your debts. Any debt with over 10 months left to pay off is a long-term debt and will be used in qualifying. Revolving debt is always used when there is a balance. VA may require a minimum payment based on past average balance even if there is a zero balance on a revolving credit account.

4. How much **cash** do you have for the down payment and the closing costs (and possibly two months residual house payments on conventional loans)?

    Where is it (bank, stocks, sale of property, gift, and so on)?

    Will there be any cash left after closing, and if so, how much?

    What other liquid assets do you own?

5. Do you have your two most recent bank/account statements; most recent paystubs for a 30-day period; past two years' W-2s; past 2 years' federal tax returns (all pages) if you are self-employed or have income requiring returns to verify? These are the basic documentation necessary for alternate documentation and required by computer underwriting.

It is a good idea to get a blank application form from a local lender and use it to fill in all of the above information. There is a copy of the Uniform Residential Loan Application on pages 185–187 in the Appendix or you can go online.

QUALIFYING RATIOS
Conventional Loans

1. Take the total gross monthly income (GMI) and multiply it by **28%**. This number will be the approximate maximum total monthly house payment that you can afford (PITI/MI/HOA). On ARMs with a 2% yearly cap, use the maximum second-year payment if the down payment is less than 20%. ARMs with a 1% yearly cap and three- and five-year ARMs qualify at the initial rate.

2. Multiply the GMI by **36%**. This number will be the maximum total house payment and long-term monthly debt payment that you can afford (PITI/MI/HOA/LTD). Subtract your monthly debts from this total. If the remainder is less than 28% of GMI, the lower amount will be used for the maximum allowable total house payment. (That is, if your debts are more than the 8% of

your GMI allowed by the 28%/36% ratios, the house payment for which you will qualify will be less than 28%. For example, let us say you have qualifying ratios of 24% and 36%. The 24% is the maximum percent of GMI that you can use for the house payment.) Remember, some lenders and/or loans will allow higher ratios, such as 33% and 38%.

FHA Loans

1. Use **29%** of GMI for the total housing expense (PITI/MIP/HOA).

2. Use **41%** of GMI for the total housing expense and long-term debt. FHA uses any debt with over 10 months to pay off as long-term debt.

3. Qualifying ratios for energy efficient homes can go up to 31% and 43%. In most areas the local electric company will certify the house as energy efficient. Otherwise, FHA has a formula, available from a lender, that can be used to determine if the house is energy efficient.

Use the Conventional/FHA Qualifying Form in the Appendix on page 190.

VA Loans

1. Use the VA Net Income Residual Qualifying sheet (page 201, Appendix) to determine if you have sufficient income. You will need to know the federal and state tax and social security withholding information for your income, and estimates of the maintenance, utilities, and residual figures. You can get the withholding information from your pay stub. A local lender can give you the current maintenance and utilities figures as long as you know the approximate finished square footage of the house and the type of heat. The lender can also provide the withholding figures if you give them your gross salary and number of dependents.

2. Use **41%** of GMI to determine the total housing expense and long-term debt payment. The VA uses all debts with over 10 months remaining. This ratio does have some flexibility if there are sufficient compensating factors.

COMPENSATING FACTORS

Remember, almost all loans have some flexibility, but for basic qualifying, assume none. Then, list everything that you feel might be a compensating factor to help you qualify. Here is a short list that lenders will consider.

1. No debt or little debt.
2. Excellent long-term credit, including previous mortgage and/or rent payments and high credit scores.
3. Proven ability to pay debts in excess of allowable ratios.
4. Large amount of liquid assets left after closing.
5. Proven ability to save.
6. Long-term job stability.
7. Good potential for increase in income.
8. Possess an advanced degree, or are working toward one.
9. Large down payment, low LTV loan.
10. Ability of nonworking co-borrower to obtain a job in which he or she has a background.
11. Potential for a large amount of overtime or a bonus.
12. Shorter loan term.
13. Little or no increase in housing expense.
14. Other income not used in qualifying.

COMPUTER UNDERWRITING

All of the exercises above will help to give you an idea of how much of a loan for which you can qualify. But, with computer underwriting, everything can change significantly. I cannot stress too much that it is possible for you to qualify for much higher ratios, and loan amounts, with:

1. Excellent credit and high credit scores
2. A large amount of assets remaining after closing
3. Lower LTV
4. Little or no debt

Each one of these by themselves and in combination can raise your qualifying amounts. I have seen 90% LTV loans with 45%/70% ratios and 95% with 38/65. Conversely, I have seen borrowers with few or none of the above (they will almost always have low credit scores) who will not qualify with the normal ratios. There are currently two predominant underwriting systems. They are the proprietary software of Fannie and Freddie. There are other systems, and they may be used more frequently in the future, but the two I am going to discuss are the main ones now used. Fannie's system is called **Desktop Underwriting, or DU.** for short. Freddie's system is called **Loan Prospector, or LP.** All conforming conventional loans can be run through these systems. In addition, FHA can also be approved through computer underwriting. VA is run through LP, but VA still requires an underwriter to review and give final approval. Many of the state revenue bond authorities can now be run through a computer underwriting system.

How do these systems work? The system will look at the things I listed above, along with other factors, to determine if the borrower qualifies. A loan application is taken by computer, the credit report is pulled and merged into the loan application, and the application is downloaded to a main computer. From there, the loan officer will send the loan through one of the systems. And, usually within five minutes, the system will give an answer with any conditions, for a grand total of 1 to 1.5 hours from application to approval. If the loan is approved, it will say **Approve/Eligible.** (LP findings are slightly different in wording.) Sometimes the borrower themselves are acceptable, but some part of the loan does not meet the Fannie/Freddie guidelines. In those instances, the loan will receive an **Approve/Ineligible.** These findings can normally be corrected unless the loan is too far off the guidelines chart. If there is something that keeps the system from giving a finding, it may say **Refer/Eligible,** which means an underwriter will have to approve it. If it is not approved, the system will say **Refer/Ineligible.** In all cases, it will give the main reasons for approval/referral/or ineligible. And don't worry if the loan doesn't go through the first time. Or the second or third time, if there is a problem with the download or software itself. The lender can correct problems and run the application through the system as many times as it takes to get a correct answer.

With Approve/Eligible, the approval will give the maximum interest rate to which the borrower is approved and all required conditions. If you receive a paystub, it will normally ask for the

most recent paystubs for a 30-day period, last year's W-2, and a **verbal verification of employment.** If the credit scores and LTV are good enough, it may just ask for a verbal verification. Even **self-employed** people may not need to give tax returns with high scores and low LTV. Normally, they will need to provide **last year's returns (occasionally the past two years)** but no P&L statement. The lender will do a verbal verification to make sure the business is still in existence. One thing you do need to keep in mind: The lender will normally be required to do another verbal verification within 30 days of closing. And, if the closing is a long enough time after the initial approval, an updated credit report, more recent paystubs and statements may be needed. If there is **child support and/or alimony** used to qualify, the system will ask for verification of up to 12 months of receipts of these payments, again depending on credit scores and LTV. A copy of the separation/divorce agreement will also be required. The approval will ask for the **most recent month's bank statement,** or the statement of any and all accounts (all pages) listed on the application, from which the necessary funds will be drawn. **Bankruptcies** shown will require copies of the bankruptcy and discharge papers. **Collections and judgments** will normally need to be paid prior to closing, although not always. Rarely will the borrower be required to give written explanations of late payments. The **appraisal requirements** can range from a full interior/exterior appraisal to a drive-by inspection. High LTVs will normally have the interior/exterior or an exterior appraisal. If the property is in **a PUD,** the system will specify if it needs to be approved by the lender and, if so, what will need to be provided. High-quality loans often do not need any type of approval or review of the PUD.

As you can see, the process can be, and normally is, very painless and quick. If the borrower brings all the documents to loan application that required for approval, about all that is left is the appraisal or inspection.

Many lenders have **a quality control or safety system** in place to protect against fraud or unintentional errors. My company has a person designated as the Data Integrity Specialist (DIS) who will review the file to make sure everything is input correctly and that all required documents are in the file. I use the example of mistakenly inputting $30,000 per month income, instead of the $3,000 per month the borrower actually earns. And, it is possible for the appraisal to not be acceptable, although I have not had that happen in several years. The DIS can also add conditions that DU or LP may not ask for specifically, but the information must be verified per Fannie or Freddie guidelines. It will then give the section under which these guidelines can be found. This does not happen on a regular basis.

If the findings from DU or LP come back **Refer/Eligible,** there is something in the application that the system cannot get by to issue an approval. It could be credit scores that are not quite high enough or several recent late payments or not enough verified funds. If the credit report is incorrect, and as a result lates and lower scores are reported, it takes about 30 to 90 days for the corrections to be made and put into the credit reporting system. (Hopefully, this system of correcting credit will be streamlined in the near future.) Until then, nothing can make the computer change its mind. If the loan is within the normal parameters of the loan guidelines, and the mistakes can be verified, a human underwriter can approve the loan. But, if the borrower needs higher ratios, they will need to wait until the problem is corrected, and hope the resulting higher credit scores are sufficient to generate an approval.

Refer/Ineligible findings are a plain old thumbs down. Unless there is something wrong that caused this refer, the loan is not eligible for a Fannie/Freddie loan. Here is where a really good lender is essential. There may be a way to fix it, or there may be another type of loan that the borrower can use to purchase the property. Order-takers with little or no experience who sit in front of a computer will cause more problems than the savings they advertise. I have personally taken loans rejected or messed up by web-based or centralized companies with no local representation and had the borrowers approved and closed using a Fannie/Freddie or FHA loan. You get what you pay for.

And, if DU rejects the loan, LP may accept it. Or visa versa. Each system has certain differences. Also, if one type of loan is rejected, such as a one-year ARM, another type, such as a 30-year fixed rate or FHA, may be approved. Computers make it quicker and easier. They do not necessarily make it simpler. The lender is the key.

GETTING YOUR LOAN FROM THE WEB
Do You Really Know With Whom You Are Dealing?

It seems everyone thinks the web is the be all and end all of mortgage lending. But, there are significant differences in how the use of the web is perceived. There are those who think the web will be the demise of all mortgage lenders as we know them. All loans will be submitted through a web site with a faceless, and sometimes voiceless, lender. Or, the lender will speak to you, and may even send you friendly emails. No more going into a lender's office and wasting precious time. In a perfect world, this could happen. Of all the loans I originate each year, about one-fourth to one-third are perfect-world loans. And most of those still need some type of tweaking and guidance that can only be provided by an experienced mortgage lender.

Others think the web is a fad, and borrowers will ultimately come back to the comfort of dealing with a friendly face. The truth lies somewhere in between. The World Wide Web is here to stay, and it is a major tool in the mortgage lending industry. Just how it is used is still evolving. My company has, in my humble opinion, the best combination. We have branch offices in many states, but not everywhere. We are always upgrading our technology to provide the borrower with the best advances in lending. We take loan applications face-to-face, over the telephone, and through our web site. The big advantage is that we will always have an experienced loan officer handling the loan. The borrower and Realtor know where to find me. Or, as one Realtor told me recently, she knows where to come if I mess up the loan and cause the borrower, and her, any pain. This comment came after a web lender delayed one of her sales significantly and the borrower ultimately went to a local lender. Even if I take the loan by telephone or through our web site, I will be in contact by telephone, mail, and e-mail. If the borrower is buying locally and applying from afar, they know I will be available in person after they move. The web site is a great tool for the borrower who does not have time, or is too far away, to come into the office. They can apply in the middle of the night, naked. Once the loan is downloaded, I will call them to confirm and to get any additional information necessary for the approval. And to make sure they are applying for the best loan to serve their needs.

At the very least, anytime you use an on line lender, they should meet certain standards:

1. They should be well-known, established, and well-funded.

2. They should provide all fees and costs up front before the borrower applies for the loan.

3. They should have experienced people handling all the loans.

4. They should be readily accessible by telephone, at the very least, and preferably at a local or regional office.

5. They should be familiar with the area or have a local contact who does know the area.

6. They should have enough variety of loan products to make sure all possible ways to finance the property are available. And the lender needs to know how to use them.

7. Their application site should be very user-friendly and capable of answering basic questions. It also should have a toll-free number to call if the borrower wants to talk to a person before making any type of application.

There are other services that should be offered, but if they meet the aforementioned standards the borrower will at least have a reasonable chance of getting the best loan. But I wouldn't count on it. Even lenders where you can go right to the office have a hard time getting good knowledgeable people. A lender far away and handling a large volume of loans from a central site will not be able to have anywhere near enough experienced personnel. I don't know anything about the markets in California, other than the fact the state is slowly slipping into the Pacific. Why would you expect someone in California to know anything about the markets in Virginia, or the costs associated with closing a loan there?

At the time this book was revised in 2000, several on line lenders had failed, leaving many borrowers to frantically search for another lender. One Realtor friend of mine who lists several builder's houses told me he had a large number of purchasers who decided to apply on line, and every one of the loans had been a nightmare. Of course, most of the worst ones will eventually be weeded out. You just want to make sure your lender has staying power.

WHERE TO GO ON THE WEB TO FIND INFORMATION

Fannie Mae:	*www.fanniemae.com*
Freddie Mac:	*www.freddiemac.com*
FHA and HUD:	*www.hud.gov*
VA:	*www.homeloans.va.gov*

Nehemiah:	*www.nehemiahprogram.com*
Realtors:	*www.realtor.com*
National Association of Mortgage Bankers:	*www.mbaa.com*
National Association of Mortgage Brokers:	*www.namb.org*
Mortgage Insurance:	*www.PrivateMI.com*
Frazier Bell (e-mail):	*wfbell@rlc.net* or *wfbell@columbianational.com*

The Fannie and Freddie sites can tell you about their different loans and special ones for certain borrowers. They also have the updated maximum loan limits. FHA and HUD (one and the same) can give you the maximum loan limits in your area and anywhere else in the United States, along with detailed information on types of loans and buying HUD foreclosures. VA is similar to the HUD site and can help a veteran find out his or her eligibility. The Nehemiah site is listed because I personally think it is a great program to help deserving buyers. There are other similar programs, but Nehemiah is the best I have found. The Realtors site is full of information, plus (unfortunately) it has quite a few industry-related links, such as specific mortgage lenders, which could lead the borrower to believe these are main information sites on the web. All lenders have web sites and some are much better than others. The sites for the mortgage bankers and mortgage brokers have various information for the members and the public, including where to find their local members. The Mortgage Insurance Companies of America site is great for those who want to understand MI and how to remove it. The last e-mail address is self-explanatory. I will answer anyone's questions to the best of my ability. Local laws in Iowa are not my forte, but I may be able to find someone who can answer those questions.

Obviously, these sites are just a few of the thousands pertaining to mortgages. If you plug mortgages or loans into your search engine, the hits are bewildering, and not necessarily what you were expecting to find. I typed in "bonds" once to find out what was out there about mortgage bonds and securities. One of the hits was "bondage." Kinky lending. All of the sites listed above can give you just about any information you may need regarding mortgages.

15

THE MAXIMUM LOAN AMOUNT

To calculate the maximum amount of loan for which you qualify, you must first answer two questions.

1. How much cash do you have for down payment and closing costs?
2. What will be the LTV?

CONVENTIONAL LOANS

1. The maximum Loan-to-Value (LTV) is **95% to 97%** (3% to 5% down).

2. There will be mortgage insurance on loans with less than 20% down payment (over 80% LTV).

3. Conforming Fannie Mae and Freddie Mac loans have maximum loan limits that depend on the number of dwelling units (single, duplex, triplex, quadruplex). The loan limits can change each year. Ask a lender for the current amounts, or check the Fannie/Freddie web sites.

4. Nonconforming or jumbo loans are any loan amounts over the conforming limits.

5. As noted previously, there are loan products that will allow 100%–107% LTV or TLTV. These are not conforming loan products.

Table 15.1

Loan Type	Purchase/Refinance/ Cash Out	Occupancy	Units	LTV	CLTV
Fixed Rate	Purchase/Refinance	Owner	1–2	95%	95%
	Limited Cash out Refinance			95%	95%
	Purchase (Flex/Alt 97)		1	97%	97%
	Cash out Refinance			90%	90%
	Purchase/Refinance		3–4	80%	80%
	Cash out Refinance			75%	75%
	Purchase	Second Home	1	95%	95%
	Refinance			95%	95%
	Cash out Refinance			90%	90%
	Purchase/Refinance	Investment	1–2	90%	90%
	Cash out Refinance			85%	85%
	Purchase/Refinance		3–4	75%	75%
	Cash out Refinance			70%	70%
	Purchase/Refinance	Co-ops	1	90%	90%
Balloon	Purchase/Refinance	Owner	1–2	95%	95%
	Cash out Refinance			90%	90%
	Purchase/Refinance		3–4	80%	80%
	Cash out Refinance			75%	75%
	Purchase/Refinance	Second Home	1	95%	95%
	Cash out Refinance			90%	90%
	Purchase/Refinance	Investment	1–2	90%	90%
	Cash out Refinance			85%	85%
	Purchase/Refinance		3–4	75%	75%
	Cash out Refinance			70%	70%
A.R.M.	Purchase/Refinance	Owner	1	95%	95%
	Purchase(Flex/Alt 97): 7/1 & 10/1		1	97%	97%
	Cash out Refinance			90%	90%
	Purchase/Refinance		2	95%	95%
	Cash out Refinance			75%	75%
	Purchase/Refinance		3–4	80%	80%
	Cash out Refinance			75%	75%
	Purchase/Refinance	Second Home	1	95%	95%
	Cash out Refinance			90%	90%
	Purchase	Investment	N/A		

Note: These percentages do change occasionally. In addition, some lenders can make loans at higher LTVs and CLTVs by their contracts with Fannie and Freddie. You will need to check with your lender to get their maximum LTVs. Go to the Fannie/Freddie web sites to find their current normal maximums.

FHA LOANS

1.   The FHA sets maximum loan limits for different regions of the country. Just like conventional loans, the maximum loan amount will depend on the number of dwelling units up to a quadraplex. They change periodically. Call a lender for the limits in your area, or look on the HUD web site. See the section on FHA loans for the maximum LTV.

2.   FHA loans will always have Mortgage Insurance Premium (MIP) regardless of LTV. This is financed on top of the loan amount, plus the annual premium escrowed into the payment.

VA LOANS

1.   The VA will guarantee a 100% no-cash-down loan if the veteran qualifies. To determine the maximum 100% loan, multiply the veteran's available entitlement by 4, or use VA Exhibit A on page 202 in the Appendix if there is only partial entitlement. The usable entitlement will be on the Certificate of Eligibility. If you do not have one, call the nearest VA office to request it.

2.   The VA Funding Fee can be financed into the loan as long as the total does not exceed the maximum loan amount (full entitlement × 4), which is currently $203,000. Entitlement and/or cash down must equal 25% of the loan.

3.   You can use the **VA Conventional Loan** combination to borrow up to the maximum Fannie/Freddie loan limits. You will have to put some cash down, normally around 4% to 6%, but you qualify using VA guidelines and no MI. Check to see if your lender offers this program.

16

USING YOUR HIGH
SCHOOL MATH

TO FIND THE HOUSE PAYMENT

If you know the maximum payment you can afford, how do you translate that into a maximum loan amount? You use a very simple equation:

$$A \times B = C$$

where

    A = Loan amount (in thousands of dollars)

    B = Factor for interest rate amortization per thousand dollars (from tables)

    C = Principal and interest payment

Let us consider an example of a $100,000 purchase with an $80,000 loan at 10% for 30 years. The per thousand payment factor for 10% 30-year amortization is $8.78 (from the amortization tables).

$$A \times B = C$$

$$80 \times \$8.78 = \$702.40 \text{ PI}$$

TO FIND THE LOAN AMOUNT

What if you know the payment, and you want to know the loan amount it represents?

$$C \div B = A$$

$$\$702.40 \div \$8.78 = 80 \text{ (or } \$80,000\text{)}$$

TO FIND THE PER THOUSAND FACTOR

Or, what if you know the payment and loan amount, but want to know the factor?

$$C \div A = B$$

$$\$702.40 \div 80 = \$8.78.$$

TAXES, HOMEOWNER'S INSURANCE, MORTGAGE INSURANCE, AND HOMEOWNER'S ASSOCIATION FEES

Remember, you have to add an estimate for monthly taxes and insurance to the full house payment. Use one twelfth of the taxes on the property and $2.50 per thousand dollars of sales price, divided by 12, for the monthly homeowner's insurance.

If there is mortgage insurance, use factors (per hundred dollars of sales price) of .72 for 95% LTV, .52 for 90%, and .32 for 85%. Divide this amount by 12. (For example, consider a $90,000 loan on a $100,000 house. .52 × 900 = $468 annual renewal premium, divided by 12 months = $39.00 escrowed into the monthly house payment, PITI/MI.) These figures will be higher or lower than what you may actually pay, depending on the mortgage insurance company and the loan type, but they should get you within $5 to $10 of the true amount. These are based on monthly mortgage insurance premiums. Financed premiums are different. Get a lender to help you with these (see Chapter 4).

Also, add any required monthly homeowner's association or condo fees. These fees are not escrowed by the lender, but they are counted in qualifying, PITI/MI/HOA.

AN EXAMPLE

To carry our example out to the full PITI payment, we start with the principal and interest.

$$\$702.40 = PI$$

In our area, taxes are $0.72 per hundred dollars of assessed value, which would be 1000 (based on our sales price or assessed value of $100,000) × 0.72 = $720/year taxes, divided by 12 months = $60 per month.

$$T = \$60$$

The estimate of homeowner's insurance would be $\$2.50 \times 100$ (per thousand dollars of sales price) = $\$250$/year, divided by $12 = \$21$.

$$I = \$21$$

Thus,

$$PITI = \$702.40\ PI + 60\ T + 21\ I$$

$$= \$783.40\ \text{total house payment}$$

The qualifying is based on this total.

ADDITIONAL CONSIDERATIONS

Now, let's add a few more factors into the qualifying math game:

A = Gross monthly income (GMI)

B = Housing ratio (28% conventional loan, 29% FHA)

C = Maximum house payment (PITI/MI/HOA)

D = Total payments ratio (36% conventional loan, 41% FHA)

E = Total long-term monthly debts

To find the *maximum allowable house payment* (PITI/MI/HOA),

$$A \times B = C$$

$\$2,798$ (income) $\times 28\% = \$783.44$ PITI/MI/HOA

To find the *necessary GMI* for a given house payment,

$$C \div B = A$$

$\$783.44$ PITI $\div 28\% = \$2,798$ per month minimum income

To find the *borrower's housing ratio* for a given house payment,

$$C \div A = B$$

$\$783.44$ PITI $\div \$2,798$ (income) $= 28\%$

To find the *borrower's total payments ratio* for a given house payment,

$$(C + E) \div A = D$$

($783.44 PITI + 223.84 [debt]) ÷ $2,798 (income) = 36%

The value $223.84 is the maximum monthly debt to stay within 36%.

To find the *borrower's maximum allowable total payments* (house + debts),

$$A \times D = C + E$$

$2,798 (income) × 36% = $1,007.28
= $783.44 PITI + $223.84 debts

To find the borrower's *maximum house payment when the total payments exceed 36%,*

$$A \times D - E = C$$

$2,798 (income) × 36% − (debts payments) = $1,007.28
−$400 (for this example = $607.28
PITI/MI/HOA

If the long-term monthly debts were $400, the total debt would be $1,183.44 (= $400 + $783.44). But $1,183.44 PITI/MI/HOA/LTD divided by $2,798 income equals 42%. To get the total debt ratio back to 36%, you determine the difference between $1,183.44 and $1,007.28 as excess monthly debt, or $176.16. This excess debt would have to be eliminated, or the total house payment reduced.

C (Proposed PITI/MI/HOA) + E − A × D (36%) =

C (Maximum allowable PITI/MI/HOA)

Because the total payment ratio of 42% is over the maximum of 36%, the maximum allowable house payment will be lowered until the house payment and total monthly debts are no more than 36% of the borrower's GMI. This is done by calculating 36% of the borrower's GMI and then subtracting the monthly debt payments. The remainder is the maximum allowable house payment.

CALCULATIONS FOR YOUR OWN CASE

Just substitute your income for A, your proposed house payment for C, and your monthly debt payments for E to find your own qualifying ratios, payments, and necessary income. The ratio you use depends on the loan type (conventional or FHA) and the LTV.

The more monthly income, the more debt that the borrower can have, or the more the borrower qualifies for if there is less debt. Don't worry about getting it to the dollar. As long as it is within $10–$15, more or less, you will be safe. You can also round up or down to get rid of the cents. No lender is going to worry about being 40 cents over. I kept the cents in the example so your answers would come out to the penny if you tried it with your calculator. Remember, DU and LP will allow higher ratios with compensating factors, so this example is only to show you the basics.

17

IF YOU ARE TURNED DOWN FOR THE LOAN

What can you do if the lender turns you down? There are several options available.

Just because you were denied the loan does not mean that your chances are absolutely finished. Ask the lender to detail exactly why you were turned down. It may be something that can be corrected so the loan can be resubmitted to the underwriter and approved. If the lender is not willing to try to correct the problem, or if it is not correctable, you will receive a written statement of credit denial that will give the reason(s).

If you feel that you can still get the loan, go to another lender and give them the facts and the reason why you were denied. The original lender may even help you to find another source. If another lender thinks the loan can be done, you can request that your original loan package be transferred from the first lender. Except for FHA and VA loans, the lender is not obligated to transfer the package. But if the lender values its good name in the community, it will do everything possible to assist you.

As a mortgage banker, I had to reject one loan that I knew could be approved by another lender I called the other lender and explained the situation. Then I advised the borrowers to transfer their package, which I sent in its entirety. The borrowers got their loan and I received a very warm thank-you note—and several referrals, which more than made up for my lost time and costs. Today, with all the different types of loans offered by most lenders, including subprime, about the only way a loan cannot be found is if you have bad credit and no money. The progression should go from the preferred loan for which you applied, to the next best loan, and so on down the list until the lender finds one that fits your situation or runs out of options for you to qualify.

If the problem is such that no lender can make you the loan, sit down with your lender and find out exactly what you need to do to correct it and how long after that before you can make application again. Few borrowers are completely hopeless.

What do you lose by being rejected? Normally, you will have paid the credit report and appraisal fee at application. These are not refundable. Some lenders will collect a fee for processing or underwriting (garbage fees). Others might collect an application fee that will include the cost of the appraisal and credit report, and some fee income to the lender itself. The application fee is usually nonrefundable. If any fees are required for loan application, find out if any or all of the fees are refundable if the lender denies the loan, and get it in writing.

Potentially the most expensive fee that you may have to pay arises if the lender charges you to transfer the loan package. The lender may try to hit you with 0.5% up to the full 1% of the origination fee. If the lender approved the loan and you wanted to transfer it, then I agree that you should pay. But, if the lender cannot do the loan, the whole matter comes back to reputation and integrity. Any lender should be more than willing to help you if it cannot make the loan. If the lender wants to charge you for transferring the package, it may be cheaper to start over with another lender than to pay 1% in additional cost.

Will the loan denial affect your credit? No. Being turned down for a loan is not in itself bad credit, although it may very well be the result of having bad credit. Nothing on your credit report will ever show that you were turned down for a home loan.

18

SUMMARY-Caveat Emptor

Buyer Beware. That is the best advice to anyone when purchasing a home and obtaining a mortgage. Nothing is simple, or free. The lending business changes so abruptly in relatively short periods that even those of us who are exposed to it daily are often caught not knowing the answer to a question. Because real estate financing is a dynamic, ever-changing industry, there will never be a source book that can completely and concisely cover financing and still remain 100% reliable for any extended length of time. Existing loan programs will change or no longer be offered, while other innovative loan products will be developed to meet the current demands of the market. There are also many regional programs for homebuyers, such as the revenue bond authorities, that I could not begin to cover in detail. The secondary market will also change its underwriting guidelines from time to time. When the market is down or stable, the secondary market will relax its rules, only to tighten them up again when things heat up or start to get beyond its ability to control the market. Never assume that any guideline is absolute. The 28%/36% qualifying ratios are not written in stone. And, not a month goes by without some story appearing about how FHA or VA is going to change its loan program.

This book has explained the basics of borrowing and the guidelines that direct them, so that you can understand the loan process. In this way, you can approach the financing of real estate with a degree of knowledge and, as a result, you will not feel overwhelmed and intimidated by the lender. If you do not agree with what the lender tells you, or you are not sure you have received the best advice, seek a second opinion from another lender. It doesn't cost you anything to ask questions. Remember, always ask further questions if you are unsure of the answer. It is better to *feel* stupid for asking than it is to *be* stupid for not having asked. Questions can save you valuable time and money.

APPENDIX
FORMS

APPLICATION CHECKLIST

EMPLOYMENT & INCOME(2 Years):
[ ]   *All Employers: Names, addresses, dates of employment. Most recent paystubs for a
30 day period. W-2s for past 2 years.
[ ]   *Social Security & Retirement Income: copies of most recent awards letter and/or copies of past 2 – 6
months bank statements showing receipt.
[ ]   *Interest & Dividend Income: Copies of most recent account statements, past 2 years 1099s and/or tax
returns.
[ ]   *Rental Income: Copies of current leases. May require past years tax returns with schedule E.
[ ]   *Alimony/Child Support: Copy of complete executed separation or divorce agreement. Evidence of
receipt of payments by past 3 – 12 months bank statements showing deposit.

SELF-EMPLOYED and/or COMMISSIONED INCOME:
[ ]   *Copies of past 1 – 2 years tax returns, all pages, signed
[ ]   *Copy of K-1, if received.
[ ]   *Copy of 1099s, if received.
[ ]   *Copies of Corporate and/or Partnership returns for past 1 – 2 years, signed.
[ ]   *P & L may be requested.

CASH AND LIQUID ASSETS:
[ ]   *Copies of your 1 – 2 most recent months account statements, all pages.
[ ]   *Explanation of any large deposits and proof of source.
[ ]   *Sale of Property: copy of sales contract and/or copy of closing statement.
[ ]   *Gift: Signed gift letter(form provided by lender). Proof of Donor's ability to give may be required. Copy
of gift check, copy of deposit slip, copy or print-out of statement showing deposit. Copy of canceled gift
check.(All prior to closing unless waived by lender.)

DEBTS:
[ ]   *Most debts will show on the credit report. Any that do not show must be verified. The lender will need:
Name, address, phone number, account number, payment, approximate balance.
[ ]   *Alimony/Child Support: Copy of separation/divorce agreement.

OTHER:
[ ]   *Copy of signed purchase contract, if buying. Copy of Deed if refinancing.
[ ]   *Copy of multiple listing agreement, if available and applicable.
[ ]   *Copy of earnest money check. If it is a large amount needed to qualify, a copy of the canceled check will
be needed prior to closing.
[ ]   *Addresses of where you have lived for the past 2 years and the names, addresses, & phone numbers of all
landlords for the same period.
[ ]   *Year, make, value of all cars.

[ ]   V.A.: Original Certificate of Eligibility, copy of DD214, most recent Earnings and Leave statement if still
enlisted.

FOR D.U. or L.P. UNDERWRITING: The normal documentation will be 30 days paystubs, past 1 – 2 yrs. W-2s,
Past 1 – 2 years tax returns, if necessary, and most recent 1 – 2 months account statements for funds needed
to close and qualify.

For all employers it is very helpful to have a contact person who can verify your employment.

This is a list of the most common information needed to apply for a loan. The type of loan and the lender may have
additional requirements. Ask the lender exactly what they will need prior to meeting with them.

Uniform Residential Loan Application

This application is designed to be completed by the applicant(s) with the Lender's assistance. Applicants should complete this form as "Borrower" or "Co-Borrower," as applicable. Co-Borrower information must also be provided (and the appropriate box checked) when ☐ the income or assets of a person other than the "Borrower" (including the Borrower's spouse) will be used as a basis for loan qualification or ☐ the income or assets of the Borrower's spouse will not be used as a basis for loan qualification, but his or her liabilities must be considered because the Borrower resides in a community property state, the security property is located in a community property state, or the Borrower is relying on other property located in a community property state as a basis for repayment of the loan.

I. TYPE OF MORTGAGE AND TERMS OF LOAN

| Mortgage Applied for: | ☐ VA   ☐ Conventional   ☐ Other: | | Agency Case Number | | Lender Case Number |
| ☐ FHA   ☐ FmHA | | | | | |

| Amount | Interest Rate | No. of Months | Amortization Type: | ☐ Fixed Rate   ☐ Other (explain): |
| $ | % | | | ☐ GPM   ☐ ARM (type): |

II. PROPERTY INFORMATION AND PURPOSE OF LOAN

| Subject Property Address (street, city, state, ZIP) | No. of Units |

| Legal Description of Subject Property (attach description if necessary) | Year Built |

| Purpose of Loan | ☐ Purchase   ☐ Construction   ☐ Other (explain): | Property will be: |
| | ☐ Refinance   ☐ Construction-Permanent | ☐ Primary Residence   ☐ Secondary Residence   ☐ Investment |

Complete this line if construction or construction-permanent loan.

| Year Lot Acquired | Original Cost | Amount Existing Liens | (a) Present Value of Lot | (b) Cost of Improvements | Total (a + b) |
| | $ | $ | $ | $ | $ |

Complete this line if this is a refinance loan.

| Year Acquired | Original Cost | Amount Existing Liens | Purpose of Refinance | Describe Improvements ☐ made ☐ to be made |
| | $ | $ | | Cost: $ |

Title will be held in what Name(s)	Manner in which Title will be held	Estate will be held in:
		☐ Fee Simple
Source of Down Payment, Settlement Charges and/or Subordinate Financing (explain)		☐ Leasehold (show expiration date)

III. BORROWER INFORMATION

| Borrower | Co-Borrower |

| Borrower's Name (include Jr. or Sr. if applicable) | Co-Borrower's Name (include Jr. or Sr. if applicable) |

| Social Security Number | Home Phone (incl. area code) | Age | Yrs. School | Social Security Number | Home Phone (incl. area code) | Age | Yrs. School |

| ☐ Married   ☐ Unmarried (include single, divorced, widowed)   ☐ Separated | Dependents (not listed by Co-Borrower) no.   ages | ☐ Married   ☐ Unmarried (include single, divorced, widowed)   ☐ Separated | Dependents (not listed by Borrower) no.   ages |

| Present Address (street, city, state, ZIP) ☐ Own ☐ Rent ____ No. Yrs. | Present Address (street, city, state, ZIP) ☐ Own ☐ Rent ____ No. Yrs. |

If residing at present address for less than two years, complete the following:

| Former Address (street, city, state, ZIP) ☐ Own ☐ Rent ____ No. Yrs. | Former Address (street, city, state, ZIP) ☐ Own ☐ Rent ____ No. Yrs. |

| Former Address (street, city, state, ZIP) ☐ Own ☐ Rent ____ No. Yrs. | Former Address (street, city, state, ZIP) ☐ Own ☐ Rent ____ No. Yrs. |

IV. EMPLOYMENT INFORMATION

| Borrower | Co-Borrower |

| Name & Address of Employer ☐ Self Employed | Yrs. on this job | Name & Address of Employer ☐ Self Employed | Yrs. on this job |
| | Yrs. employed in this line of work/profession | | Yrs. employed in this line of work/profession |

| Position/Title/Type of Business | Business Phone (incl. area code) | Position/Title/Type of Business | Business Phone (incl. area code) |

If employed in current position for less than two years or if currently employed in more than one position, complete the following:

| Name & Address of Employer ☐ Self Employed | Dates (from - to) | Name & Address of Employer ☐ Self Employed | Dates (from - to) |
| | Monthly Income $ | | Monthly Income $ |

| Position/Title/Type of Business | Business Phone (incl. area code) | Position/Title/Type of Business | Business Phone (incl. area code) |

| Name & Address of Employer ☐ Self Employed | Dates (from - to) | Name & Address of Employer ☐ Self Employed | Dates (from - to) |
| | Monthly Income $ | | Monthly Income $ |

| Position/Title/Type of Business | Business Phone (incl. area code) | Position/Title/Type of Business | Business Phone (incl. area code) |

| Borrower's Signature: X | Date |

| Co-Borrower's Signature: X | Date |

VMP-21 (9210).07   VMP MORTGAGE FORMS - (800)521-7291   Freddie Mac Form 65 10/92   Fannie Mae Form 1003 10/92

V. MONTHLY INCOME AND COMBINED HOUSING EXPENSE INFORMATION

Gross Monthly Income	Borrower	Co-Borrower	Total	Combined Monthly Housing Expense	Present	Proposed
Base Empl. Income*	$	$	$	Rent	$	
Overtime				First Mortgage (P&I)		$
Bonuses				Other Financing (P&I)		
Commissions				Hazard Insurance		
Dividends/Interest				Real Estate Taxes		
Net Rental Income				Mortgage Insurance		
Other (before completing, see the notice in "describe other income," below)				Homeowner Assn. Dues		
				Other:		
Total	$	$	$	Total	$	$

* Self Employed Borrower(s) may be required to provide additional documentation such as tax returns and financial statements.

Describe Other Income   Notice: Alimony, child support, or separate maintenance income need not be revealed if the Borrower (B) or Co-Borrower (C) does not choose to have it considered for repaying this loan.

B/C		Monthly Amount
		$

VI. ASSETS AND LIABILITIES

This Statement and any applicable supporting schedules may be completed jointly by both married and unmarried Co-Borrowers if their assets and liabilities are sufficiently joined so that the Statement can be meaningfully and fairly presented on a combined basis; otherwise separate Statements and Schedules are required. If the Co-Borrower section was completed about a spouse, this Statement and supporting schedules must be completed about that spouse also.

Completed ☐ Jointly ☐ Not Jointly

ASSETS Description	Cash or Market Value	Liabilities and Pledged Assets. List the creditor's name, address and account number for all outstanding debts, including automobile loans, revolving charge accounts, real estate loans, alimony, child support, stock pledges, etc. Use continuation sheet, if necessary. Indicate by (*) those liabilities which will be satisfied upon sale of real estate owned or upon refinancing of the subject property.	Monthly Pmt. & Mos. Left to Pay	Unpaid Balance
Cash deposit toward purchase held by:	$	**LIABILITIES**		
		Name and address of Company	$ Pmt./Mos.	$
List checking and savings accounts below				
Name and address of Bank, S&L, or Credit Union				
		Acct. no.		
		Name and address of Company	$ Pmt./Mos.	$
Acct. no.	$			
Name and address of Bank, S&L, or Credit Union				
		Acct. no.		
		Name and address of Company	$ Pmt./Mos.	$
Acct. no.	$			
Name and address of Bank, S&L, or Credit Union				
		Acct. no.		
		Name and address of Company	$ Pmt./Mos.	$
Acct. no.	$			
Name and address of Bank, S&L, or Credit Union				
		Acct. no.		
		Name and address of Company	$ Pmt./Mos.	$
Acct. no.	$			
Stocks & Bonds (Company name/number & description)	$			
		Acct. no.		
		Name and address of Company	$ Pmt./Mos.	$
Life insurance net cash value	$			
Face amount: $				
Subtotal Liquid Assets	$			
Real estate owned (enter market value from schedule of real estate owned)	$	Acct. no.		
Vested interest in retirement fund	$	Name and address of Company	$ Pmt./Mos.	$
Net worth of business(es) owned (attach financial statement)	$			
Automobiles owned (make and year)	$			
		Acct. no.		
		Alimony/Child Support/Separate Maintenance Payments Owed to:	$	
Other Assets (itemize)	$	Job Related Expense (child care, union dues, etc.)	$	
		Total Monthly Payments	$	
Total Assets a.	$	**Net Worth** (a minus b) ▶ $	**Total Liabilities b.**	$

Borrower's Signature:	Date	Co-Borrower's Signature:	Date
X		X	

UMP-21 (9210).07

Fannie Mae Form 1003 10/92
Freddie Mac Form 65 10/92

VI. ASSETS AND LIABILITIES (cont.)

Schedule of Real Estate Owned (If additional properties are owned, use continuation sheet.)

Property Address (enter S if sold, PS if pending sale or R if rental being held for income) ▼	Type of Property	Present Market Value	Amount of Mortgages & Liens	Gross Rental Income	Mortgage Payments	Insurance, Maintenance, Taxes & Misc.	Net Rental Income
		$	$	$	$	$	$
Totals		$	$	$	$	$	$

List any additional names under which credit has previously been received and indicate appropriate creditor name(s) and account number(s):

Alternate Name	Creditor Name	Account Number

VII. DETAILS OF TRANSACTION

a. Purchase price	$
b. Alterations, improvements, repairs	
c. Land (if acquired separately)	
d. Refinance (incl. debts to be paid off)	
e. Estimated prepaid items	
f. Estimated closing costs	
g. PMI, MIP, Funding Fee	
h. Discount (if Borrower will pay)	
i. Total costs (add items a through h)	
j. Subordinate financing	
k. Borrower's closing costs paid by Seller	
l. Other Credits (explain)	
m. Loan amount (exclude PMI, MIP, Funding Fee financed)	
n. PMI, MIP, Funding Fee financed	
o. Loan amount (add m & n)	
p. Cash from/ to Borrower (subtract j, k, l & o from i)	

VIII. DECLARATIONS

If you answer "Yes" to any questions a through i, please use continuation sheet for explanation.

	Borrower Yes	Borrower No	Co-Borrower Yes	Co-Borrower No
a. Are there any outstanding judgments against you?	☐	☐	☐	☐
b. Have you been declared bankrupt within the past 7 years?	☐	☐	☐	☐
c. Have you had property foreclosed upon or given title or deed in lieu thereof in the last 7 years?	☐	☐	☐	☐
d. Are you a party to a lawsuit?	☐	☐	☐	☐
e. Have you directly or indirectly been obligated on any loan which resulted in foreclosure, transfer of title in lieu of foreclosure, or judgment? (This would include such loans as home mortgage loans, SBA loans, home improvement loans, educational loans, manufactured (mobile) home loans, any mortgage, financial obligation, bond, or loan guarantee. If "Yes," provide details, including date, name and address of Lender, FHA or VA case number, if any, and reasons for the action.)	☐	☐	☐	☐
f. Are you presently delinquent or in default on any Federal debt or any other loan, mortgage, financial obligation, bond, or loan guarantee? If "Yes," give details as described in the preceding question.	☐	☐	☐	☐
g. Are you obligated to pay alimony, child support, or separate maintenance?	☐	☐	☐	☐
h. Is any part of the down payment borrowed?	☐	☐	☐	☐
i. Are you a co-maker or endorser on a note?	☐	☐	☐	☐
j. Are you a U.S. citizen?	☐	☐	☐	☐
k. Are you a permanent resident alien?	☐	☐	☐	☐
l. Do you intend to occupy the property as your primary residence? If "Yes," complete question m below.	☐	☐	☐	☐
m. Have you had an ownership interest in a property in the last three years? (1) What type of property did you own -- principal residence (PR), second home (SH), or investment property (IP)? (2) How did you hold title to the home -- solely by yourself (S), jointly with your spouse (SP), or jointly with another person (O)?	☐	☐	☐	☐

IX. ACKNOWLEDGMENT AND AGREEMENT

The undersigned specifically acknowledge(s) and agree(s) that: (1) the loan requested by this application will be secured by a first mortgage or deed of trust on the property described herein; (2) the property will not be used for any illegal or prohibited purpose or use; (3) all statements made in this application are made for the purpose of obtaining the loan indicated herein; (4) occupation of the property will be as indicated above; (5) verification or reverification of any information contained in the application may be made at any time by the Lender, its agents, successors and assigns, either directly or through a credit reporting agency, from any source named in this application, and the original copy of this application will be retained by the Lender, even if the loan is not approved; (6) the Lender, its agents, successors and assigns will rely on the information contained in the application and I/we have a continuing obligation to amend and/or supplement the information provided in this application if any of the material facts which I/we have represented herein should change prior to closing; (7) in the event my/our payments on the loan indicated in this application become delinquent, the Lender, its agents, successors and assigns, may, in addition to all their other rights and remedies, report my/our name(s) and account information to a credit reporting agency; (8) ownership of the loan may be transferred to successor or assign of the Lender without notice to me and/or the administration of the loan account may be transferred to an agent, successor or assign of the Lender with prior notice to me; (9) the Lender, its agents, successors and assigns make no representations or warranties, express or implied, to the Borrower(s) regarding the property, the condition of the property, o the value of the property.

Certification: I/We certify that the information provided in this application is true and correct as of the date set forth opposite my/our signature(s) on this application and acknowledge my/our understanding that any intentional or negligent misrepresentation(s) of the information contained in this application may result in civil liability and/or criminal penalties including, but not limited to, fine or imprisonment or both under the provisions of Title 18, United States Code, Section 1001, et seq. and liability for monetary damages to the Lender, its agents, successors and assigns, insurers and any other person who may suffer any loss due to reliance upon any misrepresentation which I/we have made on this application.

Borrower's Signature	Date	Co-Borrower's Signature	Date
X		X	

X. INFORMATION FOR GOVERNMENT MONITORING PURPOSES

The following information is requested by the Federal Government for certain types of loans related to a dwelling, in order to monitor the Lender's compliance with equal credit opportunity, fair housing and home mortgage disclosure laws. You are not required to furnish this information, but are encouraged to do so. The law provides that a Lender may neither discriminate on the basis of this information, nor on whether you choose to furnish it. However, if you choose not to furnish it, under Federal regulations this Lender is required to note race and sex on the basis of visual observation or surname. If you do not wish to furnish the above information, please check the box below. (Lender must review the above material to assure that the disclosures satisfy all requirements to which the Lender is subject under applicable state law for the particular type of loan applied for.)

BORROWER ☐ I do not wish to furnish this information

Race/National Origin: ☐ American Indian or Alaskan Native ☐ Asian or Pacific Islander ☐ Black, not of Hispanic origin ☐ White, not of Hispanic origin ☐ Hispanic ☐ Other (specify)

Sex: ☐ Female ☐ Male

CO-BORROWER ☐ I do not wish to furnish this information

Race/National Origin: ☐ American Indian or Alaskan Native ☐ Asian or Pacific Islander ☐ Black, not of Hispanic origin ☐ White, not of Hispanic origin ☐ Hispanic ☐ Other (specify)

Sex: ☐ Female ☐ Male

To be Completed by Interviewer
This application was taken by:
☐ face-to-face interview
☐ by mail
☐ by telephone

Interviewer's Name (print or type)	Name and Address of Interviewer's Employer
Interviewer's Signature	Date	
Interviewer's Phone Number (incl. area code)	

LENDER NAME AND ADDRESS

MORTGAGE SERVICING TRANSFER DISCLOSURE

NOTICE TO MORTGAGE LOAN APPLICANTS: THE RIGHT TO COLLECT YOUR MORTGAGE LOAN PAYMENTS MAY BE TRANSFERRED. FEDERAL LAW GIVES YOU CERTAIN RIGHTS. READ THIS STATEMENT AND SIGN IT ONLY IF YOU UNDERSTAND ITS CONTENTS.

Because you are applying for a mortgage loan covered by the Real Estate Settlement Procedures Act (RESPA) (12 U.S.C. §2601 et seq.) you have certain rights under that Federal law. This statement tells you about those rights. It also tells you what the chances are that the servicing for this loan may be transferred to a different loan servicer. "Servicing" refers to collecting your principal, interest and escrow account payments. If your loan servicer changes, there are certain procedures that must be followed. This statement generally explains those procedures.

Transfer Practices and Requirements
If the servicing of your loan is assigned, sold, or transferred to a new servicer, you must be given written notice of that transfer. The present loan servicer must send you notice in writing of the assignment, sale or transfer of the servicing not less than 15 days before the date of the transfer. The new loan servicer must also send you notice within 15 days after the date of the transfer. Also, a notice of prospective transfer may be provided to you at settlement (when title to your new property is transferred to you) to satisfy these requirements. The law allows a delay in the time (not more than 30 days after a transfer) for servicers to notify you under certain limited circumstances, when your servicer is changed abruptly. This exception applies only if your servicer is fired for cause, is in bankruptcy proceedings, or is involved in a conservatorship or receivership initiated by a Federal agency.

Notices must contain certain information. They must contain the effective date of the transfer of the servicing of your loan to the new servicer, the name, address, and toll-free or collect call telephone number of the new servicer, and toll-free or collect call telephone numbers of a person or department for both your present servicer and your new servicer to answer your questions about the transfer of servicing. During the 60-day period following the effective date of the transfer of the loan servicing, a loan payment received by your old servicer before its due date may not be treated by the new loan servicer as late, and a late fee may not be imposed on you.

Complaint Resolution
Section 6 of RESPA (12 U.S.C. §2605) gives you certain consumer rights, whether or not your loan servicing is transferred. If you send a "qualified written request" to your loan servicer concerning the servicing of your loan, your servicer must provide you with a written acknowledgment within 20 business days of receipt of your request. A "qualified written request" is a written correspondence, other than notice on a payment coupon or other payment medium supplied by the servicer, which includes your name and account number, and your reasons for the request. Not later than 60 business days after receiving your request, your servicer must make any appropriate corrections to your account, and must provide you with a written clarification regarding any dispute. During this 60-day period, your servicer may not provide information to a consumer reporting agency concerning any overdue payment related to such period or qualified written request.

Damages and Costs
Section 6 of RESPA also provides for damages and costs for individuals or classes of individuals in circumstances where servicers are shown to have violated the requirements of that Section.

Servicing Transfer Estimates by Original Lender
The following is the best estimate of what will happen to the servicing of your mortgage loan:

1. ☐ We do not service mortgage loans. We intend to assign, sell, or transfer the servicing of your loan to another party. You will be notified at settlement regarding the servicer.

   OR

2. ☐ We are able to service this loan and presently intend to do so. However, that may change in the future. For all the loans that we make in the 12-month period after your loan is funded, we estimate that the chances that we will transfer the servicing of those loans is between:

   ☐ 0 to 25%   ☐ 26 to 50%   ☐ 51 to 75%   ☐ 76 to 100%

   This is only our best estimate and it is not binding.
   Business conditions or other circumstances may affect our future transferring decisions.

3. This is our record of transferring the servicing of the loans we have made in the past:

YEAR	PERCENTAGE OF LOANS TRANSFERRED (Rounded to Nearest Quartile - 0%, 25%, 50%, 75% or 100%)
19	%
19	%
19	%

The estimates in 2. and 3. above do not include transfers to affiliates or subsidiaries. If the servicing of your loan is transferred to an affiliate or subsidiary in the future, you will be notified in accordance with RESPA.

_____   _____
LENDER (Signature not Mandatory)   DATE

ACKNOWLEDGMENT OF MORTGAGE LOAN APPLICANT

I/we have read this disclosure form, and understand its contents, as evidenced by my/our signature(s) below.

_____   _____
APPLICANT'S SIGNATURE   DATE

_____
CO-APPLICANT'S SIGNATURE

INSTRUCTIONS TO PREPARER: For applications received in calendar year 1991 after the effective date of this Notice, the information in 3. above will be for calendar year 1990 only; for applications received in 1992, this information will be for calendar years 1990 and 1991; and for applications received in 1993 and thereafter, this information will be for the previous three calendar years.

CONVENTIONAL/F.H.A. QUALIFYING FORM

This is only to give you a reasonable idea of the loan amount and payment for which you may qualify. D.U., L.P., and other computer based underwriting systems can approve you for significantly more than the benchmark qualifying ratios. In addition, certain loans, such as the Flex & Alt. 97, will have higher allowable ratios.

		BORROWER	CO-BORROWER	
GROSS MONTHLY INCOME:				
	BASE INCOME:	$_____	$_____	
OTHER:	OVERTIME	$_____	$_____	
	BONUS:	$_____	$_____	
	COMMISSION:	$_____	$_____	
	INTEREST/DIV.:	$_____	$_____	
	_____ :	$_____	$_____	
[A]	**TOTAL G.M.I.:**	$_____	$_____ =	$_____

TOTAL HOUSE PAYMENT:			
	PRINCIPAL & INTEREST:	$_____	
	TAXES:	$_____	
	HOMEOWNER'S INSURANCE:	$_____	
	*MORTGAGE INSURANCE:	$_____	
	*ASSOCIATION/CONDO FEES:	$_____	
	*OTHER:	$_____	
	(*If required)		
[B]	**TOTAL HOUSING EXPENSE:**	$_____ =	$_____

[C] HOUSING EXPENSE RATIOS: CONVENTIONAL: **28%+ OF G.M.I.**
                             F.H.A.:   **29%+ OF G.M.I.**

[B] $_____ divided by [A] $_____ = HOUSE PAYMENT RATIO: _____%

DEBTS:

Creditor:	Balance	Remaining Months		Payment
_____	$_____	_____	@	$_____
_____	$_____	_____	@	$_____
_____	$_____	_____	@	$_____
_____	$_____	_____	@	$_____
_____	$_____	_____	@	$_____
_____	$_____	_____	@	$_____
TOTAL:	$_____			$_____ = $_____

(Count all long term debt with over 10 months remaining and add all minimum payments on revolving debt)

[D] **TOTAL HOUSING EXPENSE AND LONG-TERM MONTHLY DEBTS:** $_____

[E] TOTAL PAYMENT RATIOS: CONVENTIONAL: **36%+ OF G.M.I.**
                           F.H.A.:   **41%+ OF G.M.I.**

[D] $_____ divided by [A] $_____ = TOTAL PAYMENTS RATIO: _____%

NOTE: On one year ARMs with a yearly cap of 2%, use the maximum second year rate to qualify. Lower LTVs and higher credit scores will allow higher qualifying ratios on most loans.

Good Faith Estimate

The below figures are estimates provided in good faith by the Lender and based upon the sales price, mortgage amount, interest rate, and discount points in effect or reasonably assumed at the time of preparation. The actual interest rate and discount points charged will be determined by the terms of the Financing Agreement.

Date: 00/00/0000

Applicant(s):   blank

Sales Price
Loan Amount:
Loan Program:
Property:

ITEMS PAYABLE WITH LOAN AND OTHER CHARGES

801	Loan Origination Fee	(0.0000%)	0.00
802	Loan Discount	(0.0000%)	0.00
803	Appraisal Fee(POC)		0.00
804	Credit Report Fee(POC)		0.00
805	Lender's Inspection Fee		0.00
806	Flood Certificate		0.00
807	Document Preparation/Review		0.00
808	Application Fee(APP)		0.00
809	Underwriting Fee		0.00
810	Tax Service Fee		0.00
814	Courier Fee		0.00
815	Rate Protection Fee		0.00
1107	Attorney Fees		0.00
1108	Title Insurance		0.00
1110	Owner's Coverage		0.00
1201	Recording Fee/Stamps		0.00
1301	Survey		0.00
1302	Pest Inspection		0.00

Total Costs   **0.00**

INTEREST RATE: 0.000%

TOTAL ESTIMATED MONTHLY PAYMENTS

Principal & Interest	0.00
Real Estate Taxes	0.00
City Taxes	0.00
School Taxes	
Hazard Insurance	0.00
Flood Insurance	0.00
Monthly PMI	0.00
Other: Ground Rent	0.00
Other: Front Foot	0.00
HOA	0.00
Secondary Financing	0.00
Total Monthly Payment	**0.00**

ITEMS REQUIRED TO BE PAID IN ADVANCE

901 Interest		0.00
Daily Interest	0.00	
Number of Days	0	
902 Mortgage Ins (0 mos)		0.00
903 Hazard Ins (12 mos)		0.00
906 County Tax (0 mos)		0.00
904 Flood Ins (0 mos)		0.00
905 FHA UFMIP		0.00
905 VA Funding Fee		0.00
910 Other:		0.00

RESERVES DEPOSITED WITH LENDER

1001 Hazard Ins (3 Mos)	0.00
1002 Mortgage Ins (0 Mos)	0.00
1004 County Tax (3 Mos)	0.00
1005 City Tax (0 Mos)	0.00
1006 School Tax (0Mos)	0.00
1007 Ground Rent (0 Mos)	0.00
1008 Front Foot (0 Mos)	0.00
1009 Flood Insurance (0 Mos)	0.00
Aggregate Escrow Adj.	0.00
Total Prepaids/Reserves	**0.00**

ESTIMATE OF FUNDS TO CLOSE

Purchase Price	0.00
Alterations, Improvements	0.00
Land	0.00
Est. Payoff (Refi Only)	0.00
Estimated Escrow Prepaids	0.00
Estimated Closing Costs	0.00
PMI, MIP, Funding Fee	0.00
Estimated Funds to Close	**0.00**

CREDITS

Subordinate Financing	0.00
Closing Cost pd by Seller	0.00
Closing Cost pd by Lender	0.00
Other:	0.00
Other:	0.00
Paid at application	0.00
Paid Outside of Closing	0.00
Earnest Money Deposit	0.00
Base Loan Amount	0.00
PMI, MIP Financed	0.00
Loan Amount	0.00
Total Funds for Closing	**0.00**

DESIGNATED PROVIDERS: Costs estimated above for the appraisal, credit report, flood insurance certification and private mortgage insurance are based on the typical costs imposed by lender designated third-party service providers. This lender has repeatedly used the services of these providers within the past 12 months. A list of these providers is available upon request.

NOTE: This calculation represents the median amount of interest you could be required to pay at settlement. The actual amount will be determined by which day of the month your settlement is conducted. To determine the amount you will have to pay, multiply the number of days remaining in the month in which your loan settles, times the daily rate shown above.

SETTLEMENT AGENT

In connection with this loan application, the undersigned applicant(s): (Check Applicable boxes)
1) [ ]   Have no preference as to who conducts settlement and issues the required Mortgagee Title Policy.
2) [ ]   Has chosen the following attorney or title company to represent me/us at time of closing. _____
NOTE: Lender requires such settlement agent to provide at no cost to lender an "Insured Closing Letter" from a reputable title insurer. Lender must be notified in writing of any change in above selection. Lender reserves the right to disapprove the recommended title insurer and/or settlement agent for reasonable cause.)
3) [ ]   Lender Attorney: Lender's designated attorney will provide review of file, closing of mortgage loan transaction, assembly of and transmittal of the completed loan package. Lender's estimate is based on the charges of the designated provider.
NOTICE: Each loan applicant must personally attend settlement or obtain advance approval from Lender for Special Power of Attorney .

ACKNOWLEDGEMENT

Date Prepared:	00/00/0000	Prepared By:	Frazier Bell
Date Mailed, if applicable: _____		Sent by:	Frazier Bell

I/We acknowledge receipt of a copy of this completed form and the following booklets, as applicable:
HUD's "Settlement Cost and You"   Consumer Handbook on Adjustable Rate Mortgages prepared by FRB/FHLBB

_____   _____
Applicant   Date   Co-Applicant   Date

FannieMae

Request for Verification of Employment

Part I - Request

1. To (Name and address of employer)

2. From (Name and address of lender)

I certify that this verification has been sent directly to the employer and has not passed through the hands of the applicant or any other interested party.

3. Signature of Lender	4. Title	5. Date	6. Lender's No. (Optional)

I have applied for a mortgage loan and stated that I am now or was formerly employed by you. My signature below authorizes verification of this information.

7. Name and Address of Applicant (include employee or badge number)

8. Signature of Applicant

X

Part II - Verification of Present Employment

9. Applicant's Date of Employment	10. Present Position	11. Probability of Continued Employment

12A. Current Gross Base Pay (Enter Amount and Check Period)
Annual, Weekly, Other (Specify), Monthly, Hourly
$_____

13. For Military Personnel Only Pay Grade, Type, Monthly Amount

14. If Overtime or Bonus is Applicable, Is Its Continuance Likely? Overtime Yes/No Bonus Yes/No

15. If paid hourly - average hours per week

12B. Gross Earnings

Type	Year To Date	Past Year	Past Year		
Base Pay	Thru____ $	$	$	Base Pay $	Rations $
Overtime	$	$	$	Flight or Hazard $	Clothing $
Commissions	$	$	$	Quarters $	Pro Pay $
Bonus	$	$	$	Overseas or Combat $	
Total	$	$	$	Variable Housing Allowance $	

16. Date of applicant's next pay increase
17. Projected amount of next pay increase
18. Date of applicant's last pay increase
19. Amount of last pay increase

20. Remarks (If employee was off work for any length of time, please indicate time period and reason)

Part III - Verification of Previous Employment

21. Date Hired	23. Salary/Wage at Termination Per (Year) (Month) (Week)
22. Date Terminated	Base ____ Overtime ____ Commissions ____ Bonus ____
24. Reason for Leaving	25. Position Held

Part IV - Authorized Signature - Federal statutes provide severe penalties for any fraud, intentional misrepresentation, or criminal connivance or conspiracy purposed to influence the issuance of any guaranty or insurance by the VA Secretary, the USDA, FmHA/FHA Commissioner, or the HUD/CPD Assistant Secretary.

26. Signature of Employer	27. Title (Please print or type)	28. Date

29. Print or type name signed in item 26

30. Phone No.

Fannie Mae
Form 1005 Mar. 90

FannieMae — Request for Verification of Deposit

Privacy Act Notice: This information is to be used by the agency collecting it or its assignees in determining whether you qualify as a prospective mortgagor under its program. It will not be disclosed outside the agency except as required and permitted by law. You do not have to provide this information, but if you do not your application for approval as a prospective mortgagor or borrower may be delayed or rejected. The information requested in this form is authorized by Title 38, USC, Chapter 37 (if VA); by 12 USC, Section 1701 et. seq. (if HUD/FHA); by 42 USC, Section 1452b (if HUD/CPD); and Title 42 USC, 1471 et. seq., or 7 USC, 1921 et. seq. (if USDA/FmHA).

Instructions: Lender - Complete items 1 through 8. Have applicant(s) complete item 9. Forward directly to depository named in item 1.
Depository - Please complete items 10 through 18 and return DIRECTLY in item 2.
The form is to be transmitted directly to the lender and is not to be transmitted through the applicant(s) or any other party.

Part I - Request

1. To (Name and address of depository)	2. From (Name and address of lender)

I certify that this verification has been sent directly to the bank or depository and has not passed through the hands of the applicant or any other party.

3. Signature of Lender	4. Title	5. Date	6. Lender's No. (Optional)

▶ 7. Information To Be Verified

Type of Account	Account in Name of	Account Number	Balance
			$
			$
			$
			$

To Depository: I/We have applied for a mortgage loan and stated in my financial statement that the balance on deposit with you is as shown above. You are authorized to verify this information and to supply the lender identified above with the information requested in items 10 through 13. Your response is solely a matter of courtesy for which no responsibility is attached to your institution or any of your officers.

8. Name and Address of Applicant(s)	9. Signature of Applicant(s)
	X
	X

To Be Completed by Depository
Part II - Verification of Depository

10. Deposit Accounts of Applicant(s)

Type of Account	Account Number	Current Balance	Average Balance For Previous Two Mos.	Date Opened
		$	$	
		$	$	
		$	$	
		$	$	

11. Loans Outstanding To Applicant(s)

Loan Number	Date of Loan	Original Amount	Current Balance	Installments(Monthly/Quarterly)	Secured By	No. of Late Pmts.
		$	$	$ per		
		$	$	$ per		
		$	$	$ per		

12. Please include any additional information which may be of assistance in determination of credit worthiness. (Please include information on loans paid-in-full in item 11 above.)

13. If the name(s) on the account(s) differ from those listed in item 7, please supply the name(s) on the account(s) as reflected by your records.

Part III - Authorized Signature - Federal statutes provide severe penalties for any fraud, intentional misrepresentation, or criminal connivance or conspiracy purposed to influence the issuance of any guaranty or insurance by the VA Secretary, the USDA, FmHA/PHA Commissioner, or the HUD/CPD Assistant Secretary.

14. Signature of Depository Representative	15. Title (Please print or type)	16. Date

17. Please print or type name signed in item 14

18. Phone No.

Fannie Mae
Form 1006 Mar. 90

GIFT LETTER

I/We _____ am/are
Clearly PRINT donor(s) name

making a bona fide gift of $ _____ to our _____
Relationship

for the purchase of the property located at

_____
Address

It is expressly understood that this is an outright gift from a relative and was not made available to the donor from any person or entity with an interest in the sale of the property including the seller, real estate agent or broker, builder, loan officer, or any entity associated with them.

It is also understood that the gift is not a loan in any form and that repayment, either in the form of services or cash, is not expected at this time or any time in the future.

I/We further certify that the funds used for this gift were not provided by anyone who directly or indirectly has any financial interest in the sale and/or conveyance of the above-mentioned property.

Notice to Borrower and Gift Donor

You and the donor should read the following "Gift Instructions" carefully and be prepared to follow these instructions <u>exactly</u>. It is important to prove transfer of the gift funds from the donor's account to your account before settlement or to prove the gift came from the donor when the gift funds are brought to settlement. If it is not possible to provide this documentation, please contact your Loan Officer or Mortgage Specialist to discuss available options.

By signing below, both borrower(s) and donor(s) acknowledge receipt of Gift Instructions.

_____.
Date

_____   _____
Donor's Signature   Donor's Signature

_____   _____
Donor's Address   Donor's Phone Number

_____   _____
Recipient's Signature   Recipient's Signature

(Tear here for copy of instructions)

GIFT INSTRUCTIONS

These requirements are subject to change if your loan type or product guidelines change.

Donor Information

☐ Provide donor's name, address, telephone number, and relationship to borrower and amount of gift. (*Conv. automated underwriting; FHA: automated underwriting and gift is already in borrower's account.*)

☐ Provide completed Gift Letter, signed by borrowers and donors (*Conv non-automated underwriting; FLEX 97; VA; FHA: non-automated underwriting or if gift not already in borrower's account.*)

Receipt of Gift Funds

If Gift Funds are to be provided prior to closing:
Provide cashier's check (or canceled personal check) from donor for the amount of the gift. The cashier's check must reference the donor's name as purchaser and be made payable to the borrower.

☐ (Applicable if checked.) If cashier's check is provided, also provide a withdrawal slip with donor's account number, name, and gift amount. If the withdrawal slip does not reference the donor's name, provide a blank deposit slip from the donor's account that shows the donor's name and account number. *(FHA)*

If Gift Funds are to be provided at closing:
Bring cashier's check from donor for the amount of the gift to the closing. The cashier's check must reference the donor's name as purchaser and be made payable to the closing agent.

☐ (Applicable if checked.) Also provide a withdrawal slip with donor's account number, name, and gift amount. If the withdrawal slip does not reference the donor's name, provide a blank deposit slip from the donor's account that shows the donor's name and account number. *(FHA.)*

Mortgage Insurance Premiums

These premiums and coverages will vary by company and
underwriting findings.

They also change periodically.

Monthly Premiums (per $1000 of loan amount /12)

LTV	COVERAGE	FIXED RATES 30 YEAR	15 YEAR	A.R.M.s 30 YEAR	15 YR
95.01–100%	35%	.96	.85	1.21	1.10
96.01–97%	18%	.59	.48	N/A	N/A
Flex 97	18%	.50	.45	N/A	N/A
90.01–95%	30%	.78	.67	.92	.81
85.01–90%	25%	.52	.41	.65	.54
80.01–85%	12%	.32	.21	.37	.26

There are one-time premiums available which can be financed or paid in cash.
Check with your lender for rates.

US Department of Housing
and Urban Development
Office of Housing
Federal Housing Commissioner

OMB Approval No: 2502-0538
(exp. 11/30/99)

For Your Protection: Get a Home Inspection

Name of Buyer _____

Property Address _____

What the FHA Does for Buyers... and What We Don't Do

What we do: FHA helps people become homeowners by insuring mortgages for lenders. This allows lenders to offer mortgages to first-time buyers and others who may not qualify for conventional loans. Because the FHA insures the loan for the lender, the buyer pays only a very low down-payment.

What we don't do: FHA does not guarantee the value or condition of your potential new home. If you find problems with your new home after closing, we can not give or lend you money for repairs, and we can not buy the home back from you.

That's why it's so important for you, the buyer, to get an independent home inspection. Ask a qualified home inspector to inspect your potential new home and give you the information you need to make a wise decision.

Appraisals and Home Inspections are Different

As part of our job insuring the loan, we require that the lender conduct an FHA appraisal. An appraisal is different from a home inspection. Appraisals are for lenders; home inspections are for buyers. The lender does an appraisal for three reasons:

· to estimate the value of a house
· to make sure that the house meets FHA minimum property standards
· to make sure that the house is marketable

Appraisals are not home inspections.

Why a Buyer Needs a Home Inspection

A home inspection gives the buyer more detailed information than an appraisal—information you need to make a wise decision. In a home inspection, a qualified inspector takes an in-depth, unbiased look at your potential new home to:

· evaluate the physical condition: structure, construction, and mechanical systems
· identify items that need to be repaired or replaced
· estimate the remaining useful life of the major systems, equipment, structure, and finishes

What Goes into a Home Inspection

A home inspection gives the buyer an impartial, physical evaluation of the overall condition of the home and items that need to be repaired or replaced. The inspection gives a detailed report on the condition of the structural components, exterior, roofing, plumbing, electrical, heating, insulation and ventilation, air conditioning, and interiors.

Be an Informed Buyer

It is your responsibility to be an informed buyer. Be sure that what you buy is satisfactory in every respect. You have the right to carefully examine your potential new home with a qualified home inspector. You may arrange to do so before signing your contract, or may do so after signing the contract as long as your contract states that the sale of the home depends on the inspection.

I understand the importance of getting an independent home inspection. I have thought about this before I signed a contract with the seller for a home.

X_____   X_____
Signature & Date   Signature & Date

Important Notice to Homebuyers

U.S. Department of Housing and Urban Development
Office of Housing – Federal Housing Commissioner 03303536

You must read this entire document at the time you apply for the loan.
Return one copy to lender as proof of notification and keep one copy for your records.

Condition of Property

The property you are buying is not HUD/FHA approved and HUD/FHA does not warrant the condition or the value of the property. An appraisal will be performed to estimate the value of the property, but this appraisal does not guarantee that the house is free of defects. You should inspect the property yourself very carefully or hire a professional inspection service to inspect the property for you. If you have a professional home inspection service perform an inspection of the property, you may include some of the cost of the inspection in your mortgage.

Interest Rate and Discount Points

- HUD does not regulate the interest rate or the discount points that may be paid by you or the seller or other third party. You should shop around to be sure you are satisfied with the loan terms offered and with the service reputation of the lender you have chosen.

- The interest rate, any discount points and the length of time the lender will honor the loan terms are all negotiated between you and the lender.

- The seller can pay the discount points, or a portion thereof, if you and the seller agree to such an arrangement.

- Lenders may agree to guarantee or "lock-in" the loan terms for a definite period of time (i.e., 15, 30, 60 days, etc.) or may permit your loan to be determined by future market conditions, also known as "floating." Lenders may require a fee to lock in the interest rate or the terms of the loan, but must provide a written agreement covering a minimum of 15 days before the anticipated closing. Your agreement with the lender will determine the degree, if any, that the interest rate and discount points may rise before closing.

- If the lender determines you are eligible for the mortgage, your agreement with the seller may require you to complete the transaction or lose your deposit on the property.

Don't Commit Loan Fraud

It is important for you to understand that you are required to provide complete and accurate information when applying for a mortgage loan.

- Do not falsify information about your income or assets.

- Disclose all loans and debts (including money that may have been borrowed to make the downpayment).

- Do not provide false letters-of-credit, cash-on-hand statements, gift letters or sweat equity letters.

- Do not accept funds to be used for your downpayment from any other party (seller, real estate salesperson, builder, etc.).

- Do not falsely certify that a property will be used for your primary residence when you are actually going to use it as a rental property.

- Do not act as a "strawbuyer" (somebody who purchases a property for another person and then transfers title of the property to that person), nor should you give that person personal or credit information for them to use in any such scheme.

- Do not apply for a loan by assuming the identity of another person.

- Do not sign documents in "blank."

Penalties for Loan Fraud: Federal laws provide severe penalties for fraud, misrepresentation, or conspiracy to influence wrongly the issuance of mortgage insurance by HUD. You can be subject to a possible prison term and fine of up to $10,000 for providing false information. Additionally, you could be prohibited from obtaining a HUD-insured loan for an indefinite period.

Report Loan Fraud: If you are aware of any fraud in HUD programs or if an individual tries to persuade you to make false statements on a loan application, you should report the matter by calling your nearest HUD office or the HUD Regional Inspector General, or call the HUD Hotline on 1(800) 347-3735.

Warning: It is a crime to knowingly make false statements to the United States Government on this or any similar form. Penalties upon conviction can include a fine and imprisonment. For details see: Title 18 U.S. Code Section 1001 and Section 1010.

Discrimination

If you believe you have been subject to discrimination because of race, color, religion, sex, handicap, familial status, or national origin, you should call HUD's **Fair Housing & Equal Opportunity Complaint Hotline: 1 (800) 669-9777.**

About Prepayment

This notice is to advise you of the requirements that must be followed to accomplish a prepayment of your mortgage, and to prevent accrual of any interest after the date of prepayment.

You may prepay any or all of the outstanding indebtedness due under your mortgage at any time, without penalty. However, to avoid the accrual of interest on any prepayment, the prepayment must be received on the installment due date (the first day of the month) if the lender stated this policy in its response for a payoff figure.

Otherwise, you may be required to pay interest on the amount prepaid through the end of the month. The lender can refuse to accept prepayment on any date other than the installment due date.

Form **HUD – 92900-B** (5/97)
ref. Handbooks 4150.1 & 4155.1

Note: If you are a first-time homebuyer and you received approved homeownership counseling, you may be entitled to a reduced up front mortgage insurance premium. Ask your lender for details.

Who May be Eligible for a Refund?

Premium Refund: You may be eligible for a refund of a portion of the insurance premium if you paid an up front mortgage insurance premium at settlement.
Review your settlement papers or check with your mortgage company to determine if you paid an up front premium.

Exceptions:

Assumptions: When a FHA insured loan is assumed the insurance remains in force (the seller receives no refund). The owner(s) of the property at the time the insurance is terminated is entitled to any refund.

FHA to FHA Refinance: When a FHA insured loan is refinanced, the refund from the old premium may be applied toward the up front premium required for the new loan.

Claims: When a mortgage company submits a claim to HUD for insurance benefits, no refund is due the homeowner.

How are Refunds Determined?

The FHA Commissioner determines how much of the up front premium is refunded when loans are terminated. Refunds are based on the number of months the loan is insured. After 84 months (7 years) no refund is due the homeowner.

How are Refunds Processed?

1. Mortgage company notifies HUD of insurance termination.

2. If you are eligible for a refund, HUD will either request Treasury to issue you a check directly or will send you an Application for Premium Refund (form HUD-27050-B).

3. Read the application carefully, sign, have it notarized, and attach proof of ownership at insurance termination.

4. Return application to the address shown on the HUD-27050-B.

5. HUD will request Treasury to issue a check if no additional information is needed.

How to Follow-Up

If you do not receive an application within 45 days after you have paid off your loan, check with your mortgage company to confirm that they have sent HUD a request for termination. If they confirm that the correct termination information was sent, contact HUD.

If you do not receive a refund or any other documentation from HUD within 60 days from the date you mailed your application, contact HUD immediately.

How to Contact HUD

By Phone:
800-697-6967
8:30 AM to 8:30 PM (EST)
Monday through Friday

By Mail:
U.S. Department of Housing & Urban Development
PO Box 23699
Washington, DC 20026-3699

Note: All inquiries should include your name, 10-digit FHA case number, paid in full date, property address, and a daytime phone number. Record your FHA case number here for future reference.

Important: The rules governing the eligibility for the premium refunds are based on the financial status of the FHA insurance fund and are subject to change.

SI USTED HABLA ESPANOL Y TIENE DIFICULTAD LEYENDO O HABLANDO INGLES, POR FAVOR LLAME A ESTE NUMERO TELEFONICO 800-697-6967.

You, the borrower(s), must be certain that you understand the transaction. Seek professional advice if you are uncertain.

Acknowledgement: I acknowledge that I have read and received a copy of this notice at the time of loan application. This notice does not constitute a contract or binding agreement. It is designed to provide current HUD/FHA policy regarding refunds.

X_____
Signature and Date

X_____
Signature and Date

X_____
Signature and Date

X_____
Signature and Date

INFORMED CONSUMER CHOICE DISCLOSURE NOTICE

In addition to an FHA-insured mortgage, you may also qualify for other mortgage products offered by your lender. To assure that you are aware of possible choices in financing, your lender has prepared a comparison of the typical costs of alternative conventional mortgage product(s) below, using representative loan amounts and costs (the actual loan amounts and associated costs shown below will vary from your own mortgage loan transaction). You should study the comparison carefully, ask questions, and determine which product is best for you. The information provided below was prepared as of May 2000.

Neither your lender nor FHA warrants that you actually qualify for any mortgage loan offered by your lender. This notice is provided to you to identify the key differences between these mortgage products offered by your lender. **This disclosure is not a contract and does not constitute loan approval.** Actual mortgage approval can only be made following a full underwriting analysis by your mortgage lender.

		FHA Financing 203(b) Fixed Rate	Conventional Financing 97% with Mortgage Insurance (MI)
1	Sales Price	$100,000	$100,000
2	Mortgage Amount	$97,750 ($99,950 w/ Upfront Mortgage Insurance Premium)	$97,000
3	Closing Costs	$2,000	$3,455
4	Downpayment Needed	$2,250	$3,000
5	Interest Rate and Term of Loan in Years	8.00%/30 Year Loan	8.00%/30 Year Loan
6	Monthly Payment (principal and interest only)	$733	$712
7	Loan-to-Value	99.95%	97%
8	Monthly Mortgage Insurance Premium (first year)	$41.65[1]	$40.42
9	Maximum Number of Years of Monthly Insurance Premium Payments	30 Years	Approx. 13 Years
10	Upfront Mortgage Insurance Premium (if applicable)	$2200[2] (Included in Mortgage Amount, line 2)	N/A

[1]Monthly mortgage insurance premiums are calculated on the average annual principal balance, i.e., as the amount you owe on the loan decreases each year, so does the amount of the monthly premium.
[2]Based on an upfront mortgage insurance premium rate available for first-time homebuyers who obtain housing counseling.

FHA Mortgage Insurance Premium Information:

If you paid an upfront mortgage insurance premium, you will also be charged a monthly mortgage insurance premium for the period of time shown below, based on the initial loan-to-value and term of your mortgage. You are required to make these payments on your FHA-insured loan for the time shown unless you refinance or the mortgage is otherwise paid in full. (If you were *not* charged an upfront premium, as for example on condominiums, you will pay the monthly premium for the life of the mortgage.)

If the term of your mortgage will be greater than 15 years and with a loan-to-value ratio:	You will make mortgage insurance premium payments for:
Of 89.99 or Less	7 Years
Between 90.00 and 95.00	12 Years
Of 95.01 and Greater	30 Years

If the term of your mortgage will be 15 years or less and with a loan-to-value ratio:	You will make mortgage insurance premium payments for:
Of 89.99 or Less	None Required
Between 90.00 and 95.00	4 Years
Of 95.01 and Greater	8 Years

I/We have received a copy of this disclosure.

_____   _____   _____   _____
Borrower   Date   Borrower   Date

_____   _____   _____   _____
Borrower   Date   Borrower   Date

DISCLOSURE BOOKLET ACKNOWLEDGEMENT

Borrower's Certification & Authorization

Authorization to Release Information

Privacy Act Statement (If VA loan) – This information is to be used by the Department of Veteran Affairs (VA) in determining whether you qualify as a prospective mortgagor for mortgage or guaranty. This information will not be disclosed outside the Department without your consent except to financial institutions for verification of your deposits and as required and permitted by law. You do not have to give us this information, but, if you do not, your application for approval as a prospective mortgagor for mortgage guaranty may be delayed or rejected. This information request is authorized by Title 38, U.S.C., Chapter 37.

Privacy Act Statement (If HUD/FHA loan) – **Notice to Borrowers:** This is notice to you as required by the Right to Financial Privacy Act of 1978 that HUD/FHA has a right of access to financial records held by financial institutions in connection with the consideration or administration of assistance to you. Financial records involving your transaction will be available to HUD/FHA without further notice or authorization but will not be disclosed or released by this institution to another Government Agency or Department without your consent except as required or permitted by law.

Certification

1.   I/We have applied for a mortgage loan from   . ("Lender"). In applying for the loan, I/we have completed a loan application containing various information on the purpose of the loan, the amount and source of the downpayment, employment and income information, and assets and liabilities. I/We certify that all of the information is true and complete. I/We made no misrepresentations in the loan application or other documents, nor did I/we omit any pertinent information.

2.   I/We understand and agree that Lender reserves the right to change the mortgage loan review process to a full documentation program. This would mean that a limited documentation program may be changed to a full documentation program which would include verifying the information provided on the application with the employer and/or financial institution.

3.   I/We have not been induced by Lender, or any of its employees, to leave any answers blank or conceal or misrepresent, in any way, any information required to be provided on the loan application.

4.   I/We fully understand that it is a Federal crime punishable by fine or imprisonment, or both, to knowingly make any false statements when applying for this mortgage, as applicable under the provisions of Title 18, United States Code (USC), Section 1014.

To whom it may concern:

1.   I/We have applied for a mortgage loan from   ("Lender"). As part of the application process, Lender and any investor to whom it may sell my loan may verify information contained in my/our loan application and in other documents required in connection with the loan either before the loan is closed or as part of its quality control program. This includes relevant tax information from the IRS. If this information is to be used in connection with the processing of my mortgage loan application, I authorize Lender to certify my past and present employment earning records, bank accounts, stock holdings and any other asset balances that are needed to process my mortgage loan application. I further authorize Lender to order a residential mortgage credit report and verify other credit information, including past and present mortgage and landlord references.

2.   In an effort to maintain quality lending standards, and in compliance with federal-agency regulations, Lender reviews a random sample of real estate loans settled. I understand the need for a quality control review and if my loan is selected, I authorize the release to Lender and to any investor that purchased the loan from it, and to the mortgage guaranty insurer (if any), any and all information relating to my creditworthiness including, but not limited to, information from my employer(s), financial institutions where I have assets on deposit, a credit agency, income tax returns or my creditors.

3.   Lender, or any investor that purchases the loan, may address this authorization to any party named in the loan application.

4.   A copy of this authorization may be accepted as original.

5.   Mortgage guaranty insurer (if any): _____

I acknowledge the receipt of the following disclosures:

Partial Interest Payment Disclosure.. I do _____   I do not _____ wish to participate in the   program.
                  Privacy Policy... I do _____   I do not _____ wish to have my name and address made available to third party vendors.
Residential Loan Application Addendum
HUD Important Notice to Homebuyers (if applicable)
HUD Informed Consumer Choice Disclosure
Reinsurance Disclosure Form (if applicable)
Hazard Insurance Information
Mortgage Transfer Disclosure Statement
Accidental Death Insurance Information
Borrower's Certification & Authorization
Financing Agreement
Settlement Costs and Helpful Information Booklet

FOR INTERNAL USE ONLY	
Loan #:	_____
Loan Type:	_____
Product:	_____
Borrower:	_____
Budget Center:	_____

I acknowledge receipt for the fees collected:

$_____	Application Fee*	$_____	Other Fee _____
$_____	Appraisal Fee	$_____	Other Fee _____
$_____	Credit Report Fee	$_____	Other Fee _____

Property Address: _____

X _____   X _____
    Applicant – Signature and Date   Co-Applicant – Signature and Date

X _____   X _____
    Co-Applicant – Signature and Date   Co-Applicant – Signature and Date

X _____
    Lender's Representative – Signature and Date

*Application Fee may be used to pay for appraisal and credit reports   Original to Lender; Copy to Borrower

F.H.A. ASSUMPTION CHART

	INVESTOR ASSUMING FROM INVESTOR	INVESTOR ASSUMING FROM OWNER-OCCUPANT	OWNER-OCCUPANT ASSUMING FROM INVESTOR	OWNER-OCCUPANT ASSUMING FROM OWNER-OCCUPANT
MORTGAGE ORIGINATED* PRIOR TO 12/01/86				
PAYDOWN TO 75% LTV?	NO	NO	NO	NO
CREDITWORTHINESS REVIEW NECESSARY?**	NO	NO	NO	NO
MORTGAGE ORIGINATED* ON OR AFTER 12/01/86 BUT PRIOR TO 02/05/88				
PAY DOWN TO 75% LTV?	NO	NO	NO	NO
CREDIT WORTHINESS REVIEW NECESSARY?**	THE FIRST 24 MONTHS AFTER SETTLEMENT.	THE FIRST 12 MONTHS AFTER SETTLEMENT.	THE FIRST 24 MONTHS AFTER SETTLEMENT.	THE FIRST 12 MONTHS AFTER SETTLEMENT.
MORTGAGE ORIGINATED* ON OR AFTER 02/05/88 BUT PRIOR TO 12/15/89				
PAY DOWN TO 75% LTV?	YES, IF ORIGINAL BORROWER IS RELEASED.	YES, IF ORIGINAL BORROWER IS RELEASED.	N/A	NO
CREDIT WORTHINESS REVIEW NECESSARY?**	THE FIRST 24 MONTHS AFTER SETTLEMENT.	THE FIRST 12 MONTHS AFTER SETTLEMENT.	THE FIRST 24 MONTHS AFTER SETTLEMENT.	THE FIRST 12 MONTHS AFTER SETTLEMENT.
MORTGAGE ORIGINATED* ON OR AFTER 12/15/89				
PAY DOWN TO 75% LTV?	NOT ELIGIBLE	NOT ELIGIBLE	N/A	NO
CREDIT WORTHINESS REVIEW NECESSARY?	NOT ELIGIBLE	NOT ELIGIBLE	N/A	FOR THE LIFE OF THE MORTGAGE.

*ORIGINATION DATE REFERS TO THE FOLLOWING:
    12/01/86: DATE APPLICATION WAS SIGNED.
    02/05/88 and 12/15/89: DATE APPRAISED VALUE WAS APPROVED BY THE D.E. UNDERWRITER OR THE
                CONDITIONAL COMMITMENT WAS ISSUED.

**PLEASE NOTE THAT THE CREDITWORTHINESS REVIEW IS ALWAYS REQUIRED IF THERE IS A REQUEST BY THE SELLER TO BE
RELEASED FROM LIABILITY.

```
                    V.A. NET INCOME RESIDUAL QUALIFYING
-----------------------------------------------------------------------------
INCOME:
        Borrower's Base Monthly Income:......................+$_____

        Other:...............................................+$_____

        Co-Borrower's Base Monthly Income:...................+$_____

        Other:...............................................+$_____

        Real Estate Income:..................................+$_____
            (VA=80% of Gross rent, 90% on subject property)
        Total Monthly Effective Income:......................+$_____

        Minus Federal Taxes(monthly withholding)..............-$_____
        (Do not count rental income, child support or tax free
        income in taxable income).
        NET EFFECTIVE INCOME:............................(A)=$_____
HOUSING EXPENSE:                                               --------------
        Principal and Interest:..............................+$_____

        Hazard(Homeowner's) Insurance(1/12th):...............+$_____

        Property Taxes(1/12th):..............................+$_____

        TOTAL MORTGAGE PAYMENT(PITI):.......................=$_____

        Maintenance and common Expense(get from lender or VA).+$_____

        Utilities(get from lender or VA):....................+$_____

        TOTAL HOUSING EXPENSE:...........................(B)=$_____
DEBTS:                                                        --------------
        State and Local Income Tax(monthly withholding):.....+$_____

        Social Security(monthly withholding):................+$_____

        Total Recurring Installment Payments(6 months+).......+$_____

        Child Support and/or Child Care(monthly):............+$_____

        TOTAL RECURRING DEBTS:..............................=$_____

        Add Total Housing Expense(B):........................+$_____

        TOTAL FIXED PAYMENTS:............................(C)=$_____
RESIDUAL INCOME:                                              --------------
        Net Effective Income(A):.............................+$_____

        Minus Total Fixed Payments(C):.......................-$_____
        RESIDUAL INCOME:(see Chart in section on VA):.......(D)=$_____
-----------------------------------------------------------------------------
        PROPOSED HOUSE PAYMENT(PITI):........................+$_____

        LONG TERM MONTHLY DEBT PAYMENTS:.....................+$_____

        TOTAL MONTHLY HOUSE AND DEBT PAYMENTS:...............=$_____

        DIVIDED BY GROSS MONTHLY INCOME......................./$_____
        SHOULD NOT EXCEED 41%................................=$_____
        (This can be exceeded with compensating factors.)     --------------
```

Worksheet for Computing Guaranty
Under Public Law 100-198

HOME LOANS

1. Proposed Loan Amount: $_____
   If loan is $45,000 or less, complete item 2.
   If loan is over $45,000, complete item 3.

2. If item 1 is $45,000 or less, multiply item 1
   by 0.50 and show product here and in item 4: $_____
   (Skip to item 4).

3. If item 1 is over $45,000, multiply item 1
   by 0.40 and show product: $_____

   (a) If product is less than $22,500,
        enter $22,500 in item 4.

   (b) If product is greater than $22,500,
        but does not exceed $36,000, enter
        the amount in item 4.

   (c) If product is over $36,000, enter
        $36,000 in item 4.

4. Preliminary guaranty amount: $_____

5. Show the amount of guaranty used by the
   veteran that has not been restored: $_____

6. Final guaranty amount: $_____
   (Subtract item 5 from item 4).

7. Percentage of loan to be guaranteed: _____%
   (Divide the amount in item 6 by the amount in
   item 1).

U.S. DEPARTMENT OF HOUSING AND URBAN DEVELOPMENT

WATCH OUT FOR LEAD-BASED PAINT POISONING

NOTIFICATION

TO: PURCHASERS OF HOUSING CONSTRUCTED BEFORE 1978

If the building was constructed before 1978, there is a possibility that it may contain lead-based paint.

PLEASE READ THE FOLLOWING INFORMATION CONCERNING LEAD PAINT POISONING

The interiors of older homes and apartments often have layers of lead-based paint on the walls, ceilings, window sills and door frames. Lead-based paint and primers may also have been used on outside porches, railings, garages, fire escapes and lamp posts. When the paint chips, flakes or peels off, there may be a real danger for babies and young children.

Children may eat paint chips or chew on painted railings, window sills or other items when parents are not around. Children can also ingest lead even if they do not specifically eat paint chips. For example, when children play in an area where there are loose paint or dust particles containing lead, they may get these particles on their hands, put their hands into their mouths, and ingest a dangerous amount of lead.

Has your child been especially cranky or irritable? Is he or she eating normally? Does your child have stomachaches and vomiting? Does he or she complain about headaches? Is your child unwilling to play? These may be signs of lead poisoning, although many times there are no symptoms at all. Lead poisoning can eventually cause mental retardation, blindness and even death.

If you suspect that your child has eaten chips of paint or someone told you this, you should take your child to the doctor or clinic for testing. If the test shows that your child has an elevated blood lead level, treatment is available. Contact your doctor or local health department for help or more information. Lead screening and treatment are available through the Medicaid Program for those who are eligible.

Inform other family members and baby-sitters of the dangers of lead-poisoning. You can safeguard your child from lead poisoning by preventing him or her from eating paint that may contain lead.

Look at your walls, ceilings, door frames, window sills. Are there places where the paint is peeling, flaking or chipping? If so, there are some things you can do immediately to protect your child:

    (1) Cover all furniture and appliances;

    (2) Get a broom or stiff brush and remove all loose pieces of paint from walls, woodwork and ceilings;

    (3) Sweep up all pieces of paint and plaster and put them in a paper bag or wrap them in newspaper. Put these packages in the trash can. DO NOT BURN THEM;

    (4) Do not leave paint chips on the floor. Damp mop floors in and around the work area to remove all dust and paint particles. Keeping the floor clear of paint chips, dust and dirt is easy and very important; and

    (5) Do not allow loose paint to remain within your children's reach since children may pick loose paint off the lower part of the walls.

AS A HOMEOWNER:

You should keep your home in good shape. Water leaks from faulty plumbing, defective roofs or exterior holes and breaks may admit rain or dampness into the interior of your home, damaging walls or ceilings, causing paint to peel, crack or flake. These conditions should be corrected immediately. Before repainting, all surfaces that are peeling, chipping or loose should be thoroughly cleaned by washing, sanding, or brushing the loose paint from the surface; then repaint with two (2) coats of non-leaded paint; or cover the surface with other material such as wallpaper or paneling. SIMPLY PAINTING OVER DETERIORATED PAINTED SURFACES DOES NOT REMOVE THE HAZARD.

When lead-based paint is removed by scraping or sanding, a dust is created, which may be hazardous. The dust can enter the body either by breathing or swallowing it. The use of heat or paint removers could create a vapor or fume which may cause poisoning if inhaled over a long period of time. The removal of lead-based paint should not be undertaken by amateurs and every precaution should be taken to safeguard workers and occupants during the removal process. Whenever possible, the removal of lead based paint should take place when there are no children and pregnant women on the premises.

I have received a copy of the Notice entitled "Watch Out for Lead Paint Poisoning".

          DATE   SIGNATURE

Form 4720 (8711)

Self-Employed Income Analysis

Borrower Name

Property Address

General Instructions: This form is to be used as a guide in Underwriting the Self-employed borrower. The underwriter has a choice in analyzing the Individual Tax return by either the Schedule Analysis Method or the Adjusted Gross Income (AGI) Method. The Schedule Analysis Method derives only self-employed income by analyzing Schedules C, D, F, K-1, and 2106. Non-business income such as dividends, interest, and rental income should be summarized separately on the loan application.

Schedule Analysis Method

		19__	19__	19__
A.	Individual Tax Return (Form 1040)			
1.	Schedule C:			
	a. Net Profit or Loss			
	b. Depletion	(+)		
	c. Depreciation	(+)		
	d. Less: 20% Exclusion for Meals and Entertainment	(−)		
2.	Schedule D			
	Recurring Capital Gains	(+)		
3.	Schedule F			
	a. Net Profit or Loss			
	b. Depreciation	(+)		
4.	Schedule K-1			
	a. Form 1065, Partnership Ordinary Income (Loss) +Guaranteed Payments			
	b. Form 1120-s Ordinary Income (Loss) + Other Income (Loss)			
5.	Schedule 2106			
	Total Expenses	(−)		
6.	W-2 income from Corporation	(+)		
7.	Total			

Complete sections B, C, and D only if the borrower needs more income to qualify for the loan than is shown in section A and the borrower has the legal right to draw additional income from the business to qualify for the loan.

		19__	19__	19__
B.	Corporate Tax Return Form (1120) - Corporate income to qualify the borrower will be considered only if the borrower can provide evidence of access to the funds			
1.	Taxable Income (Tax and Payments Section)	(+)		
2.	Total Tax (Tax and Payments Section)	(−)		
3.	Depreciation (Deductions Section)	(+)		
4.	Depletion (Deductions Section)	(+)		
5.	Mortgages, notes, bonds payable in less than one year (Balance Sheets Section)	(−)		
6.	Subtotal			
7.	Times individual percentage of ownership	X ____ %	X ____ %	X ____ %
8.	Subtotal			
9.	Dividend Income reflected on borrower's individual income tax returns	(−)		
10.	Total Income available to borrower			

C.	S Corporation Tax Returns (Form 1120s) or Partnership Tax Returns (Form 1065) - Partnership or S Corporation income to qualify the borrower will be considered only if the borrower can provide evidence of access to the funds.			
1.	Depreciation (Deductions Section)	(+)		
2.	Depletion (Deductions Section)	(+)		
3.	Mortgages, notes, bonds payable in less than one year (Balance Sheets Section)	(−)		
4.	Subtotal			
5.	Times individual percentage of ownership	X ____ %	X ____ %	X ____ %
6.	Total income available to borrower			
	Total Income Available (add A, B, C)	I	II	III

D. Year-to-Date Profit and Loss
Year-to-date income to qualify the borrower will be considered only if that income is in line with the previous year's earnings or if audited financial statements are provided.

1.	Salary/Draws to Individual				$ ____
2.	Total Allowable add back	$ ____	X ____	% of individual ownership =	$ ____
3.	Total net profit	$ ____	X ____	% of individual ownership =	$ ____
4.	Total				$ ____

Combined Total I, II, III, YTD = $ _____ divided by _____ months = $ _____ Monthly Average

This form is only a reference to help organize information from the tax returns. You must refer to the selling guide for our complete underwriting requirements on the self-employed.

A. **Settlement Statement**

U.S. Department of Housing and Urban Development

OMB Approval No. 2502-0265

B. Type of Loan

1. ☐ FHA 2. ☐ FmHA 3. ☐ Conv. Unins. 4. ☐ VA 5. ☐ Conv. Ins.	6. File Number: 7. Loan Number: 8. Mortgage Insurance Case Number:

C. Note: This form is furnished to give you a statement of actual settlement costs. Amounts paid to and by the settlement agent are shown. Items marked "(p.o.c.)" were paid outside the closing; they are shown here for informational purposes and are not included in the totals.

D. Name & Address of Borrower:	E. Name & Address of Seller:	F. Name & Address of Lender:

G. Property Location:	H. Settlement Agent:
	Place of Settlement: I. Settlement Date:

J. Summary of Borrower's Transaction		**K. Summary of Seller's Transaction**	
100. Gross Amount Due From Borrower		**400. Gross Amount Due To Seller**	
101. Contract sales price		401. Contract sales price	
102. Personal property		402. Personal property	
103. Settlement charges to borrower (line 1400)		403.	
104.		404.	
105.		405.	
Adjustments for items paid by seller in advance		**Adjustments for items paid by seller in advance**	
106. City/town taxes to		406. City/town taxes to	
107. County taxes to		407. County taxes to	
108. Assessments to		408. Assessments to	
109.		409.	
110.		410.	
111.		411.	
112.		412.	
120. Gross Amount Due From Borrower		**420. Gross Amount Due To Seller**	
200. Amounts Paid By Or In Behalf Of Borrower		**500. Reductions In Amount Due To Seller**	
201. Deposit or earnest money		501. Excess deposit (see instructions)	
202. Principal amount of new loan(s)		502. Settlement charges to seller (line 1400)	
203. Existing loan(s) taken subject to		503. Existing loan(s) taken subject to	
204.		504. Payoff of first mortgage loan	
205.		505. Payoff of second mortgage loan	
206.		506.	
207.		507.	
208.		508.	
209.		509.	
Adjustments for items unpaid by seller		**Adjustments for items unpaid by seller**	
210. City/town taxes to		510. City/town taxes to	
211. County taxes to		511. County taxes to	
212. Assessments to		512. Assessments to	
213.		513.	
214.		514.	
215.		515.	
216.		516.	
217.		517.	
218.		518.	
219.		519.	
220. Total Paid By/For Borrower		**520. Total Reduction Amount Due Seller**	
300. Cash At Settlement From/To Borrower		**600. Cash At Settlement To/From Seller**	
301. Gross Amount due from borrower (line 120)		601. Gross amount due to seller (line 420)	
302. Less amounts paid by/for borrower (line 220)	( )	602. Less reductions in amt. due seller (line 520)	( )
303. Cash ☐ From ☐ To Borrower		**603. Cash** ☐ To ☐ From Seller	

Section 5 of the Real Estate Settlement Procedures Act (RESPA) requires the following: • HUD must develop a Special Information Booklet to help persons borrowing money to finance the purchase of residential real estate to better understand the nature and costs of real estate settlement services; • Each lender must provide the booklet to all applicants from whom it receives or for whom it prepares a written application to borrow money to finance the purchase of residential real estate; • Lenders must prepare and distribute with the Booklet a Good Faith Estimate of the settlement costs that the borrower is likely to incur in connection with the settlement. These disclosures are manadatory.

Section 4(a) of RESPA mandates that HUD develop and prescribe this standard form to be used at the time of loan settlement to provide full disclosure of all charges imposed upon the borrower and seller. These are third party disclosures that are designed to provide the borrower with pertinent information during the settlement process in order to be a better shopper.

The Public Reporting Burden for this collection of information is estimated to average one hour per response, including the time for reviewing instructions, searching existing data sources, gathering and maintaining the data needed, and completing and reviewing the collection of information.

This agency may not collect this information, and you are not required to complete this form, unless it displays a currently valid OMB control number.

The information requested does not lend itself to confidentiality.

L. Settlement Charges

			Paid From Borrowers Funds at Settlement	Paid From Seller's Funds at Settlement
700.	**Total Sales/Broker's Commission based on price $** @ % =			
	Division of Commission (line 700) as follows:			
701.	$ to			
702.	$ to			
703.	Commission paid at Settlement			
704.				
800.	**Items Payable In Connection With Loan**			
801.	Loan Origination Fee %			
802.	Loan Discount %			
803.	Appraisal Fee to			
804.	Credit Report to			
805.	Lender's Inspection Fee			
806.	Mortgage Insurance Application Fee to			
807.	Assumption Fee			
808.				
809.				
810.				
811.				
900.	**Items Required By Lender To Be Paid In Advance**			
901.	Interest from to @$ /day			
902.	Mortgage Insurance Premium for months to			
903.	Hazard Insurance Premium for years to			
904.	years to			
905.				
1000.	**Reserves Deposited With Lender**			
1001.	Hazard insurance months @ $ per month			
1002.	Mortgage insurance months @ $ per month			
1003.	City property taxes months @ $ per month			
1004.	County property taxes months @ $ per month			
1005.	Annual assessments months @ $ per month			
1006.	months @ $ per month			
1007.	months @ $ per month			
1008.	months @ $ per month			
1100.	**Title Charges**			
1101.	Settlement or closing fee to			
1102.	Abstract or title search to			
1103.	Title examination to			
1104.	Title insurance binder to			
1105.	Document preparation to			
1106.	Notary fees to			
1107.	Attorney's fees to			
	(includes above items numbers:)			
1108.	Title insurance to			
	(includes above items numbers:)			
1109.	Lender's coverage $			
1110.	Owner's coverage $			
1111.				
1112.				
1113.				
1200.	**Government Recording and Transfer Charges**			
1201.	Recording fees: Deed $; Mortgage $; Releases $			
1202.	City/county tax/stamps: Deed $; Mortgage $			
1203.	State tax/stamps: Deed $; Mortgage $			
1204.				
1205.				
1300.	**Additional Settlement Charges**			
1301.	Survey to			
1302.	Pest inspection to			
1303.				
1304.				
1305.				
1400.	**Total Settlement Charges (enter on lines 103, Section J and 502, Section K)**			

TRUTH-IN-LENDING DISCLOSURE STATEMENT
(THIS IS NEITHER A CONTRACT NOR A COMMITMENT TO LEND)

LENDER OR LENDER'S AGENT:

[X] Preliminary [ ] Final
DATE:
LOAN NO.:
Type of Loan: Purchase
Conventional
Primary

BORROWERS:

ADDRESS:
CITY/STATE/ZIP:
PROPERTY:

ANNUAL PERCENTAGE RATE	FINANCE CHARGE	Amount Financed	Total of Payments
The cost of your credit as a yearly rate.	The dollar amount the credit will cost you.	The amount of credit provided to you or on your behalf.	The amount you will have paid after you have made all payments as scheduled.
8.3867	559,148.46	319,828.81	878,977.27

PAYMENT SCHEDULE:

NUMBER OF PAYMENTS	AMOUNT OF PAYMENTS	PAYMENTS ARE DUE BEGINNING	NUMBER OF PAYMENTS	AMOUNT OF PAYMENTS	PAYMENTS ARE DUE BEGINNING
359	2,441.62	11/1/00			
1	2,435.69	10/1/2030			

DEMAND FEATURE: [X] This loan does not have a Demand Feature. [ ] This loan has a Demand Feature as follows:

VARIABLE RATE FEATURE:
[ ] This Loan has a Variable Rate Feature. Variable Rate Disclosures have been provided to you earlier.

SECURITY: You are giving a security interest in the property located at:

ASSUMPTION: Someone buying this property [X] cannot assume the remaining balance due under original mortgage terms
[ ] may assume, subject to lender's conditions, the remaining balance due under original mortgage terms.

FILING / RECORDING FEES: $

PROPERTY INSURANCE: [X] Property hazard insurance in the amount of $ 0.00 with a mortgagee clause to the lender
is a required condition of this loan. Borrower may purchase this insurance from any insurance company acceptable to the lender.
Hazard insurance [ ] is [X] is not available through the lender at an estimated cost of for a year term.

LATE CHARGES: If your payment is more than 15 days late, you will be charged a late charge of 5.00 % of the overdue payment.

PREPAYMENT: If you pay off your loan early, you
[ ] may [X] will not have to pay a penalty.
[ ] may [X] will not be entitled to a refund of part of the finance charge.

See your contract documents for any additional information regarding non-payment, default, required repayment in full before scheduled date, and prepayment refunds and penalties.
e means estimate

I/We hereby acknowledge reading and receiving a complete copy of this disclosure.

95%

_____ | _____
BORROWER/DATE | BORROWER/DATE

_____ | _____
BORROWER/DATE | BORROWER/DATE

NOTICE OF RIGHT TO CANCEL

YOUR RIGHT TO CANCEL:

You are entering into a transaction that will result in a security interest in your home. You have a legal right under federal law to cancel this transaction, without cost, within three business days from whichever of the following three events occurs last:

(1) the date of the transaction which is _____ ; or

(2) the date you received your Truth in Lending disclosures; or

(3) the date you received this notice of your right to cancel.

The box indicated below, if checked, applies only to you if your loan is to increase the amount of credit already provided to you.

☐ If this is a new transaction to increase the amount of credit provided to you, your cancellation will apply only to the increase in the amount of credit. It will not affect the amount you presently owe or the security interest we already have in your home.

HOW TO CANCEL:

If you decide to cancel this transaction, you may do so by notifying us, in writing, at

_____

You may use any written statement that is signed, dated and states your intention to cancel this transaction, or you may use this notice by dating and signing below. If you use this notice, you may want to make a copy since it contains important information about your rights and it is proof of when you cancelled.

If you cancel by mail or telegram, the notice must be sent no later than midnight of _____ or midnight of the third business day after the latest of the three events listed above. If you use any other means to cancel, it must be delivered to the above address no later than that time.

I HEREBY CANCEL THIS TRANSACTION _____

(Customer's Signature)   (Date)

If you cancel the transaction, the security interest is also cancelled. Within 20 days of receiving of your notice, we must take the steps necessary to reflect the fact that the security interest in your home has been cancelled and we must return to you any money or property you have given to us or to anyone else in connection with this transaction. If we have given you any money or property, you may keep it until we have performed our obligations. You must then offer to return the money or property; if the return of the property itself is impractical or unfair, you must offer its reasonable value. You may offer to return the property at your home or at the location of the property. Money must be returned to the address indicated above. If we do not take possession of the money or property within 20 days of your offer, you may keep it without further obligation.

CUSTOMER'S CERTIFICATION

I HEREBY CERTIFY THAT I HAVE RECEIVED TWO COPIES OF THE ABOVE NOTICE

A Summary Appraisal Report
Property Description

UNIFORM RESIDENTIAL APPRAISAL REPORT

File No. sample

Property Address				City		State VA	Zip Code
Legal Description						County	
Assessor's Parcel No.				Tax Year	R.E. Taxes $	Special Assessments $	

Borrower		Current Owner			Occupant:	Owner	Tenant	Vacant

Property rights appraised [ ] Fee Simple [ ] Leasehold   Project Type [ ] PUD [ ] Condominium (HUD/VA only) HOA$ /Mo.

Neighborhood or Project Name _____ Map Reference _____ Census Tract _____

Sale Price $	Date of Sale	Description and $ amount of loan charges/concessions to be paid by seller
Lender/Client		Address

Appraiser Heritage Appraisal Services   Address 1340 Seminole Trail, Charlottesville, Virginia 22901

Location	Urban	Suburban	Rural	Predominant	Single family housing		Present land use %	Land use change
					PRICE $(000)	AGE (yrs)		
Built up	Over 75%	25-75%	Under 25%	occupancy			One family	Not likely Likely
Growth rate	Rapid	Stable	Slow	Owner	Low		2-4 family	In process
Property values	Increasing	Stable	Declining	Tenant	High		Multi-family	To:
Demand/supply	Shortage	In balance	Over supply	Vacant (0-5%)	Predominant		Commercial	
Marketing time	Under 3 mos.	3-6 mos.	Over 6 mos.	Vacant (over 5%)			Vacant	

Note: Race and the racial composition of the neighborhood are not appraisal factors.

Neighborhood boundaries and characteristics: _____

Factors that affect the marketability of the properties in the neighborhood (proximity to employment and amenities, employment stability, appeal to market, etc.): _____

Market conditions in the subject neighborhood (including support for the above conclusions related to the trend of property values, demand/supply, and marketing time - - such as data on competitive properties for sale in the neighborhood, description of the prevalence of sales and financing concessions, etc.): _____

Project Information for PUDs (If applicable) - - Is the developer/builder in control of the Home Owner's Association (HOA)?   [ ] Yes [ ] No

Approximate total number of units in the subject project _____   Approximate total number of units for sale in the subject project _____

Describe common elements and recreational facilities: _____

Dimensions		Topography	
Site area		Size	
Specific zoning classification and description	Corner Lot [ ] Yes [ ] No	Shape	
Zoning compliance [ ] Legal [ ] Legal nonconforming (Grandfathered use) [ ] Illegal [ ] No zoning		Drainage	
Highest & best use as improved: [ ] Present use [ ] Other use (explain)		View	

Utilities	Public	Other	Off-site Improvements	Type	Public	Private	Landscaping	
Electricity			Street				Driveway surface	
Gas			Curb/gutter				Apparent easements	
Water			Sidewalk				FEMA Special Flood Hazard Area [ ] Yes [ ] No	
Sanitary sewer			Street lights				FEMA Zone ___ Map Date ___	
Storm sewer			Alley				FEMA Map No.	

Comments (apparent adverse easements, encroachments, special assessments, slide areas, illegal or legal nonconforming zoning use, etc.): _____

GENERAL DESCRIPTION	EXTERIOR DESCRIPTION	FOUNDATION	BASEMENT	INSULATION
No. of Units	Foundation	Slab	Area Sq. Ft.	Roof
No. of Stories	Exterior Walls	Crawl Space	% Finished	Ceiling
Type (Det./Att.)	Roof Surface	Basement	Ceiling	Walls
Design (Style)	Gutters & Dwnspts.	Sump Pump	Walls	Floor
Existing/Proposed	Window Type	Dampness	Floor	None
Age (Yrs.)	Storm/Screens	Settlement	Outside Entry	Unknown
Effective Age (Yrs.)	Manufactured House	Infestation		

ROOMS	Foyer	Living	Dining	Kitchen	Den	Family Rm.	Rec. Rm.	Bedrooms	# Baths	Laundry	Other	Area Sq. Ft.
Basement												
Level 1												
Level 2												

Finished area **above** grade contains: _____ Rooms; _____ Bedroom(s); _____ Bath(s); _____ Square Feet of Gross Living Area

INTERIOR	Materials/Condition	HEATING	KITCHEN EQUIP.	ATTIC	AMENITIES	CAR STORAGE:
Floors		Type	Refrigerator	None	Fireplace(s) #	None
Walls		Fuel	Range/Oven	Stairs	Patio	Garage # of cars
Trim/Finish		Condition	Disposal	Drop Stair	Deck	Attached
Bath Floor		COOLING	Dishwasher	Scuttle	Porch	Detached
Bath Wainscot		Central	Fan/Hood	Floor	Fence	Built-In
Doors		Other	Microwave	Heated	Pool	Carport
		Condition	Washer/Dryer	Finished		Driveway

Additional features (special energy efficient items, etc.): _____

Condition of the improvements, depreciation (physical, functional and external), repairs needed, quality of construction, remodeling/additions, etc.: _____

Adverse environmental conditions (such as, but not limited to, hazardous wastes, toxic substances, etc.) present in the improvements, on the site, or in the immediate vicinity of the subject property: _____

HERITAGE APPRAISAL SERVICES

Valuation Section   **File No.** sample

COST APPROACH

ESTIMATED SITE VALUE . . . . = $ _____

ESTIMATED REPRODUCTION COST-NEW-OF IMPROVEMENTS:

Dwelling _____ Sq. Ft. @ _____ = $ _____

_____ Sq. Ft. @ _____ = _____

= _____

Garage/Carport _____ Sq. Ft. @ _____ = _____

Total Estimated Cost New . . . . = $ _____

Physical   Functional   External

Less

Depreciation _____ | _____ | _____ = $ _____

Depreciated Value of Improvements . . . . = $ _____

"As-is" Value of Site Improvements . . . . = $ _____

INDICATED VALUE BY COST APPROACH . . . . = $

Comments on Cost Approach (such as, source of cost estimate, site value, square foot calculation and for HUD, VA and FmHA, the estimated remaining economic life of the property): _____

SALES COMPARISON ANALYSIS

ITEM	SUBJECT	COMPARABLE NO. 1		COMPARABLE NO. 2		COMPARABLE NO. 3	
Address							
Proximity to Subject							
Sales Price	$		$		$		$
Price/Gross Liv. Area	$	$		$		$	
Data and/or Verification Source							
VALUE ADJUSTMENTS	DESCRIPTION	DESCRIPTION	+ (-) $ Adjustment	DESCRIPTION	+ (-) $ Adjustment	DESCRIPTION	+ (-) $ Adjustment
Sales or Financing Concessions							
Date of Sale/Time							
Location							
Leasehold/Fee Simple							
Site							
View							
Design and Appeal							
Quality of Construction							
Age							
Condition							
Above Grade Room Count	Total Bdrms Baths	Total Bdrms Baths		Total Bdrms Baths		Total Bdrms Baths	
Gross Living Area	Sq. Ft.	Sq. Ft.		Sq. Ft.		Sq. Ft.	
Basement & Finished Rooms Below Grade							
Functional Utility							
Heating/Cooling							
Energy Efficient Items							
Garage/Carport							
Porch, Patio, Deck, Fireplace(s), etc.							
Fence, Pool, etc.							
Net Adj. (total)		+ -	$	+ -	$	+ -	$
Adjusted Sales Price of Comparable		% Net % Grs	$	% Net % Grs	$	% Net % Grs	$

Comments on Sales Comparison (including the subject property's compatibility to the neighborhood, etc.): _____

ITEM	SUBJECT	COMPARABLE NO. 1	COMPARABLE NO. 2	COMPARABLE NO. 3
Date, Price, and Data Source, for prior sales within year of appraisal				

Analysis of any current agreement of sale, option, or listing of the subject property and analysis of any prior sales of subject and comparables within one year of the date of appraisal: _____

INDICATED VALUE BY SALES COMPARISON APPROACH . . . . $ _____

INDICATED VALUE BY INCOME APPROACH (If Applicable) Estimated Market Rent $ _____ /Mo. x Gross Rent Multiplier _____ = $ n/a

RECONCILIATION

This appraisal is made ☐ "as is" ☐ subject to repairs, alterations, inspections or conditions listed below ☐ subject to completion per plans and specifications.

Conditions of Appraisal: _____

Final Reconciliation: _____

The purpose of this appraisal is to estimate the market value of the real property that is the subject of this report, based on the above conditions and the certification, contingent and limiting conditions, and market value definition that are stated in the attached Freddie Mac Form 439/Fannie Mae Form 1004B (Revised 6/93 _____).

I (WE) ESTIMATE THE MARKET VALUE, AS DEFINED, OF THE REAL PROPERTY THAT IS THE SUBJECT OF THIS REPORT, AS OF _____

(WHICH IS THE DATE OF INSPECTION AND THE EFFECTIVE DATE OF THIS REPORT) TO BE $ _____

APPRAISER:	SUPERVISORY APPRAISER (ONLY IF REQUIRED):	
Signature	Signature	☐ Did ☐ Did Not
Name	Name	Inspect Property
Date Report Signed	Date Report Signed	
State Certification #	State Certification #	
Or State License #	Or State License #	

State _____   State VA   State _____

DEFINITION OF MARKET VALUE: The most probable price which a property should bring in a competitive and open market under all conditions requisite to a fair sale, the buyer and seller, each acting prudently, knowledgeably and assuming the price is not affected by undue stimulus. Implicit in this definition is the consummation of a sale as of a specified date and the passing of title from seller to buyer under conditions whereby: (1) buyer and seller are typically motivated; (2) both parties are well informed or well advised, and each acting in what he considers his own best interest; (3) a reasonable time is allowed for exposure in the open market; (4) payment is made in terms of cash in U. S. dollars or in terms of financial arrangements comparable thereto; and (5) the price represents the normal consideration for the property sold unaffected by special or creative financing or sales concessions* granted by anyone associated with the sale.

*Adjustments to the comparables must be made for special or creative financing or sales concessions. No adjustments are necessary for those costs which are normally paid by sellers as a result of tradition or law in a market area; these costs are readily identifiable since the seller pays these costs in virtually all sales transactions. Special or creative financing adjustments can be made to the comparable property by comparisons to financing terms offered by a third party institutional lender that is not already involved in the property or transaction. Any adjustment should not be calculated on a mechanical dollar for dollar cost of the financing or concession but the dollar amount of any adjustment should approximate the market's reaction to the financing or concessions based on the appraiser's judgment.

STATEMENT OF LIMITING CONDITIONS AND APPRAISER'S CERTIFICATION

CONTINGENT AND LIMITING CONDITIONS: The appraiser's certification that appears in the appraisal report is subject to the following conditions:

1. The appraiser will not be responsible for matters of a legal nature that affect either the property being appraised or the title to it. The appraiser assumes that the title is good and marketable and, therefore, will not render any opinions about the title. The property is appraised on the basis of it being under responsible ownership.

2. The appraiser has provided a sketch in the appraisal report to show approximate dimensions of the improvements and the sketch is included only to assist the reader of the report in visualizing the property and understanding the appraiser's determination of its size.

3. The appraiser has examined the available flood maps that are provided by the Federal Emergency Management Agency (or other data sources) and has noted in the appraisal report whether the subject site is located in an identified Special Flood Hazard Area. Because the appraiser is not a surveyor, he or she makes no guarantees, express or implied, regarding this determination.

4. The appraiser will not give testimony or appear in court because he or she made an appraisal of the property in question, unless specific arrangements to do so have been made beforehand.

5. The appraiser has estimated the value of the land in the cost approach at its highest and best use and the improvements at their contributory value. These separate valuations of the land and improvements must not be used in conjunction with any other appraisal and are invalid if they are so used.

6. The appraiser has noted in the appraisal report any adverse conditions (such as, needed repairs, depreciation, the presence of hazardous wastes, toxic substances, etc.) observed during the inspection of the subject property or that he or she became aware of during the normal research involved in performing the appraisal. Unless otherwise stated in the appraisal report, the appraiser has no knowledge of any hidden or unapparent conditions of the property or adverse environmental conditions (including the presence of hazardous wastes, toxic substances, etc.) that would make the property more or less valuable, and has assumed that there are no such conditions and makes no guarantees or warranties, express or implied, regarding the condition of the property. The appraiser will not be responsible for any such conditions that do exist or for any engineering or testing that might be required to discover whether such conditions exist. Because the appraiser is not an expert in the field of environmental hazards, the appraisal report must not be considered as an environmental assessment of the property.

7. The appraiser obtained the information, estimates, and opinions that were expressed in the appraisal report from sources that he or she considers to be reliable and believes them to be true and correct. The appraiser does not assume responsibility for the accuracy of such items that were furnished by other parties.

8. The appraiser will not disclose the contents of the appraisal report except as provided for in the Uniform Standards of Professional Appraisal Practice.

9. The appraiser has based his or her appraisal report and valuation conclusion for an appraisal that is subject to satisfactory completion, repairs, or alterations on the assumption that completion of the improvements will be performed in a workmanlike manner.

10. The appraiser must provide his or her prior written consent before the lender/client specified in the appraisal report can distribute the appraisal report (including conclusions about the property value, the appraiser's identity and professional designations, and references to any professional appraisal organizations or the firm with which the appraiser is associated) to anyone other than the borrower; the mortgagee or its successors and assigns; the mortgage insurer; consultants; professional appraisal organizations; any state or federally approved financial institution; or any department, agency, or instrumentality of the United States or any state or the District of Columbia; except that the lender/client may distribute the property description section of the report only to data collection or reporting service(s) without having to obtain the appraiser's prior written consent. The appraiser's written consent and approval must also be obtained before the appraisal can be conveyed by anyone to the public through advertising, public relations, news, sales, or other media.

Comparison of 30- and 15-year $100,000 loans at 10% interest

30 Yr	360.00				15 Yr	180.00			
Pay #	Payment	Principal	Interest	Balance	Pay #	Payment	Principal	Interest	Balance
1	877.57	44.24	833.33	99955.76	1	1074.61	241.27	833.33	99758.73
2	877.57	44.61	832.96	99911.15	2	1074.61	243.28	831.32	99515.45
3	877.57	44.98	832.59	99866.18	3	1074.61	245.31	829.30	99270.14
4	877.57	45.35	832.22	99820.82	4	1074.61	247.35	827.25	99022.78
5	877.57	45.73	831.84	99775.09	5	1074.61	249.42	825.19	98773.37
6	877.57	46.11	831.46	99728.98	6	1074.61	251.49	823.11	98521.87
7	877.57	46.50	831.07	99682.48	7	1074.61	253.59	821.02	98268.28
8	877.57	46.88	830.69	99635.60	8	1074.61	255.70	818.90	98012.58
9	877.57	47.27	830.30	99588.32	9	1074.61	257.83	816.77	97754.75
10	877.57	47.67	829.90	99540.65	10	1074.61	259.98	814.62	97494.77
11	877.57	48.07	829.51	99492.59	11	1074.61	262.15	812.46	97232.62
12	877.57	48.47	829.10	99444.12	12	1074.61	264.33	810.27	96968.28
13	877.57	48.87	828.70	99395.25	13	1074.61	266.54	808.07	96701.75
14	877.57	49.28	828.29	99345.97	14	1074.61	268.76	805.85	96432.99
15	877.57	49.69	827.88	99296.28	15	1074.61	271.00	803.61	96161.99
16	877.57	50.10	827.47	99246.18	16	1074.61	273.26	801.35	95888.74
17	877.57	50.52	827.05	99195.66	17	1074.61	275.53	799.07	95613.21
18	877.57	50.94	826.63	99144.72	18	1074.61	277.83	796.78	95335.38
19	877.57	51.37	826.21	99093.36	19	1074.61	280.14	794.46	95055.23
20	877.57	51.79	825.78	99041.56	20	1074.61	282.48	792.13	94772.76
21	877.57	52.23	825.35	98989.34	21	1074.61	284.83	789.77	94487.92
22	877.57	52.66	824.91	98936.68	22	1074.61	287.21	787.40	94200.72
23	877.57	53.10	824.47	98883.58	23	1074.61	289.60	785.01	93911.12
24	877.57	53.54	824.03	98830.04	24	1074.61	292.01	782.59	93619.11
25	877.57	53.99	823.58	98776.05	25	1074.61	294.45	780.16	93324.66
26	877.57	54.44	823.13	98721.61	26	1074.61	296.90	777.71	93027.76
27	877.57	54.89	822.68	98666.72	27	1074.61	299.37	775.23	92728.39
28	877.57	55.35	822.22	98611.37	28	1074.61	301.87	772.74	92426.52
29	877.57	55.81	821.76	98555.56	29	1074.61	304.38	770.22	92122.13
30	877.57	56.28	821.30	98499.28	30	1074.61	306.92	767.68	91815.21
31	877.57	56.74	820.83	98442.54	31	1074.61	309.48	765.13	91505.73
32	877.57	57.22	820.35	98385.32	32	1074.61	312.06	762.55	91193.68
33	877.57	57.69	819.88	98327.63	33	1074.61	314.66	759.95	90879.02
34	877.57	58.17	819.40	98269.45	34	1074.61	317.28	757.33	90561.74
35	877.57	58.66	818.91	98210.79	35	1074.61	319.92	754.68	90241.82
36	877.57	59.15	818.42	98151.65	36	1074.61	322.59	752.02	89919.23
37	877.57	59.64	817.93	98092.00	37	1074.61	325.28	749.33	89593.95
38	877.57	60.14	817.43	98031.87	38	1074.61	327.99	746.62	89265.96
39	877.57	60.64	816.93	97971.23	39	1074.61	330.72	743.88	88935.24
40	877.57	61.14	816.43	97910.08	40	1074.61	333.48	741.13	88601.76
41	877.57	61.65	815.92	97848.43	41	1074.61	336.26	738.35	88265.50
42	877.57	62.17	815.40	97786.26	42	1074.61	339.06	735.55	87926.44
43	877.57	62.69	814.89	97723.57	43	1074.61	341.88	732.72	87584.56
44	877.57	63.21	814.36	97660.37	44	1074.61	344.73	729.87	87239.82
45	877.57	63.74	813.84	97596.63	45	1074.61	347.61	727.00	86892.22
46	877.57	64.27	813.31	97532.36	46	1074.61	350.50	724.10	86541.71
47	877.57	64.80	812.77	97467.56	47	1074.61	353.42	721.18	86188.29
48	877.57	65.34	812.23	97402.22	48	1074.61	356.37	718.24	85831.92
49	877.57	65.89	811.69	97336.33	49	1074.61	359.34	715.27	85472.58
50	877.57	66.44	811.14	97269.90	50	1074.61	362.33	712.27	85110.25
51	877.57	66.99	810.58	97202.91	51	1074.61	365.35	709.25	84744.89
52	877.57	67.55	810.02	97135.36	52	1074.61	368.40	706.21	84376.50
53	877.57	68.11	809.46	97067.25	53	1074.61	371.47	703.14	84005.03
54	877.57	68.68	808.89	96998.57	54	1074.61	374.56	700.04	83630.47
55	877.57	69.25	808.32	96929.32	55	1074.61	377.68	696.92	83252.78
56	877.57	69.83	807.74	96859.50	56	1074.61	380.83	693.77	82871.95
57	877.57	70.41	807.16	96789.09	57	1074.61	384.01	690.60	82487.94
58	877.57	71.00	806.58	96718.09	58	1074.61	387.21	687.40	82100.74
59	877.57	71.59	805.98	96646.50	59	1074.61	390.43	684.17	81710.31
60	877.57	72.18	805.39	96574.32	60	1074.61	393.69	680.92	81316.62
61	877.57	72.79	804.79	96501.53	61	1074.61	396.97	677.64	80919.65
62	877.57	73.39	804.18	96428.14	62	1074.61	400.27	674.33	80519.38
63	877.57	74.00	803.57	96354.14	63	1074.61	403.61	670.99	80115.77
64	877.57	74.62	802.95	96279.52	64	1074.61	406.97	667.63	79708.79
65	877.57	75.24	802.33	96204.28	65	1074.61	410.37	664.24	79298.43
66	877.57	75.87	801.70	96128.41	66	1074.61	413.78	660.82	78884.64
67	877.57	76.50	801.07	96051.91	67	1074.61	417.23	657.37	78467.41
68	877.57	77.14	800.43	95974.77	68	1074.61	420.71	653.90	78046.70
69	877.57	77.78	799.79	95896.98	69	1074.61	424.22	650.39	77622.49

Comparison of 30- and 15-year $100,000 loans at 10% interest (continued)

70	877.57	78.43	799.14	95818.55	70	1074.61	427.75	646.85	77194.73
71	877.57	79.08	798.49	95739.47	71	1074.61	431.32	643.29	76763.42
72	877.57	79.74	797.83	95659.73	72	1074.61	434.91	639.70	76328.51
73	877.57	80.41	797.16	95579.32	73	1074.61	438.53	636.07	75889.97
74	877.57	81.08	796.49	95498.24	74	1074.61	442.19	632.42	75447.79
75	877.57	81.75	795.82	95416.49	75	1074.61	445.87	628.73	75001.91
76	877.57	82.43	795.14	95334.06	76	1074.61	449.59	625.02	74552.32
77	877.57	83.12	794.45	95250.94	77	1074.61	453.34	621.27	74098.99
78	877.57	83.81	793.76	95167.12	78	1074.61	457.11	617.49	73641.87
79	877.57	84.51	793.06	95082.61	79	1074.61	460.92	613.68	73180.95
80	877.57	85.22	792.36	94997.39	80	1074.61	464.76	609.84	72716.19
81	877.57	85.93	791.64	94911.47	81	1074.61	468.64	605.97	72247.55
82	877.57	86.64	790.93	94824.82	82	1074.61	472.54	602.06	71775.01
83	877.57	87.36	790.21	94737.46	83	1074.61	476.48	598.13	71298.53
84	877.57	88.09	789.48	94649.37	84	1074.61	480.45	594.15	70818.08
85	877.57	88.83	788.74	94560.54	85	1074.61	484.45	590.15	70333.62
86	877.57	89.57	788.00	94470.97	86	1074.61	488.49	586.11	69845.13
87	877.57	90.31	787.26	94380.66	87	1074.61	492.56	582.04	69352.57
88	877.57	91.07	786.51	94289.59	88	1074.61	496.67	577.94	68855.90
89	877.57	91.82	785.75	94197.77	89	1074.61	500.81	573.80	68355.10
90	877.57	92.59	784.98	94105.18	90	1074.61	504.98	569.63	67850.12
91	877.57	93.36	784.21	94011.82	91	1074.61	509.19	565.42	67340.93
92	877.57	94.14	783.43	93917.68	92	1074.61	513.43	561.17	66827.50
93	877.57	94.92	782.65	93822.75	93	1074.61	517.71	556.90	66309.79
94	877.57	95.72	781.86	93727.04	94	1074.61	522.02	552.58	65787.76
95	877.57	96.51	781.06	93630.52	95	1074.61	526.37	548.23	65261.39
96	877.57	97.32	780.25	93533.21	96	1074.61	530.76	543.84	64730.63
97	877.57	98.13	779.44	93435.08	97	1074.61	535.18	539.42	64195.45
98	877.57	98.95	778.63	93336.13	98	1074.61	539.64	534.96	63655.80
99	877.57	99.77	777.80	93236.36	99	1074.61	544.14	530.47	63111.66
100	877.57	100.60	776.97	93135.76	100	1074.61	548.67	525.93	62562.99
101	877.57	101.44	776.13	93034.32	101	1074.61	553.25	521.36	62009.74
102	877.57	102.29	775.29	92932.03	102	1074.61	557.86	516.75	61451.89
103	877.57	103.14	774.43	92828.90	103	1074.61	562.51	512.10	60889.38
104	877.57	104.00	773.57	92724.90	104	1074.61	567.19	507.41	60322.19
105	877.57	104.86	772.71	92620.04	105	1074.61	571.92	502.68	59750.27
106	877.57	105.74	771.83	92514.30	106	1074.61	576.69	497.92	59173.58
107	877.57	106.62	770.95	92407.68	107	1074.61	581.49	493.11	58592.09
108	877.57	107.51	770.06	92300.17	108	1074.61	586.34	488.27	58005.75
109	877.57	108.40	769.17	92191.77	109	1074.61	591.22	483.38	57414.53
110	877.57	109.31	768.26	92082.46	110	1074.61	596.15	478.45	56818.38
111	877.57	110.22	767.35	91972.24	111	1074.61	601.12	473.49	56217.26
112	877.57	111.14	766.44	91861.11	112	1074.61	606.13	468.48	55611.13
113	877.57	112.06	765.51	91749.04	113	1074.61	611.18	463.43	54999.95
114	877.57	113.00	764.58	91636.05	114	1074.61	616.27	458.33	54383.68
115	877.57	113.94	763.63	91522.11	115	1074.61	621.41	453.20	53762.27
116	877.57	114.89	762.68	91407.22	116	1074.61	626.59	448.02	53135.68
117	877.57	115.84	761.73	91291.38	117	1074.61	631.81	442.80	52503.88
118	877.57	116.81	760.76	91174.57	118	1074.61	637.07	437.53	51866.80
119	877.57	117.78	759.79	91056.78	119	1074.61	642.38	432.22	51224.42
120	877.57	118.77	758.81	90938.02	120	1074.61	647.73	426.87	50576.69
121	877.57	119.75	757.82	90818.26	121	1074.61	653.13	421.47	49923.55
122	877.57	120.75	756.82	90697.51	122	1074.61	658.58	416.03	49264.98
123	877.57	121.76	755.81	90575.75	123	1074.61	664.06	410.54	48600.91
124	877.57	122.77	754.80	90452.98	124	1074.61	669.60	405.01	47931.32
125	877.57	123.80	753.77	90329.18	125	1074.61	675.18	399.43	47256.14
126	877.57	124.83	752.74	90204.35	126	1074.61	680.80	393.80	46575.34
127	877.57	125.87	751.70	90078.49	127	1074.61	686.48	388.13	45888.86
128	877.57	126.92	750.65	89951.57	128	1074.61	692.20	382.41	45196.66
129	877.57	127.98	749.60	89823.59	129	1074.61	697.97	376.64	44498.69
130	877.57	129.04	748.53	89694.55	130	1074.61	703.78	370.82	43794.91
131	877.57	130.12	747.45	89564.43	131	1074.61	709.65	364.96	43085.26
132	877.57	131.20	746.37	89433.23	132	1074.61	715.56	359.04	42369.70
133	877.57	132.29	745.28	89300.94	133	1074.61	721.52	353.08	41648.18
134	877.57	133.40	744.17	89167.54	134	1074.61	727.54	347.07	40920.64
135	877.57	134.51	743.06	89033.03	135	1074.61	733.60	341.01	40187.04
136	877.57	135.63	741.94	88897.40	136	1074.61	739.71	334.89	39447.33
137	877.57	136.76	740.81	88760.64	137	1074.61	745.88	328.73	38701.45
138	877.57	137.90	739.67	88622.74	138	1074.61	752.09	322.51	37949.36
139	877.57	139.05	738.52	88483.69	139	1074.61	758.36	316.24	37191.00
140	877.57	140.21	737.36	88343.49	140	1074.61	764.68	309.92	36426.32
141	877.57	141.38	736.20	88202.11	141	1074.61	771.05	303.55	35655.27

Comparison of 30- and 15-year $100,000 loans at 10% interest (continued)

142	877.57	142.55	735.02	88059.56	142	1074.61	777.48	297.13	34877.79
143	877.57	143.74	733.83	87915.82	143	1074.61	783.96	290.65	34093.83
144	877.57	144.94	732.63	87770.88	144	1074.61	790.49	284.12	33303.34
145	877.57	146.15	731.42	87624.73	145	1074.61	797.08	277.53	32506.26
146	877.57	147.37	730.21	87477.36	146	1074.61	803.72	270.89	31702.54
147	877.57	148.59	728.98	87328.77	147	1074.61	810.42	264.19	30892.13
148	877.57	149.83	727.74	87178.94	148	1074.61	817.17	257.43	30074.96
149	877.57	151.08	726.49	87027.86	149	1074.61	823.98	250.62	29250.98
150	877.57	152.34	725.23	86875.52	150	1074.61	830.85	243.76	28420.13
151	877.57	153.61	723.96	86721.91	151	1074.61	837.77	236.83	27582.36
152	877.57	154.89	722.68	86567.02	152	1074.61	844.75	229.85	26737.61
153	877.57	156.18	721.39	86410.84	153	1074.61	851.79	222.81	25885.81
154	877.57	157.48	720.09	86253.36	154	1074.61	858.89	215.72	25026.92
155	877.57	158.79	718.78	86094.56	155	1074.61	866.05	208.56	24160.88
156	877.57	160.12	717.45	85934.45	156	1074.61	873.26	201.34	23287.61
157	877.57	161.45	716.12	85773.00	157	1074.61	880.54	194.06	22407.07
158	877.57	162.80	714.77	85610.20	158	1074.61	887.88	186.73	21519.19
159	877.57	164.15	713.42	85446.05	159	1074.61	895.28	179.33	20623.91
160	877.57	165.52	712.05	85280.53	160	1074.61	902.74	171.87	19721.17
161	877.57	166.90	710.67	85113.63	161	1074.61	910.26	164.34	18810.91
162	877.57	168.29	709.28	84945.33	162	1074.61	917.85	156.76	17893.06
163	877.57	169.69	707.88	84775.64	163	1074.61	925.50	149.11	16967.57
164	877.57	171.11	706.46	84604.53	164	1074.61	933.21	141.40	16034.36
165	877.57	172.53	705.04	84432.00	165	1074.61	940.99	133.62	15093.37
166	877.57	173.97	703.60	84258.03	166	1074.61	948.83	125.78	14144.55
167	877.57	175.42	702.15	84082.61	167	1074.61	956.73	117.87	13187.81
168	877.57	176.88	700.69	83905.72	168	1074.61	964.71	109.90	12223.10
169	877.57	178.36	699.21	83727.37	169	1074.61	972.75	101.86	11250.36
170	877.57	179.84	697.73	83547.52	170	1074.61	980.85	93.75	10269.51
171	877.57	181.34	696.23	83366.18	171	1074.61	989.03	85.58	9280.48
172	877.57	182.85	694.72	83183.33	172	1074.61	997.27	77.34	8283.21
173	877.57	184.38	693.19	82998.95	173	1074.61	1005.58	69.03	7277.63
174	877.57	185.91	691.66	82813.04	174	1074.61	1013.96	60.65	6263.68
175	877.57	187.46	690.11	82625.57	175	1074.61	1022.41	52.20	5241.27
176	877.57	189.03	688.55	82436.55	176	1074.61	1030.93	43.68	4210.34
177	877.57	190.60	686.97	82245.95	177	1074.61	1039.52	35.09	3170.82
178	877.57	192.19	685.38	82053.76	178	1074.61	1048.18	26.42	2122.64
179	877.57	193.79	683.78	81859.97	179	1074.61	1056.92	17.69	1065.72
180	877.57	195.41	682.17	81664.56	180	1074.61	1065.72	8.88	0.00
181	877.57	197.03	680.54	81467.53					
182	877.57	198.68	678.90	81268.85					
183	877.57	200.33	677.24	81068.52					
184	877.57	202.00	675.57	80866.52					
185	877.57	203.68	673.89	80662.84					
186	877.57	205.38	672.19	80457.46					
187	877.57	207.09	670.48	80250.36					
188	877.57	208.82	668.75	80041.55					
189	877.57	210.56	667.01	79830.99					
190	877.57	212.31	665.26	79618.67					
191	877.57	214.08	663.49	79404.59					
192	877.57	215.87	661.70	79188.72					
193	877.57	217.67	659.91	78971.06					
194	877.57	219.48	658.09	78751.58					
195	877.57	221.31	656.26	78530.27					
196	877.57	223.15	654.42	78307.12					
197	877.57	225.01	652.56	78082.11					
198	877.57	226.89	650.68	77855.22					
199	877.57	228.78	648.79	77626.44					
200	877.57	230.68	646.89	77395.76					
201	877.57	232.61	644.96	77163.15					
202	877.57	234.55	643.03	76928.60					
203	877.57	236.50	641.07	76692.10					
204	877.57	238.47	639.10	76453.63					
205	877.57	240.46	637.11	76213.18					
206	877.57	242.46	635.11	75970.71					
207	877.57	244.48	633.09	75726.23					
208	877.57	246.52	631.05	75479.71					
209	877.57	248.57	629.00	75231.14					
210	877.57	250.65	626.93	74980.49					
211	877.57	252.73	624.84	74727.76					
212	877.57	254.84	622.73	74472.92					
213	877.57	256.96	620.61	74215.95					

30-year $100,000 at 10% interest (continued)

214	877.57	259.11	618.47	73956.85
215	877.57	261.26	616.31	73695.58
216	877.57	263.44	614.13	73432.14
217	877.57	265.64	611.93	73166.51
218	877.57	267.85	609.72	72898.65
219	877.57	270.08	607.49	72628.57
220	877.57	272.33	605.24	72356.24
221	877.57	274.60	602.97	72081.64
222	877.57	276.89	600.68	71804.74
223	877.57	279.20	598.37	71525.55
224	877.57	281.53	596.05	71244.02
225	877.57	283.87	593.70	70960.15
226	877.57	286.24	591.33	70673.91
227	877.57	288.62	588.95	70385.29
228	877.57	291.03	586.54	70094.26
229	877.57	293.45	584.12	69800.81
230	877.57	295.90	581.67	69504.91
231	877.57	298.36	579.21	69206.55
232	877.57	300.85	576.72	68905.70
233	877.57	303.36	574.21	68602.34
234	877.57	305.89	571.69	68296.45
235	877.57	308.43	569.14	67988.02
236	877.57	311.00	566.57	67677.01
237	877.57	313.60	563.98	67363.42
238	877.57	316.21	561.36	67047.21
239	877.57	318.84	558.73	66728.36
240	877.57	321.50	556.07	66406.86
241	877.57	324.18	553.39	66082.68
242	877.57	326.88	550.69	65755.80
243	877.57	329.61	547.96	65426.19
244	877.57	332.35	545.22	65093.84
245	877.57	335.12	542.45	64758.72
246	877.57	337.92	539.66	64420.80
247	877.57	340.73	536.84	64080.07
248	877.57	343.57	534.00	63736.50
249	877.57	346.43	531.14	63390.06
250	877.57	349.32	528.25	63040.74
251	877.57	352.23	525.34	62688.51
252	877.57	355.17	522.40	62333.34
253	877.57	358.13	519.44	61975.22
254	877.57	361.11	516.46	61614.10
255	877.57	364.12	513.45	61249.98
256	877.57	367.16	510.42	60882.83
257	877.57	370.21	507.36	60512.61
258	877.57	373.30	504.27	60139.31
259	877.57	376.41	501.16	59762.90
260	877.57	379.55	498.02	59383.36
261	877.57	382.71	494.86	59000.65
262	877.57	385.90	491.67	58614.75
263	877.57	389.12	488.46	58225.63
264	877.57	392.36	485.21	57833.27
265	877.57	395.63	481.94	57437.65
266	877.57	398.92	478.65	57038.72
267	877.57	402.25	475.32	56636.47
268	877.57	405.60	471.97	56230.87
269	877.57	408.98	468.59	55821.89
270	877.57	412.39	465.18	55409.50
271	877.57	415.83	461.75	54993.67
272	877.57	419.29	458.28	54574.38
273	877.57	422.79	454.79	54151.60
274	877.57	426.31	451.26	53725.29
275	877.57	429.86	447.71	53295.43
276	877.57	433.44	444.13	52861.99
277	877.57	437.06	440.52	52424.93
278	877.57	440.70	436.87	51984.23
279	877.57	444.37	433.20	51539.86
280	877.57	448.07	429.50	51091.79
281	877.57	451.81	425.76	50639.99
282	877.57	455.57	422.00	50184.41
283	877.57	459.37	418.20	49725.05
284	877.57	463.20	414.38	49261.85
285	877.57	467.06	410.52	48794.79

30-year $100,000 at 10% interest (continued)

286	877.57	470.95	406.62	48323.85
287	877.57	474.87	402.70	47848.97
288	877.57	478.83	398.74	47370.14
289	877.57	482.82	394.75	46887.32
290	877.57	486.84	390.73	46400.48
291	877.57	490.90	386.67	45909.58
292	877.57	494.99	382.58	45414.59
293	877.57	499.12	378.45	44915.47
294	877.57	503.28	374.30	44412.19
295	877.57	507.47	370.10	43904.72
296	877.57	511.70	365.87	43393.02
297	877.57	515.96	361.61	42877.06
298	877.57	520.26	357.31	42356.80
299	877.57	524.60	352.97	41832.20
300	877.57	528.97	348.60	41303.23
301	877.57	533.38	344.19	40769.85
302	877.57	537.82	339.75	40232.03
303	877.57	542.30	335.27	39689.72
304	877.57	546.82	330.75	39142.90
305	877.57	551.38	326.19	38591.52
306	877.57	555.98	321.60	38035.54
307	877.57	560.61	316.96	37474.94
308	877.57	565.28	312.29	36909.66
309	877.57	569.99	307.58	36339.66
310	877.57	574.74	302.83	35764.92
311	877.57	579.53	298.04	35185.39
312	877.57	584.36	293.21	34601.03
313	877.57	589.23	288.34	34011.80
314	877.57	594.14	283.43	33417.66
315	877.57	599.09	278.48	32818.57
316	877.57	604.08	273.49	32214.49
317	877.57	609.12	268.45	31605.37
318	877.57	614.19	263.38	30991.18
319	877.57	619.31	258.26	30371.87
320	877.57	624.47	253.10	29747.39
321	877.57	629.68	247.89	29117.72
322	877.57	634.92	242.65	28482.79
323	877.57	640.21	237.36	27842.58
324	877.57	645.55	232.02	27197.03
325	877.57	650.93	226.64	26546.10
326	877.57	656.35	221.22	25889.74
327	877.57	661.82	215.75	25227.92
328	877.57	667.34	210.23	24560.58
329	877.57	672.90	204.67	23887.68
330	877.57	678.51	199.06	23209.17
331	877.57	684.16	193.41	22525.01
332	877.57	689.86	187.71	21835.15
333	877.57	695.61	181.96	21139.54
334	877.57	701.41	176.16	20438.13
335	877.57	707.25	170.32	19730.87
336	877.57	713.15	164.42	19017.73
337	877.57	719.09	158.48	18298.64
338	877.57	725.08	152.49	17573.55
339	877.57	731.13	146.45	16842.43
340	877.57	737.22	140.35	16105.21
341	877.57	743.36	134.21	15361.85
342	877.57	749.56	128.02	14612.29
343	877.57	755.80	121.77	13856.49
344	877.57	762.10	115.47	13094.39
345	877.57	768.45	109.12	12325.94
346	877.57	774.86	102.72	11551.08
347	877.57	781.31	96.26	10769.77
348	877.57	787.82	89.75	9981.95
349	877.57	794.39	83.18	9187.56
350	877.57	801.01	76.56	8386.55
351	877.57	807.68	69.89	7578.86
352	877.57	814.41	63.16	6764.45
353	877.57	821.20	56.37	5943.25
354	877.57	828.04	49.53	5115.20
355	877.57	834.94	42.63	4280.26
356	877.57	841.90	35.67	3438.36
357	877.57	848.92	28.65	2589.44

30-year $100,000 at 10% interest (continued)

358	877.57	855.99	21.58	1733.45
359	877.57	863.13	14.45	870.32
360	877.57	870.32	7.25	0.00

FACTORS FOR MONTHLY PRINCIPAL & INTEREST PAYMENTS
The factors are per thousand of the loan amount and are rounded.
The resulting payment may be a few cents off of the actual payment.

RATE	15 YEARS	20 YEARS	30 YEARS
5.000%	7.9079	6.5995	5.3682
5.125%	7.9732	6.6688	5.4449
5.250%	8.0388	6.7384	5.5220
5.375%	8.1047	6.8085	5.5997
5.500%	8.1708	6.8789	5.6779
5.625%	8.2373	6.9497	5.7566
5.750%	8.3041	7.0208	5.8357
5.875%	8.3712	7.0924	5.9154
6.000%	8.4386	7.1643	5.9955
6.125%	8.5062	7.2366	6.0761
6.250%	8.5742	7.3093	6.1572
6.375%	8.6425	7.3823	6.2387
6.500%	8.7111	7.4557	6.3207
6.625%	8.7799	7.5295	6.4038
6.750%	8.8491	7.6036	6.4860
6.875%	8.9185	7.6781	6.5693
7.000%	8.9883	7.7530	6.6530
7.125%	9.0583	7.8282	6.7372
7.250%	9.1286	7.9038	6.8218
7.375%	9.1992	7.9797	6.9068
7.500%	9.2701	8.0559	6.9922
7.625%	9.3413	8.1325	7.0779
7.750%	9.4128	8.2095	7.1641
7.875%	9.4845	8.2868	7.2507
8.000%	9.5565	8.3644	7.3377
8.125%	9.6288	8.4424	7.4250
8.250%	9.7014	8.5207	7.5127
8.375%	9.7743	8.5993	7.6001
8.500%	9.8474	8.6782	7.6891
8.625%	9.9208	8.7575	7.7779
8.750%	9.9945	8.8371	7.8670
8.875%	10.0684	8.9170	7.9565
9.000%	10.1427	8.9973	8.0462
9.125%	10.2172	9.0778	8.1363
9.250%	10.2919	9.1587	8.2268
9.375%	10.3669	9.2400	8.3175
9.500%	10.4423	9.3213	8.4085
9.625%	10.5178	9.4031	8.5000
9.750%	10.5936	9.4852	8.5915
9.875%	10.6700	9.5676	8.6835
10.000%	10.7461	9.6502	8.7757
10.125%	10.8227	9.7332	8.8682
10.250%	10.9000	9.8164	8.9610
10.375%	10.9766	9.9000	9.0541
10.500%	11.0540	9.9838	9.1474
10.625%	11.1316	10.0679	9.2410
10.750%	11.2095	10.1523	9.3348
10.875%	11.2876	10.2370	9.4289
11.000%	11.3660	10.3219	9.5232
11.125%	11.4446	10.4071	9.6178
11.250%	11.5235	10.4926	9.7126
11.375%	11.6026	10.5783	9.8077
11.500%	11.6819	10.6643	9.9029
11.625%	11.7615	10.7510	9.9984
11.750%	11.8413	10.8371	10.0941
11.875%	11.9214	10.9238	10.1900
12.000%	12.0017	11.0109	10.2861
12.125%	12.0822	11.0981	10.3825
12.250%	12.1630	11.1857	10.4790
12.375%	12.2399	11.2734	10.5757
12.500%	12.3252	11.3614	10.6726
12.625%	12.4067	11.4496	10.7697
12.750%	12.4484	11.5381	10.8669
12.875%	12.5703	11.6268	10.9644
13.000%	12.6524	11.7158	11.0620
13.125%	12.7348	11.8049	11.1598
13.250%	12.8174	11.8943	11.2577
13.375%	12.9002	11.9839	11.3559
13.500%	12.9832	12.0738	11.4541
13.625%	13.0664	12.1638	11.5526
13.750%	13.1499	12.2541	11.6511
13.875%	13.2335	12.3445	11.7499
14.000%	13.3174	12.4352	11.8487
14.250%	13.4858	12.6172	12.0469
14.500%	13.6550	12.8000	12.2456
14.750%	13.8250	12.9836	12.4448
15.000%	14.9959	13.1679	12.6444

OMB Approved No. 2900-0086
Respondent Burden: 15 minutes

Department of Veterans Affairs	TO	Department of Veterans Affairs Attn: Loan Guaranty Division
REQUEST FOR A CERTIFICATE OF ELIGIBILITY		

NOTE: Please read information on reverse before completing this form. If additional space is required, attach a separate sheet.

1. FIRST-MIDDLE-LAST NAME OF VETERAN	2. DATE OF BIRTH	3. VETERAN'S DAYTIME TELEPHONE NO. (_ _)

4. ADDRESS OF VETERAN (No., street or rural route, city or P.O., State and ZIP Code)	5. MAIL CERTIFICATE OF ELIGIBILITY TO: (Complete ONLY if the Certificate is to be mailed to an address different from the one listed in Item 4)

6. MILITARY SERVICE DATA (ATTACH PROOF OF SERVICE - SEE PARAGRAPH "D" ON REVERSE)

A. ITEM	B. PERIODS OF ACTIVE SERVICE		C. NAME (Show your name exactly as it appears on your separation papers or Statement of Service)	D. SOCIAL SECURITY NUMBER	E. SERVICE NUMBER (If different from Social Security No.)	F. BRANCH OF SERVICE
	DATE FROM	DATE TO				
1.						
2.						
3.						
4.						

7A. WERE YOU DISCHARGED, RETIRED OR SEPARATED FROM SERVICE BECAUSE OF DISABILITY OR DO YOU NOW HAVE ANY SERVICE-CONNECTED DISABILITIES?

☐ YES ☐ NO (If "Yes," complete Item 7B)

7B. VA CLAIM FILE NUMBER

C-

8. PREVIOUS VA LOANS (Must answer N/A if no previous VA home loan. DO NOT LEAVE BLANK)

A. ITEM	B. TYPE (Home, Refinance, Manufactured Home, or Direct)	C. ADDRESS OF PROPERTY	D. DATE OF LOAN	E. DO YOU STILL OWN THE PROPERTY? (YES/NO)	F. DATE PROPERTY WAS SOLD (Submit a copy of HUD-1, Settlement Statement, if available)	G. VA LOAN NUMBER (If known)
1.						
2.						
3.						
4.						
5.						
6.						

I CERTIFY THAT the statements herein are true to the best of my knowledge and belief.

9. SIGNATURE OF VETERAN (Do NOT print)	10. DATE SIGNED

FEDERAL STATUTES PROVIDE SEVERE PENALTIES FOR FRAUD, INTENTIONAL MISREPRESENTATION, CRIMINAL CONNIVANCE OR CONSPIRACY PURPOSED TO INFLUENCE THE ISSUANCE OF ANY GUARANTY OR INSURANCE BY THE SECRETARY OF VETERANS AFFAIRS.

FOR VA USE ONLY

11A. DATE CERTIFICATE ISSUED	11B. SIGNATURE OF VA AGENT

VA FORM **26-1880**
FEB 2000

SUPERSEDES VA FORM 26-1880, MAR 1999,
WHICH WILL NOT BE USED.

INSTRUCTIONS FOR VA FORM 26-1880

PRIVACY ACT INFORMATION: No Certificate of Eligibility may be issued unless VA receives sufficient information to determine that you are eligible (38 U.S.C. 3702). You are not required to furnish the information, including the Social Security Number, but are urged to do so, since it is vital to proper action by VA in your case. Specifically, your Social Security Number is requested under authority of 38 U.S.C. 3702 and is requested only if the service department used your Social Security Number as a service number. Failure to provide a completed application will deprive VA of information needed in reaching decisions which could affect you. Responses may be disclosed outside VA only if the disclosure is authorized under the Privacy Act, including the routine uses identified in the VA system of records, 55VA26, Loan Guaranty Home, Condominium and Manufactured Home Loan Applicant Records, Specially Adapted Housing Applicant Records, and Vendee Loan Applicant Records - VA, published in the Federal Register.

RESPONDENT BURDEN: VA may not conduct or sponsor, and respondent is not required to respond to this collection of information unless it displays a valid OMB Control Number. Public reporting burden for this collection of information is estimated to average 15 minutes per response, including the time for reviewing instructions, searching existing data sources, gathering and maintaining the data needed, and completing and reviewing the collection of information. If you have comments regarding this burden estimate or any other aspect of this collection of information, call 1-800-827-1000 for mailing information on where to send your comments.

A. Mail this completed form, along with proof of service, to the Eligibility Center at P.O. Box 20729, Winston-Salem, NC 27120 (for veterans located in the eastern half of the country) or P.O. Box 240097, Los Angeles, CA 90024 (for veterans located in the western half of the country). Veterans stationed overseas may use either address.

B. Military Service Requirements for VA Loan Eligibility: (NOTE: Cases involving other than honorable discharges will usually require further development by VA. This is necessary to determine if the service was under other than dishonorable conditions.)

1. **Wartime Service.** If you served anytime during World War II (September 16, 1940 to July 25, 1947), Korean Conflict (June 27, 1950 to January 31, 1955), or Vietnam Era (August 5, 1964 to May 7, 1975) you must have served at least 90 days on active duty and have been discharged or released under other than dishonorable conditions. If you served less than 90 days, you may be eligible if discharged because of service-connected disability.

2. **Peacetime Service.** If your service fell entirely within one of the following periods: July 26, 1947 to June 26, 1950, or February 1, 1955 to August 4, 1964, you must have served at least 181 days of continuous active duty and have been discharged under conditions other than dishonorable. If you entered service after May 7, 1975 but prior to September 8, 1980 (enlisted) or October 17, 1981 (officer) and completed your service before August 2, 1990, 181 days service is also required. If you served less than 181 days, you may be eligible if discharged for a service-connected disability.

3. **Service after September 7, 1980 (enlisted) or October 16, 1981 (officer) and prior to August 2, 1990.** If you were separated from service which began after these dates, you must have: (a) Completed 24 months of continuous active duty for the full period (at least 181 days) for which you were called or ordered to active duty, and been discharged or released under conditions other than dishonorable; or (b) Completed at least 181 days of active duty and been discharged under the specific authority of 10 U.S.C. 1173 (hardship discharge) or 10 U.S.C. 1171 (early out discharge), or have been determined to have a compensable service-connected disability; or (c) Been discharged with less than 181 days of service for a service-connected disability. Individuals may also be eligible if they were released from active duty due to an involuntary reduction in force, certain medical conditions, or, in some instances. for the convenience of the Government.

4. **Gulf War.** If you served on active duty during the Gulf War (August 2, 1990 to a date yet to be determined), you must have: (a) Completed 24 months of continuous active duty or the full period (at least 90 days) for which you were called or ordered to active duty, and been discharged or released under conditions other than dishonorable; or (b) Completed at least 90 days of active duty and been discharged under the specific authority of 10 U.S.C. 1173 (hardship discharge), or 10 U.S.C. 1171 (early out discharge), or have been determined to have a compensable service-connected disability; or (c) Been discharged with less than 90 days of service for a service-connected disability. Individuals may also be eligible if they were released from active duty due to an involuntary reduction in force, certain medical conditions, or, in some instances, for the convenience of the Government.

5. **Active Duty Service Personnel.** If you are now on active duty, you are eligible after having served on continuous active duty for at least 181 days (90 days during the Persian Gulf War) unless discharged or separated from a previous qualifying period of active duty service.

6. **Selected Reserve Requirements for VA Loan Eligibility.** If you are not otherwise eligible and you completed a total of 6 years in the Selected Reserves or National Guard (member of an active unit, attended required weekend drills and 2-week active duty training) and (a) Were discharged with an honorable discharge; or (b) Were placed on the retired list or (c) Were transferred to the Standby Reserve or an element of the Ready Reserve other than the Selected Reserve after Service characterized as honorable service; or (d) Continue to serve in the Selected Reserve. Individuals who completed less than 6 years may be eligible if discharged for a service-connected disability. Eligibility for Selected Reservists expires September 30, 2007.

C. Unmarried surviving spouses of eligible veterans seeking determination of basic eligibility for VA Loan Guaranty benefits are NOT required to complete this form, but are required to complete VA Form 26-1817, Request for Determination of Loan Guaranty Eligibility-Unmarried Surviving Spouse.

D. Proof of Military Service

1. **"Regular" Veterans.** Attach to this request your most recent discharge or separation papers from active military duty since September 16, 1940, which show active duty dates and type of discharge. If you were separated after January 1, 1950, DD Form 214 must be submitted. If you were separated after October 1, 1979, and you received DD Form 214, Certificate of Release or Discharge From Active Duty, 1 July edition, VA must be furnished Copy 4 of the form. You may submit either original papers or legible copies. In addition, if you are now on active duty submit a statement of service signed by, or by direction of, the adjutant, personnel officer, or commander of your unit or higher headquarters showing date of entry on your current active duty period and the duration of any time lost. Any Veterans Services Representative in the nearest Department of Veterans Affairs office or center will assist you in securing necessary proof of military service.

2. **Selected Reserves/National Guard.** If you are a discharged member of the Army or Air Force National Guard you may submit a NGB Form 22, Report of Separation and Record of Service, or NGB Form 23, Retirement Points Accounting, or it's equivalent (this is similar to a retirement points summary). If you are a discharged member of the Selected Reserve you may submit a copy of your latest annual point statement and evidence of honorable service. You may submit either your original papers or legible copies. Since there is no single form used by the Reserves or National Guard similar to the DD Form 214, it is your responsibility to furnish adequate documentation of at least 6 years of honorable service. In addition, if you are currently serving in the Selected Reserve you must submit a statement of service signed by, or by the direction of, the adjutant, personnel officer or commander of your unit or higher headquarters showing the length of time that you have been a member of the unit.

GLOSSARY

adjustable rate mortgage (ARM)   A loan that allows the interest rate, and usually the payment, to adjust periodically during the life of the loan. Most ARMs start at a lower-than-market interest rate and then adjust based on a prevailing index plus margin.

amortization   The continuous regular payment of a set amount on a loan, which will reduce and pay it off in a given period of time.

annual percentage rate (APR)   The interest rate on credit as expressed by a combination of the loan interest rate and certain loan costs. The Truth-in-Lending statement of Regulation Z of the Federal Reserve requires the APR to be quoted.

balloon payment   When a debt is paid off in less than the set amortization period by paying the remaining principal balance, a balloon payment of the loan has been made. A loan with a 30 year amortization payment with the remaining principal to be paid off in five years is a balloon loan.

basis points   One basis point equals 0.01%, one hundred basis points equal 1.0%.

bond   A security for payment of an obligation. In mortgage lending, bonds are backed by mortgage loans that are pooled together and the resultant bond can be sold in the secondary market.

broker   In mortgage lending, a broker is someone who acts as an intermediary between the borrower and the actual lender. A broker is typically an independent agent representing several lending sources.

buy-down   A loan that is *bought down* below its original interest rate and/or payment. A permanent buy-down will reduce the interest rate and payment for the life of the loan, while a temporary buy-down will reduce the payments on the loan only in the beginning years.

certificate of reasonable value (C.R.V.)   The name given to a Veteran's Administration (VA) appraisal.

C.H.A.R.M. booklet Consumer Handbook on Adjustable Rate Mortgages, which must be given to any borrower who applies for an ARM. This is a federally required disclosure.

chattel Personal property that is not a part of the real estate and can be moved.

closing costs The sum of all costs in relation to the purchase and/or loan closing, excluding the down payment.

cloud A defect on the title of the property that would prevent the purchaser from obtaining a clear title.

collateral The security for a loan. Something of value against which the loan is secured. A mortgage is secured by real estate.

commitment A promise to do something. In mortgage lending, the lender will commit to make the loan, or commit to make the loan at a specific rate and points. Some lenders will require a commitment fee to guarantee the commitment.

common area Part of a property owned by all of the owners. In a condominium or planned unit development there are common areas owned by the property owners jointly.

compensating factor A positive factor that can help to influence the loan approval. Long-term good credit, a large amount of assets, or increasing income are some examples.

condominium A property where the unit is owned individually and the land and all other improvements are owned jointly with all the owners, or the condominium association.

conforming In mortgage lending, a loan that conforms to the guidelines set forth by Fannie Mae or Freddie Mac is said to be conforming.

construction loan A short-term, temporary loan, made by a lender to pay the cost of constructing a building, which is paid off upon completion by cash or a permanent mortgage. The construction loan is secured by the real estate.

conventional loan A loan that is not insured, guaranteed, or funded by the government.

covenants and restrictions The rules and regulations governing the maintenance and use of an area. Condominiums and Planned Unit Developments (PUDs) will have covenants and restrictions.

creditor A lender, or someone who lends money to a borrower (debtor).

credit scores Automated credit system which determines the quality of a borrower's credit.

D.E. underwriter A direct endorsement underwriter who is approved by the FHA to underwrite (approve/reject) FHA-insured loans. The underwriter will normally be employed by the lender making the loan.

deed The document that shows ownership in real property.

deed of trust A mortgage that secures the note by the real property, and appoints a third party trustee to act in the lender's behalf, without having to go to court to proceed with foreclosure when the borrower defaults on the loan.

default A condition of the mortgage that occurs any time the borrower is not in compliance with the terms of the loan. A late payment is a default. A default that is not corrected will result in the loan being called for payment in full.

depreciation When the value of property goes down. Some depreciation is taken as a tax write-off and is considered to be a paper loss because the actual value has not diminished.

Desktop Underwriting (DU) Fannie Mae's automated computer underwriting system.

discount points Points, expressed as a percent of the loan, that are used to buy the interest rate down. Sometimes discount points are used as fee income by the lender. If 10% is the rate with no discount points, or the rate is at par, a rate of 9.75% would have points added to buy it down from 10%. The borrower gets a discounted rate by paying additional points, or interest, up-front.

disintermediation The movement of funds from one place to another to seek a higher yield. If money is moving out of bank accounts and into higher-paying instruments, such as government bonds, this movement can create a shortage of funds, or higher interest rates.

due-on-sale clause A clause in a mortgage that requires the loan to be paid off if the property is sold or conveyed to another person.

earnest money The deposit on a contract. It is part of the consideration on a binding contract. It can be in the form of cash or a note.

encroachment   When some part of a property is on an adjoining property. If a fence or roof overhang from one property is on the other property, it is encroaching on the latter. A lender will not make a loan on the property until either the encroachment is corrected or title insurance insures against it.

equity   The value of property beyond any lien against it. That portion that is owned without liability.

escrow   Money held by the lender to pay future claims. Taxes and insurance are normally added into the monthly payment and held in escrow until they are due to be paid.

fair-market value   The value a purchaser will pay for a property; on an appraisal it is value as determined by comparing the property to similar properties that have sold in the community.

Federal Home Loan Mortgage Corporation (FHLMC or Freddie Mac)   A quasi-governmental agency that acts as a secondary market investor to buy and sell mortgage loans. It sets many of the underwriting guidelines on conventional loans, along with Fannie Mae (FNMA).

Federal Housing Administration (FHA)   A section of the U.S. Department of Housing and Urban Development that insures loans by the full faith and credit of the U.S. government. It sets the guidelines for the approval and insurance of these FHA loans.

Federal National Mortgage Association (FNMA)   A secondary market investor that was originally a government agency and is now a private corporation whose stock is traded on the N.Y. Stock Exchange. It buys and sells mortgages that meet its guidelines. Also known as Fannie Mae.

fee simple   The highest form of ownership that someone can hold in a property. This is the most common form of ownership.

first mortgage   A first lien on real estate, or a loan that has priority over other mortgages on the same property.

fixed rate mortgage (FRM)   A mortgage with an interest rate that does not change or adjust.

fixture   A part of the property that is attached and conveys with it. The opposite of chattel.

foreclosure   Legal action by the lender upon default to have the property sold to pay the securing mortgage.

front end zero   In mortgage insurance, the up-front or first year's premium is allowed to be financed into the loan so that it does not have to be paid at closing.

funding fee   The VA funding fee is a closing cost that may be paid by anyone, or financed into the mortgage as long as the total does not exceed the maximum 100% loan currently allowed by Ginnie Mae (GNMA). The fee is 1.25% on LTVs over 95% to 100% loans, 0.75% on loans over 90% LTV up to 95%, 0.50% on loans with at least 10% down, and 0.50% on assumptions.

Government National Mortgage Association (GNMA or Ginnie Mae)   A government agency that participates in the secondary market and is involved in buying, selling, and guaranteeing government loans such as FHA and VA.

grace period   The time between the due date and the past-due date of a loan during which there is no late charge.

graduated payment mortgage (GPM)   A loan that starts out with a substantially lower payment and then increases the payments each year until a level payment is reached that will pay off the loan over the remaining amortization period. There is usually negative amortization.

gross income   Total income before withholding is subtracted. Gross monthly income (GMI) is used to qualify borrowers.

growing equity mortgage (GEM)   A loan in which the normal payment is increased each year so that the amortization is accelerated, paying off the mortgage in a shorter period of time.

hazard insurance   That portion of the homeowner's insurance that protects the property against fire and other forms of destruction.

HUD (Department of Housing and Urban Development)   The government agency that governs FHA and other housing programs.

index   A figure, normally compiled from other indicators, that is used to establish rates on ARMs.

judgment   An unsecured lien filed against a borrower for nonpayment of a debt.

jumbo loans   Nonconforming loans that are higher than the loan amounts acceptable to FNMA and FHLMC.

late charge   The penalty imposed when a late payment is made or received after the grace period of a loan.

lien   A debt that is secured by something of value. A mortgage is a lien on real estate.

Loan Prospector (LP)   Freddie Mac's automated computer underwriting system.

loan-to-value (LTV)   The amount of the total value of the property that is secured by the mortgage. An $80,000 mortgage on a $100,000 property has 80% LTV. Total loan-to-value (TLTV) is the sum of all liens on a property.

lock-in   The ability to have an interest rate and/or points locked in, or guaranteed, for a specific period of time.

long-term debt (LTD)   Any debt that exceeds the maximum payoff period as set by the guidelines for individual loans.

margin   The interest added onto the index of an ARM to determine the adjustment of the interest rate.

mortgage   A legal instrument that makes real estate security for a loan.

mortgagee   The holder of a mortgage loan.

mortgagor   The borrower of a mortgage loan.

mortgage banker   A lender who deals regularly with the secondary market. A mortgage banker originates, closes, services, and sells the loans.

mortgage broker   A lender who deals with other lenders as an intermediary, or broker, of the other lender's loans.

mortgage insurance (MI)   Insurance on a mortgage that protects the lender against losses due to default and/or foreclosure. It is required on all conventional loans with less than 20% down payment. It is not life insurance. It is sometimes called Private Mortgage Insurance, or PMI.

mortgage insurance premium (MIP)   Mortgage insurance on FHA loans that is backed by the full faith and credit of the U.S. government.

negative amortization   This situation occurs when the borrowers are charged more interest than they are paying. The unpaid interest is added back into the principal amount of the loan.

nonconforming   Loans that do not conform to standard conventional loan guidelines set by Fannie Mae or Freddie Mac. Jumbo loans are nonconforming.

note The legal instrument that shows the borrower is obligated to pay the loan.

origination fee The fee the lender gets for originating and closing the loan, usually 1% of the loan amount.

PITI The basic house payment P = principal, I = interest, T = taxes, I = hazard insurance. Additional parts of the payment might be the following MI = mortgage insurance, HOA = homeowner's association fees or road maintenance fees.

planned unit development (PUD) A comprehensive development that encompasses several different sections and amenities.

points Points are a percentage of the loan amount. Discount points are charged to make up the difference between a lower loan amount and the actual required rate, which is higher. Some lenders will charge extra points as fee income. The origination fee is often included as part of the total points.

principal The amount of the loan.

private mortgage insurance The same as mortgage insurance.

Realtor A registered name for any real estate agent who belongs to the National Association of Realtors.

second mortgage Secondary financing behind or after the primary or first mortgage.

secondary market Investors who buy and sell large numbers of mortgage loans from the primary lenders. Fannie Mae, or the Federal National Mortgage Association (FNMA); and Freddie Mac, or the Federal Home Loan Mortgage Corporation (FHLMC) are two of the largest.

servicing The job of collecting the monthly house payments from a loan and making sure that they are properly credited. The loan servicer must make sure that the loans stay current, that the taxes and insurance are paid, and that the borrower is notified of the loan status and any changes.

subordination A second mortgage is subordinate to a first mortgage.

survey Most lenders will require a physical survey of the property. This is done by a registered surveyor who will measure the lot lines and show the footprint of the house and all outbuildings, roads, rights of way, easements, and water located on the property.

title   To hold title to property is to show ownership. A deed is evidence of holding title to property.

title insurance   Insurance that insures against any defects in the title that would give less than clear title to the property. Normal exceptions are mortgages, easements, and rights of way. The borrower normally pays for this as a normal closing cost. However, the seller or other third party can pay the insurance premium.

total loan-to-value (TLTV)   The total of all mortgages on the property expressed as a percentage of the value. Such as, a $100,000 house with an $80,000 first mortgage and a $10,000 second mortgage = 90% TLTV.

underwriter   A person who underwrites a mortgage loan is the one who either approves or rejects it based on certain guidelines pertaining to that loan. Some lenders approve loans by loan committees.

Veteran's Administration (VA)   This federal agency oversees the VA loan guarantee program.

value   the worth of a property, being the lesser of the sales price or appraised value.

INDEX